D0968489

EAST
ASIA
AND THE
WORLD
ECONOMY

EAST ASIA AND THE WORLD ECONOMY

Alvin Y. So
Stephen W. K. Chiu

MIBM HC 460.5 .S63 1995

So, Alvin Y., 1953-

East Asia and the world
economy

SAGE Publications
International Educational and Professional Publisher
Thousand Oaks   London   New Delhi

HELEN-JEAN MOORE LIBRARY
POINT PARK COLLEGE

Copyright © 1995 by Sage Publications, Inc.

All rights reserved. No part of this book may be reproduced or utilized in any form or by any means, electronic or mechanical, including photocopying, recording, or by any information storage and retrieval system, without permission in writing from the publisher.

For information address:

SAGE Publications, Inc.
2455 Teller Road
Thousand Oaks, California 91320
E-mail: order@sagepub.com

SAGE Publications Ltd.
6 Bonhill Street
London EC2A 4PU
United Kingdom

SAGE Publications India Pvt. Ltd.
M-32 Market
Greater Kailash I
New Delhi 110 048 India

Printed in the United States of America

Library of Congress Cataloging-in-Publication Data

So, Alvin Y., 1953-
 East Asia and the world economy / Alvin Y. So, Stephen W. K. Chiu.
  p. cm.
 Includes bibliographical references and index.
 ISBN 0-8039-4899-9 (alk. paper). — ISBN 0-8039-4900-6 (pbk.: alk. paper)
  1. East Asia—Economic conditions. 2. East Asia—Commercial policy. 3. International economic relations. 4. International trade. I. Chiu, Stephen Wing-kai. II. Title.
HC460.5.S63 1995
337.5—dc20   95-10325

This book is printed on acid-free paper.

96 97 98 99 10 9 8 7 6 5 4 3 2

Sage Project Editor: Susan McElroy

*This book is dedicated to our teachers,
colleagues, friends, and students in Hong Kong.*

Contents

Preface

Suppose there was a time machine that could take us back to the old East Asia. About 150 years ago we would observe how British hongs triumphantly took over the fishing island of Hong Kong, how the Chinese emperor was humiliated by his defeat in the Opium War, and how the "angry young men" of Japan quarreled with their shogun on how to deal with the foreigners. About 100 years ago we would watch how Japan, after destroying the Chinese navy in Korea, quickly acquired Taiwan as its colony and emerged as an imperialist power. About 50 years ago we would witness the occupation of Japan by the United States, the pending victory of the Chinese Communists against the nationalists, and a civil-war-torn Korea. About 20 years ago we would be impressed by the rising economic power of Japan, the shift from revolutionary Maoism to market socialism in China, and the rapid industrialization of Hong Kong, South Korea, and Taiwan. At present our concerns are the growing hegemonic rivalry between Japan and the United States, the precarious national reunification projects of China and Korea, and the prospect for the East Asian region as the new epicenter of global capital accumulation in the 21st century. Looking back through history, we are inevitably struck by the contrast between the old and the new East Asia.

Because East Asia has changed so much so fast, researchers have yet to provide a firm understanding of the contour of East Asian development. For example, not only was East Asia able to withstand its painful defeat in World War II, but it also quickly emerged as an economic powerhouse in the late 20th century. No one would have predicted, even

20 years ago, that the Chinese Communist Party could carry out market reforms so successfully. And no one would have predicted, even 10 years ago, that Hong Kong could continue having such robust economic growth despite the shadow of 1997.

In the literature, there are four general perspectives to explain the pattern of modern East Asian development. The neoclassical economists point to the role of the free market; the culturalists focus on the influence of Confucianism; the political scientists highlight the capacity of the state; and radical researchers from the dependency perspective stress the dark side of the East Asian miracle. Although the above four perspectives are quite useful in clarifying certain aspects of East Asian development, they tend to be unidisciplinary, adopt short historical time spans, fail to study the socialist states in East Asia, and seldom bring world-systems dynamics into their analysis. Subsequently, they are unable to provide a comprehensive review of the entire East Asian region, let alone explain the intricate linkages among Japanese industrialization; Chinese communism; the dynamics of the newly industrializing economies of Hong Kong, South Korea, and Taiwan; regional integration; and the prospect for national reunification in East Asia.

What this book offers is a world-systems analysis to explain both the origins and the transformation of the modern East Asia phenomenon. We argue that the methodology of world-systems analysis (which stresses the large-scale, long-term, and holistic approach) and the innovative concepts of such analysis (e.g., incorporation, semiperiphery, regionalization, hegemony and rivalry, and antisystemic movements) have shed new light on the study of modern East Asia.

In contrast to the literature's focuses on market, culture, state, and dependency, a world-systems analysis has pointed to the crucial role of geopolitical and regional factors in East Asian development. We argue that the peculiar pattern of East Asian incorporation into the capitalist world economy in the 19th century and the three attempts at regionalization (the Japanese empire-building projects in the first half of the 20th century, the American polarization project in the aftermath of World War II, and the two waves of organic division of labor by Japan and China in the late 20th century) have led not just to the three paths of development in East Asia (the "corization" of Japan, the Socialist transformation of China, and the capitalist industrialization of Hong Kong, South Korea, and Taiwan) but also to the upward mobility of the entire East Asian region.

Acknowledgments

The most gratifying part of writing this book is to be able to acknowledge the many debts we have incurred. Our interest in East Asian development began when we took courses from our teachers in Hong Kong. We became more and more interested in this field after taking a number of stimulating seminars from Professors Lucie Cheng and Philip C. C. Huang at UCLA, and Professors Gene Burns, Frank Dobbin, and Gilbert Rozman at Princeton. Since we have begun our teaching careers, we have benefited greatly from sharing our ideas with our colleagues: Professors Hagen Koo, Ravi Palat, and Patricia Steinhoff at the University of Hawaii, and Dr. Lui Tai-Lok at the Chinese University of Hong Kong.

Furthermore, Alvin Y. So wants to thank the graduate students in his seminar on Social Change in Developing Areas in 1993—Weihua Chen, Michael Gray, Jianliang Guo, Kathryn Hauschild, Akira Hirayama, Shiping Hua, In-Young Kim, Jun Kitamura, Andrew Ovenden, Stephen Phillon, Mariko Takagi-Kitayama, and Ida Yoshinaga—who provided weekly criticisms on the first draft of the manuscript. In particular, the detailed editing of Ida Yoshinaga and the helpful advice from Shiping Hua on romanization have greatly improved the readability of this manuscript. Dr. K. C. Ho made a significant contribution to this book by offering detailed criticisms chapter by chapter. In addition, Alvin Y. So is grateful for the support of Professor Don Topping, the director of the Social Science Research Institute at the University of Hawaii, for reducing his teaching load while he was preparing this book for publication. Stephen Chiu also would like to acknowledge his debt to the refreshing discussions with the graduate students of the Chinese University of Hong Kong, especially Kin-Chun Yau.

The editorial remarks by three anonymous reviewers for Sage Publications have been very helpful to us in our work on revising the manuscript. Giovanni Arrighi, Jerry Bentley, Wally Goldfrank, Tom Goldman, John Lie, Ravi Palat, and Mark Selden have read either some chapters or the entire manuscript and offered very helpful critical comments.

We also especially want to thank Dr. Hsin-Huang Michael Hsiao for his kind permission to use part of his coauthored paper (Hsiao & So, 1993) in the chapter on Chinese national integration. We are also grateful to Carrie Mullen, acquisitions editor at Sage, for her sympathetic understanding about the slow progress of our writing.

Because both of us grew up, received our education, and carried out much of our research in Hong Kong, we would like to take this opportunity to dedicate this book to our teachers, colleagues, friends, and students in Hong Kong. Without their academic stimulation, it is doubtful whether we would have ever embarked on a book project on East Asian development.

PART I

Theoretical Introduction

1. Current Perspectives on East Asian Development

"Why bother to write another book on East Asia," remarked a colleague, "when there are already more than a dozen such books published over the last decade?" Our response is that although, at first glance, there would seem to be an abundance of such books, very few of them actually capture and explain the peculiar pattern of East Asian development since its incorporation into the capitalist world economy in the early 19th century.

First, East Asia is the only region to produce a non-European state (Japan) that not only escaped colonization but also became an economic power challenging U.S. hegemony. Second, the largest state in East Asia (China) not only successfully transformed itself from an Asian empire to a Communist state but also attained rapid industrialization in the late 20th century. Third, East Asia is the only region where nation-states (mainland China and Taiwan; South Korea and North Korea) still divided along old Cold War lines, thus prompting the pressing problem of national reunification. Finally, in just a half century, the entire East Asian region has attained upward mobility. Not only are Taiwan, South Korea, and Hong Kong transformed into the so-called newly industrializing economies (NIEs), but the entire region has turned into an economic powerhouse in the world economy.

The so-called East Asian economic miracle, in particular, has stimulated much discussion on the underlying causes of and conditions behind the phenomenal success of the countries in the region. As in the field of development studies, several conflicting interpretations have emerged, all claiming to have discovered the true East Asian model of development. This chapter will first offer a brief review of the strengths and weaknesses of the neoclassical, the culturalist, the statist, and the dependency theories on East Asian development. Then it will focus on the world-systems analysis, whose new methodology and innovative concepts will be used to explain the peculiar pattern of modern East Asian development.

THE NEOCLASSICAL PERSPECTIVE

Theoretical Context

Many populist regimes in Latin America tried out a dev[...] [...]mental strategy of protectionism and industrialization called impo[...] [...]ution (IS) in the 1950s. This strategy speeds up the process o[...] [...]ation by substituting dor[...] [...]uction for a l[...] [...]urrent imports. Governme[...] [...]or of the industrialization pr[...] [...]s to protect domestic industries [...] [...]m & Hettne, 1984, pp. 41-42).

As a critique to this import-substituted industrialization strategy, a neoliberal or neoclassical interpretation emerged in the literature on East Asian economic development in the 1970s. Firmly rooted in the theorems of neoclassical economics, the neoclassical view has shared the following assumptions (Wade, 1992). First, neoclassical economists believe that short-run efficient resource allocation is the key to rapid long-term economic growth. Thus "getting the prices right" is a necessary and nearly a sufficient condition for maximizing the rate of long-term growth ("getting" means letting prices find their right levels; "right" refers to the relative prices established in freely operating domestic and international markets). According to this viewpoint, the problem of the Latin American countries is that their import-substituting industries are oligopolistic in structure and, therefore, suffer from excess capacity, inefficiency, high mark-up, and low-quality output.

Second, neoclassical economists believe that growth is a natural or inherent property of the market in the capitalist economies. Governments play an important role in providing the "public goods" (such as infrastructure and education) that are difficult to arrange through private contracts. But governments should not step beyond this role and adopt policies that interfere with the free workings of the market. Hence, neoclassical economists believe that the Latin American governments' control of import licensing and the rationing of foreign exchange invites corruption, smuggling, and black markets as well as inefficiency in the allocation of resources.

Third, neoclassical economists believe that the above principles are universally applicable to all countries. Hirschman (1981) has labeled this belief the "monoeconomics" claim. Hughes (1988, p. xvi) also remarks in her book on East Asian industrialization that "there seems little doubt that if other [Latin American] developing countries had followed similar economic policies they would also have grown more rapidly . . ." With respect to this claim, Haggard (1990, p. 9) points out that neoclassical economists maintain "a voluntarist view of policy making. Policy is simply a matter of making the right choices; 'incorrect' policy reflects misguided ideas or lack of political 'will.'" According to this view, the Latin American policymakers have adopted the wrong strategy of import-substituting industrialization; this explains why their economies are in trouble. How do neoclassical economists interpret East Asian devel-

Asian Development

Focusing on the East Asian newly industrializing economies (NIEs), Balassa (1988) observes that these countries (apart from Hong Kong) have also passed through the first stage of import-substituting industrialization. However, instead of following the path of the Latin American NIEs in adopting the second stage of import-substituting industrialization, the East Asian NIEs shifted to a new developmental strategy called *export-oriented industrialization.*

For Balassa (1988, pp. 280-281), it was the growth of exports in East Asian NIEs that accounted for their GDP growth rates, which were among the highest for developing countries. First, Balassa stated that "exports contribute to resource allocation according to comparative advantage. At the same time, these gains cumulate over time as the efficiency of new investment is enhanced through its orientation toward industries that correspond to the comparative advantage of the countries concerned." Second, exports make it possible for East Asian NIEs to overcome the limitations of their small domestic markets by ensuring economies of scale and full capacity utilization. Third, although import substitution often leads to protectionism and monopolies, export-oriented industrialization provides the carrot-and-stick of competition, inducing technological change in export industries that must keep up with modern technology in order to improve their position in the world market. But even if exports are the key to economic success, what explains the adoption of this policy among the East Asian NIEs?

According to Balassa (1988, pp. 286-288), the four determinants of the East Asian NIEs' favorable economic performance are: stability of the incentive system, limited government intervention, well-functioning labor and capital markets, and reliance on private capital.

First, the East Asian NIEs governments have a long tradition of encouraging exports by establishing export incentives, eliminating administrative obstacles to exports, and creating a favorable environment for exporters. In addition, the incentive system for exporters is relatively stable. For instance, East Asian NIEs' governments avoid the appreciation of the real effective exchange rate, and exporters can usually expect that the incentives that they receive will be maintained in the future. This is in contrast with the Latin American NIEs' governments, which allow the export exchange rate to fluctuate and wages to rise, thereby greatly reducing the profitability of exporters.

Second, although the governments in East Asia actively work to create a positive environment for economic growth, they rarely stray outside this limit and they do not interfere with the free workings of markets. As a result, the scope of administrative controls is much more limited in East Asia than in Latin America. In the latter case, not only are there pervasive controls over investment, prices, and imports, but decisions are also generally made on a case-by-case basis, thereby creating uncertainty from a business perspective.

Third, governments in the East Asian NIEs have instituted fewer policy-imposed distortions over labor and capital markets. Although labor markets are generally free in the East Asian NIEs, they are highly regulated in the Latin American NIEs. Balassa complained that prohibitions on discharging labor and high severance payments in the Latin American NIEs have increased their cost of labor. Moreover, capital markets are also freer in the East Asian NIEs than in the Latin American NIEs. In the East Asian NIEs, interest rates are tied to market rates, both to provide incentives for domestic saving and to discourage the outflow of capital. In the Latin American NIEs, by contrast, artificially low interest rates have reinforced the effects of overvalued currency rates in encouraging the outflow of capital.

Finally, greater reliance has been placed on the private sector in the East Asian NIEs than in the Latin American NIEs. In the East Asian NIEs, private enterprise took the lead in making the necessary investments, and, through exposure to international competition, in becoming efficient and profitable. On the other hand, public enterprise tends to play a more important role in the Latin American NIEs than in the East Asian NIEs. In the early 1980s, the outlays of public enterprise accounted for 26% of the GDP in Mexico, compared to only 4% in South Korea. Balassa argues that economic growth is negatively correlated with the size of the public sector, the share of government expenditures in the GDP, and the tax burden.

Evaluation

The neoclassical perspective contributes by pointing to the importance of export-led industrialization in East Asian development. Highlighting the factors of private enterprise, free markets, and positive but limited government intervention, this neoclassical perspective has received strong support from transnational corporations, which have sought to open markets in developing countries to allow them to move their assets worldwide in search of profit maximization (Wade, 1992, p. 319). This is because neoclassical economists' doctrines of free trade and investment, free market, and limited government intervention have enabled the transnational corporations to present their own interests as entirely consistent with the interests of developing countries.

What is missing in the neoclassical perspective, then, is its critical examination of the impact of transnational corporations, an interstate system, and regional dynamics on East Asian development. For example, how did the transnationals' shift from "Fordism" to a flexible mode of accumulation (Harvey, 1989) affect the prospect for private enterprises in East Asia? How did the advanced industrial countries' shift from free trade to protectionism affect the prospects for a free market in East Asia? And how did such changing regional dynamics as democratization and national reunification in East Asia affect its mode of government intervention in the economy?

If it was in the 1970s that the neoclassical perspective made the first claim of discovering East Asia's secret of success, then the 1980s saw the emergence of cultural and statist perspectives to either supplement or challenge this free market explanation.

THE CULTURAL PERSPECTIVE

Theoretical Context

As Rozman (1992) has stressed, the cultural perspective is not aimed at reducing economic development to a set of cultural traits or "national character" traits. The issue is not whether culture is the exclusive influential factor over development (Tai, 1989). Rather, the cultural perspective allows researchers to relate development policy choices and institutions to certain cultural antecedents that make the reasons for such choices easier to understand. In other words, the cultural perspective is aimed at providing researchers with a frame of reference within which they can see how values, attitudes, and practices have influenced the developing countries. Thus, the cultural perspective complements rather than contradicts the neoclassical economic interpretation.

In addition, the cultural perspective has revised several basic assumptions of the classical modernization school (So, 1990b). As Huntington (1976) points out, this school considers "modernity" and "tradition" to be essentially opposite concepts. For a society to move into modernity, the classical modernization school argues, the traditional structures and values must be totally replaced by a set of modern values. The economic backwardness of the developing countries, therefore, is explained by their inability to get rid of traditional cultural elements. For instance, the economic stagnation in Japan and South Korea in the early 1950s was routinely attributed to their Confucian heritage, because the formal Confucian tradition frowned on merchants and cast suspicion on easy money from unproductive activities.

However, the cultural perspective avoids treating tradition and modernity as a set of mutually exclusive concepts. From the cultural perspective, tradition and modernity not only coexist, but penetrate and intermingle with one another. Far from being an obstacle to development, tradition is seen by the culturists as highly beneficial to development. This new orientation toward tradition has opened up new research agendas for interpreting East Asian development.

East Asian Development

From the cultural perspective, what the successful East Asian (Japanese, Taiwanese, South Korean, and Hong Kongese) economies share in common is their Confucian tradition (Berger, 1986; Cho, 1994). Rozman (1992), in particular, argues that in East Asia there emerged a kind of "mass Confucianism" and "elite or merchant house Confucianism," which is a different emphasis from that of Western economic success in terms of orientation to learning and education, small family business, corporate management, and governmental services.

First of all, with respect to orientation to learning and education, Rozman (1992, p. 312) argues that Westerners and early Asian reformers had originally wrongly dismissed Confucian learning as a handicap to development, because they saw it merely as a process of training in textual memorization. Rather than closing people's minds, Confucian tradition was capable of opening them, teaching individuals to "learn how to learn," and giving them the tools to observe, interpret, and take on new knowledge. It also taught them to internalize ethical principles friendly to economic development, such as diligence, self-sacrifice, and delayed gratification. In addition, in its primary concern of improving social relations, Confucianism established a precedent for focusing on education. Individuals were urged to seek self-improvement through intense study and purification of their minds. Furthermore, education in Confucian teachings urged the most highly trained to serve their community and country and prepared the masses to view learning as a path to improving their lot in life. As Rozman (1992, p. 314) points out, such Confucian values fostered a competitive and even, within understandable premodern limitations, entrepreneurial spirit.

Second, although Western philosophy emphasized individualism, Confucianism endorsed familism and placed the family as the paramount institution within society. The path to success was not through leaving the family to find one's fortune, but through relying on and providing family assistance. Entrepreneurial skills did not normally originate in risky commercial undertakings but instead were an outgrowth of a wide range of business orientations extending from the family firms to the community. Thus small family enterprises commonly started out with family savings or credit from relatives, drew on the labor of many unpaid family members, turned sitting rooms and family bedrooms into production sites, and relied on kin to obtain contracts and markets. Family entrepreneurship, not individualism, thus became the backbone of successful East Asian economies (Rozman, 1992, p. 314).

Third, Confucianism has shaped a new pattern of personalistic corporate management that differs from the West's formal, rational, bureaucratic management. "The spiritual qualities of organizations," as Rozman (1992, p. 315) underscores, are given credit for business achievements in East Asia: "Employees are often hired through personal recommendations that praise their personality qualities and suggest that they are consistent with company needs. Particularly in Japan, orientation sessions are both long and demanding, concentrating on character building and linking work to higher social goals. The company teaches values at an abstract level and proceeds to reinforce them through many group-oriented practices." Furthermore, the Japanese company fosters a cult of ancestor worship for its founder and his successors. The history of the firm emphasizes pride in distinctive traditions over many generations, and the firm employs a set of rituals and ceremonies to smooth the way for harmonious human relations. As a result of this pattern of personalistic management, the transition from the risk-oriented founders of pioneer industries to the more cautious managers of well-established enterprises has proven relatively easy in the East Asian region.

Finally, just as there are contrasting patterns of corporate management between East Asia and the West, so are there differences in their values toward government service. For one thing, administrative elites received much higher prestige and social standing in East Asia than their counterparts in the West. Rozman (1992, p. 318) explains this by citing the "tenacity of Confucian elitist culture," which "glorified the established authority of the better educated and rationalized their claims of superiority on the basis of possessing specialized wisdom." The East Asian people believe in the justice and competence of their public administrators because they are the products of the highest-ranked universities and demanding civil-service examinations. In addition, public belief in the rhetoric of public service to the national community is far more pervasive in East Asia than in the West. Senior government officials constantly remind the public that they are serving not their own interests, but the interests of the whole nation. As a result, this positive orientation to government service facilitated the creation of what Chalmers Johnson (1987) calls a "developmental state," where the administrative elites often *rule,* but politicians only *reign.*

Evaluation

The cultural perspective contributes by highlighting the crucial role of Confucianism—especially its orientation toward learning and education, familism, personalistic management, and the high prestige of government service—in East Asian industrialization. This cultural perspective, needless to stress, has won the support of parents, teachers, domestic entrepreneurs, and administrative elites in East Asian countries (Tai, 1989).

However, the cultural perspective generally fails to examine the specific historical context and the geopolitical conditions through which different forms of Confucianism emerged (or failed to emerge) in East Asia. For example, why did the Japanese reformers blend Confucianism with Shintoism and the emperor cult during the Meiji period? Why did the Nationalist Party use Confucianism to reconstruct Chinese national culture right after it was forced to relocate its government to Taiwan in 1949? And why did mainland China, which had a strong heritage of Confucianism, turn to Communism instead of capitalist industrialization after World War II? Furthermore, the cultural perspective fails to explain the timing of the impact of Confucianism. Why, as Lie (1992b, p. 286) asks in his study of Korean industrialization, "did it only lead to economic success in the last 30 years, when Confucianism has held sway in Korea for centuries? Ironically, the same Confucian ethic was widely used to explain Korea's backwardness 30 years ago."

Like the cultural perspective, the statist perspective also seems to have downplayed the role of historical and geopolitical factors in East Asian development.

THE STATIST PERSPECTIVE

Theoretical Context

The statist perspective emerged as a critique of the neoclassical economic interpretation of developing countries. Instead of emphasizing free markets, trade liberalization, private enterprise, and the restricted role of the state, the statist perspective contends that states have a strategic role to play in taming domestic and international market forces and harnessing them to national ends. Instead of focusing on maximum profitability on the basis of current comparative advantage, the statist perspective focuses on the phenomenon of "late industrialization." In this respect, the statist perspective is still sharing the Gerschenkronian view of late development, arguing for the importance of a strong state to overcome market imperfections and the various bottlenecks of industrialization (Gerschenkron, 1962; Rueschemeyer & Evans, 1985).

Recent studies from the statist perspective, however, have gone beyond the issue of whether the state or the market is solely responsible for promoting development. As Onis (1991, p. 110) points out, the latest pertinent question of the statist perspective is how to find the appropriate mixture of market orientation and government intervention in a manner consistent with rapid and efficient late industrialization. Equally central is the issue of which set of social and political institutions is compatible with this state-economy mixture. Focusing on the mixture issue, the statist perspective's present research focuses on the complex interactions among the state, the market, and sociopolitical institutions.

Regarding East Asian development, then, the statist perspective has raised the following research questions: Why does a developmental state tend to emerge in East Asian late industrialization? What are the characteristics of this developmental state? How does it intervene in the market economy to promote late industrialization? And what is the relationship between the developmental state and other social institutions in the East Asian society?

East Asian Development

First of all, why does a developmental state tend to emerge in late industrialization? In Amsden's (1989) formulation, East Asian industrialization is characterized by its "lateness" rather than by its "newness" (as in newly industrializing economies). As latecomers, East Asian firms must compete with established Western firms that can introduce new technologies fast enough to capture "technology rents" and thereby earn higher profits. This does, of course, allow the East Asian firms to acquire, learn, or borrow, the more codified elements of a given technology from the West without having to develop them for themselves. Nevertheless, there is generally a great gap between buying, borrowing, or stealing the codified elements on one hand and mastering the technology in production on the other. As a result, developmental states are called upon to offset the disadvantages faced by East Asian firms in international competition so as to move the NIEs' industrial structure toward more technologically dynamic activities (Wade, 1992).

Second, the developmental state, according to Johnson's (1987) conception, possesses the following features: (a) As the name implies, economic development (in terms of growth, productivity, and competitiveness) is the foremost priority of state action. The state single-mindedly adheres to economic development even at the expense of other objectives, such as equality and social welfare. (b) Because the developmental state is not a socialist state, it has firm commitment to private property and the market. The market, however, is closely governed by state managers who formulate strategic industrial policy to promote development. (c) Within the state bureaucracy, a pilot agency (such as the Ministry of International Trade and Industry [MITI] in Japan) plays a key role in strategic policy formulation and implementation. This agency is given sufficient scope to take initiatives and operate effectively, and is staffed by the best managerial talent available to the state bureaucracy. Onis (1991, p. 114) suggests that "rigorous standard of entry not only ensured a high degree of bureaucratic capability, but also generated a sense of unity and common identity on the part of the bureaucratic elites. Hence the bureaucrats were imbued with a sense of mission and identified themselves with national goals derived from a position of leadership in society."

Third, with respect to how the state promotes late industrialization, Amsden's (1989) study on South Korea emphasizes the dual policies of "subsidies" and "discipline." If the First Industrial Revolution was built on laissez-faire, and the Second on infant industry protection, then Amsden argues that South Korea's late industrialization in South Korea was founded on subsidies. The allocation of subsidies has rendered the

South Korean government not merely a banker but an entrepreneur, using subsidies to decide what, when, and how much to produce, and which strategic industries to favor. Subsidies were necessary because the South Korean firms could not initially compete against Japanese products, even in such highly labor-intensive industries as cotton spinning and weaving. Needless to say, the long gestation periods and relatively low profitability (through industries' adolescent period) made capital-intensive industries even less desirable investments to South Korean firms. According to Amsden, South Korea's entry into heavy industries and the emergence of cotton textiles as its leading export industry provide graphic evidence of the need for state intervention under conditions of late industrialization.

Nevertheless, although the South Korean government subsidized strategic industrial firms, it was also not reluctant to impose discipline on them. For example, the government specified stringent performance requirements (notably in the field of exports) in return for the subsidies it provides. Such discipline exercised over private firms involved both rewarding good performers and penalizing poor ones. The carrot-and-stick took the form of granting or withholding industrial licensing, government bank loans, advanced technology acquired through the government's investing in foreign licensing and technical assistance, and so on. Because the South Korean government deliberately refrained from bailing out firms that were badly managed in otherwise profitable industries, government subsidies did not lead to a waste of resources, as they did in the case of socialist countries and many developing countries in Latin America. Thus Amsden (1989, p. 14) asserts that "Where Korea differs from most other late industrializing countries is in the discipline its state exercises over private firms."

Fourth and finally, what is the relationship between the developmental state and other social institutions in the society? Onis (1991) points out that East Asian industrializing states were unusual because they experienced both bureaucratic autonomy and public-private cooperation. On one hand, there was a high degree of bureaucratic autonomy and capacity because of meritocratic recruitment and a sense of unity and mission among state managers. This allowed the state and bureaucratic elites to develop national strategic developmental policies independent from the other powerful groups in society. On the other hand, there were close institutional links between the developmental state and private sector conglomerates, banks, and trading companies that dominated strategic sectors of the economy. This close linkage resulted from state policy, because huge business conglomerates (like the *chaebols* of South Korea) owed their phenomenal growth to special incentives provided by the state, and they remained dependent on the state for their survival. As a result, the private sector cooperated highly with the state policy of subsidies and discipline. Onis argues that this unusual mixture of bureaucratic autonomy and public-private sector cooperation caused the emergence of a strong autonomous state that was not only able to formulate strategic developmental goals but was also able to translate these broad national goals into effective policy action to promote late industrialization in East Asia.

Evaluation

The statist perspective contributes by highlighting the decisive role of the developmental state in East Asian late industrialization in the second half of the 20th century. It shows that the pattern of East Asian development is indeed quite different from those of Western industrialized countries. If the neoclassical economic perspective is used by the transnational corporations to justify their claims to opening national markets for free trade and investment, then the statist perspective is a defense used by the East Asian state managers and planners to justify protectionism and intervention in their economy.

However, the statist perspective often fails to bring in geopolitical factors and regional dynamics to explain the origins of developmental state in East Asia. For example, where did state autonomy (independence from society) and state capacity (the ability to plan and implement policy) in East Asia come from? Why were some states in East Asia able to develop strong autonomy and capacity after World War II, when other states in the Third World failed to do so?

In addition, in treating late industrialization as mostly a technical issue of learning or borrowing, and highlighting the merits of state strategic planning in promoting development, the statist perspective may unintentionally endorse the actions of authoritarian states in East Asia while overlooking the dark side of late industrialization (Lie, 1991). What is missing in the statist perspective, then, are studies of labor repression, violation of human rights, environmental degradation, conflict with foreign corporations, and economic crises. As the following discussion will reveal, these policy issues are key concerns of the dependency perspective.

THE DEPENDENCY PERSPECTIVE

Theoretical Context

The classical dependency perspective emerged as a critique of the modernization school, including the neoclassical economic and the cultural perspectives. Coming from a radical tradition, the dependency perspective is strongly influenced by neo-Marxist theories of imperialism and class domination.

The following theoretical assumptions characterize the classical dependency tradition (So, 1990b). First, with respect to the causes of the problems of developing countries, the dependency perspective offered an external explanation. Instead of pointing to such potentially negative internal factors as lack of a free market, Confucianism, and strategic state planning, the dependency perspective stressed the detrimental role played by imperialism, foreign domination, and neocolonialism in shaping the backwardness of the developing countries. Second, with respect to the links between the West and the developing countries, the dependency perspective saw these relationships as harmful rather than beneficial. Instead of claiming that Western countries are assisting the developing countries in development, the dependency perspective emphasized that Western countries are exploiting the developing countries. Third, with respect to the future direction of development, the dependency perspective was highly pessimistic. Instead of predicting that the developing countries will eventually catch up with the West and modernize themselves, the dependency perspective foresees further economic backwardness, and even bankruptcy of the developing countries, if their present exploitative links with the West remain unchallenged.

Nevertheless, recent studies from the dependency perspective have begun to recognize the possibility of economic growth in the Third World; hence the emergence of the new dependency perspective (or the "dependent development" thesis) formulated by Cardoso and Faletto (1979) and elaborated by Evans (1979, 1987). Cardoso, for instance, asserts that developing countries are entering a new phase, which has emerged as a result of the rise of transnational corporations and the immersion of industrial capital into developing economies. Thus Cardoso (1973, p. 149) argues that "to some extent, the interests of the foreign corporations become compatible with the internal prosperity of the dependent countries. In this sense, they help to promote development." Still, Cardoso insists that the process of peripheral development is ridden with contradictions because it lacks "autonomous technology and a fully developed capital-goods sector."

Based upon the above arguments, how would the dependency perspective examine the phenomenon of East Asian development?

East Asian Development

Frobel, Heinrichs, and Kreye (1980) and Landsberg (1979) argue that although East Asian NIEs have enjoyed high-speed growth for the time being, their dependence on foreign capital and markets is bound to cause acute problems in the long run. In a similar vein, instead of perceiving the East Asian NIEs as models of success, Bello and Rosenfeld (1990) highlight the following crises facing the Asian NIEs: the sluggishness of key exports, mounting inflation, faltering growth rates, working-class insurrection, capital flight, and environmental pollution.

In order to understand the unfolding crises confronting the East Asian NIEs, Bello and Rosenfeld contend that it is important to first examine the following three conditions that enabled these countries to emerge as important players in the world economy. First, the economic rise of the NIEs was closely linked to the political hegemony of the United States after World War II. South Korea and Taiwan, considered by the United States to be on the front lines of the global struggle against Communism, received $1.5 billion in economic aid as well as billions of dollars in military aid from the United States. This massive U.S. aid helped South Korea and Taiwan recover from the devastation caused by war and civil strife. In addition, the Korean War provided vital stimuli for the economies of Taiwan and South Korea in the form of American purchases of commodities, spending on recreation, and construction contracts.

Second, there was the Japan factor. As Japanese firms sought to escape the rising cost of domestic labor in the 1960s and 1970s, their first choice for relocation of production was their former colonies—Taiwan and

South Korea. As the East Asian NIEs sought to emulate Japan's export success, Japanese trading companies handled international trade for many Taiwanese and South Korean firms. Moreover, as Taiwanese and South Korean industrialization began to take off in the 1970s, Japan provided a significant portion of the capital goods, intermediate inputs, and technology that the East Asian enterprises needed to turn out goods for exports. As a result, although the NIEs ran multibillion-dollar trade surpluses with the United States, they ran multibillion-dollar trade deficits with Japan.

Third, there were the policies of what Bello and Rosenfeld call "command capitalism." Export success, not efficient resource allocation, was the overriding goal of the state technocrats in East Asia. Thus the Park Chung Hee regime in South Korea manipulated interest rates and channeled credit resources and other subsidies to South Korean conglomerates, and the Taiwanese and South Korean states forcefully intervened in the labor market to depress workers' wages below market rates in order to make East Asian exports highly competitive in the international market.

By the late 1980s, however, the NIEs' external and internal environments had been drastically transformed. Bello and Rosenfeld point out that what had been the NIEs' key assets during the earlier periods of high-speed growth began increasingly to look like liabilities. First, there was the threat of protectionism. Once the guardian of the free market, the United States had been transformed, by the late 1980s, into an aggressively protectionist power, and the NIEs became the prime targets of this protectionist offensive. Consequently, the United States revoked the tariff-free entry of selected East Asian imports, imposed voluntary export restraints on East Asian NIEs, forced the appreciation of the Taiwan dollar and the Korean *won*, and sought to open domestic markets in Taiwan and South Korea.

Second, there were social and political crises within the NIEs. The social costs of the NIEs' model became apparent by the mid-1980s, and chief among these was the high political price exacted by the imposition of export-led growth. Prosperity had not been spread around evenly; income inequality was actually worsening; and the depth of alienation created by decades of labor repression was manifested in the strikes that exploded after the democratization decree in South Korea and the lifting of martial law in Taiwan. In Taiwan, labor was calling not only for wage increases, but also for union autonomy, fair labor practices, and reform of current labor laws. In South Korea, *chaebol* (corporate conglomerate) became a dirty word, and the South Korean public began to view the state-*chaebol* relationship as increasingly corrupt.

Third, the agricultural sector in the NIEs was in trouble. Bello and Rosenfeld argue that there was serious erosion of the agricultural basis of the East Asian NIEs' economies. Since the mid-1960s, the countryside had been systematically exploited to provide capital and resources needed to fuel export-oriented industrialization. By keeping grain cheap, the government held urban wages low and thus kept the prices of Taiwanese and South Korean exports highly competitive. However, these policies caused rural incomes and the size of the rural population to decline sharply. Making a living from agriculture became so difficult that by the early 1980s only 11% of Taiwan's farmers were full-time farmers. This decline in agricultural production, together with the dumping of cheap American agricultural surplus goods, had ruined the diversified agricultural economies in Taiwan and South Korea, prompting violent protest movements by farmers against American imports.

Fourth, the environment became a prime victim of the NIEs' high-speed industrial growth strategy. Seoul's air now has one of the highest concentrations of sulphur dioxide in the world, and South Korea's tap water is unsuitable for drinking. In Taiwan, agricultural land is not only overdosed with pesticides but also heavily contaminated with metals from unregulated industrial waste dumping. This rapid ecological deterioration spawned the rise of a multiclass environmental movement in Taiwan, which helped to stop the construction of a $160-million titanium dioxide plant by DuPont and close a petrochemical plant owned by the British ICI Corporation.

Fifth and finally, the NIEs now face a structural squeeze. The NIEs risk losing their competitive edge because their labor is no longer cheap, compared with that of less industrialized nations. A militant labor movement and the drying up of labor reserves in the countryside created strong upward pressures on wages. However, instead of upgrading their industries to high-tech production, the capitalists in the NIEs preferred to move their investments to countries where wages were lower, to import workers from Southeast Asian countries, or to speculate in the

NIEs' overheated real estate market and stock exchange. Furthermore, Bello and Rosenfeld point out that even should state managers push for high-tech policies, the NIEs will still face a shortage of scientific and engineering personnel, a lack of massive financial resources to conduct high-tech research, an absence of quality suppliers, and a low capability for self-sustaining technological innovation.

Evaluation

The dependency perspective contributes by highlighting the constraints and problems—such as worldwide protectionism, social and political unrest, declining agricultural sectors, environmental degradation, the structural squeeze between high wages, and the inability to move into high-tech production—of the NIEs. Instead of trying to gain the support of transnational capitalists and domestic state managers, the dependency perspective wants to appeal to those forces that have the greatest stake in a new strategy of democratic development—namely, farmers, workers, environmentalists, and small businessmen.

However, as a result of its theoretical assumptions on Third World backwardness, the dependency perspective has failed to examine many interesting issues of East Asian development. For example, it fails to study the struggles between Japan and the United States for economic hegemony of East Asia; it does not investigate how the prospect of national reunification among mainland China, Taiwan, and Hong Kong may affect East Asian development; and it excludes mainland China and North Korea from its discussion on East Asia because they are socialist states.

More important, the dependency perspective holds a deterministic outlook that East Asian states, except Japan, are unable to solve their deep-rooted developmental problems. Thus it fails to address the issue that many East Asian states in the 1990s are not only experiencing upward mobility into advanced industrial countries but are also starting to diversify their investment in many Southeast Asian countries. If many East Asian states could overcome their external, political, and economic crises from the 1960s to the 1980s, what makes researchers predict that these states will have a developmental breakdown in the 1990s?

GENERAL CRITICISM
OF THE CURRENT PERSPECTIVES

So far, this chapter has discussed four theories of East Asian development—the neoclassical economic perspective, the cultural perspective, the statist perspective, and the dependency perspective. Each perspective has made a significant contribution to our understanding of the East Asian economic phenomenon. For instance, neoclassical economists highlight the crucial role played by the market and private enterprises; culturists bring out the impact of Confucianism on education, family enterprises, and corporate management; statists underscore the strategic industrial policies of the developmental state; and dependency theorists reveal the dark side and the crises of East Asian industrialization. Nevertheless, these four perspectives suffer from the following problems.

First, these perspectives are unidisciplinary. They focus only on factors stressed by their own disciplines, and they tend to talk past one another, arguing that the other perspectives are moving in the wrong direction by neglecting a particular factor. What is missing in the literature, then, is a comprehensive meta-perspective that examines the complex interactions among economic, political, and cultural forces in shaping East Asian development.

Second, these perspectives confine themselves to the study of capitalist states. Even when the term *East Asia* is used, it becomes clear that China and North Korea are excluded, because these countries have "a different political and social system from the rest" of East Asia (Balassa, 1988, p. 289). What is missing in the literature are the developmental experiences of East Asian socialist states.

Third, the unit of analysis of each perspective is restricted, because they all confine themselves to the study of nations. Thus their studies focus on national economies, national cultures, and nation-states. Except for the dependency perspective, the literature tends to ignore the *regional* dimension of East Asian development, and there is little discussion on the intricate interactions among the states in the East Asian region.

Fourth, as a result of their nation-state focus, these perspectives tend to take world-system dynamics for granted. There is little discussion of how such world-system dynamics as the secular trends of incorporation and world wars over the past 2 centuries have affected East Asian development.

Fifth and finally, these perspectives often adopt a short historical time span, mostly focusing on post-World War II development. But what was East Asia like before 1945? How did the pre-1945 historical legacy affect contemporary development in East Asia? In this respect, it is necessary to go beyond the 1945 dividing line and bring history back in to analyze how industrialization has unfolded in East Asia over the past two centuries.

Subsequently, although there are numerous excellent monographs on Japanese industrialization, Chinese Communism, national reunification, and the dynamics of East Asian newly industrializing economies, very few of them have provided a comprehensive review of the entire East Asian region. Although there are many outstanding political scientists, economists, sociologists, and psychologists who enlighten us about East Asia, there are hardly any efforts among social scientists to transcend their disciplinary boundaries in order to examine the complex interactions among political, economic, and cultural forces in East Asian development. Although there are many first-rate, country-specific studies on China, Japan, Taiwan, Korea, and Hong Kong, there is a lack of research that focuses the interactions among these East Asian states in the world economy. Although there are detailed historical accounts on old East Asia and there are fascinating policy analyses of contemporary East Asia, area specialists seldom try to integrate the past with the present.

What is needed, then, is a new, comprehensive perspective to go beyond disciplinary boundaries, adopt a larger unit of analysis to analyze state interactions and regional dynamics, trace a longer historical time span, and examine East Asian history from the bottom up. We will discuss the elements of this new perspective in the next section.

WORLD-SYSTEMS ANALYSIS: THEORETICAL CONTEXT

Early world-systems analysis, as formulated in Immanuel Wallerstein's (1976, 1979) studies, was strongly influenced by the dependency literature. As a result, critics have charged early world-systems analysis with presenting a reified concept of the world-system, overlooking the role of internal dynamics such as class conflict, and portraying peripheral states as passive victims of the world economy (Brenner, 1977; Koo, 1984; Petras, 1978; Shannon, 1989; Skocpol, 1977; Zeitlin, 1984).

However, at a later stage, when Wallerstein fully developed his world-systems analysis, he seemed to move beyond the domain of the dependency literature. This shift in Wallerstein's orientation may be explained by the fact that he was later strongly influenced by Fernand Braudel's French Annales school, which calls for the study of "total" history and the synthesis of history with social sciences (So, 1990b; Wallerstein, 1982a, 1986).

Methodology

In Wallerstein's (1991b) recent formulation, world-systems analysis is not a theory but a protest against the ways in which social scientific inquiry itself had been structured since its inception in the middle of the 19th century. First, Wallerstein questioned whether academic disciplines could be separated from one another in the first place. Can the economy, the polity, and the society be conceived to have, even hypothetically, autonomous activity? For instance, as markets are sociopolitical creations, can a true economic price somehow be stripped of its political and social bases? As an alternative, Wallerstein proposed a new historical social science that is *undisciplinary* and would encourage researchers to examine the interactions among these three supposedly distinctive arenas of economics, politics, and society.

Second, Wallerstein's world-systems analysis fights a war on two fronts regarding the concept of time: against the traditional historians whose task is to date such events so as to provide a narrative episodic history unique and explicable only in its own terms, and against the social scientists whose task is to search for eternal laws of human behavior that are applicable across time. To go beyond this 19th-century conception of time, Wallerstein calls for a shift of focus from the historian's "episodic time" and the social scientist's "eternal time" to the historical social scientist's study of "structural time (the *longue duree*) and cyclical time (*conjonctures*)."

Third, Wallerstein questions the treatment of the state/society as the unit of analysis. Where and when do the entities, within which social life occurs, exist? Thus, Wallerstein insists on taking the large-scale historical

world-system rather than the state/society as the unit of scientific inquiry. For Wallerstein, this is more than a mere semantic substitution,
because the term *historical world-system* rids us of the central connota-
tion that society is linked to the state and that the nation-state represents
a relatively autonomous society that develops over time.

   In sum, in contrast to the historians' concentration on the infinitely
small in space and time, and the social scientists' concentration on the
infinitely small in scope and eternal in time, Wallerstein's world-systems
analysis calls for the examination of large-scale, holistic social change
(especially the instantaneous interactions among politics, economics,
and culture) over long periods of time in historical world-systems.

Concepts

   In addition to methodological differences, there are also significant
differences in the conceptual framework and research focuses between
world-systems analysis and dependency theory.

   First of all, instead of the dependency theory's bimodal structure of
core (advanced industrial states) versus periphery (backward Third
World states), Wallerstein proposes a trimodal structure consisting of
core, semiperiphery, and periphery. Semiperipheral states are situated
between core and peripheral states, and they have a fairly even mix of
core-like and peripheral-like activities. In addition, semiperipheral states
are characterized by active intervention in the economy as well as struggles for regional domination (Martin, 1990; Smith & Lee, 1990). The
formulation of the semiperiphery concept was a theoretical breakthrough because it enabled world-systems researchers to entertain the
possibilities of upward mobility (a periphery moving to semiperipheral
status, or a semiperiphery moving to core status) and downward mobility (a core moving to semiperipheral status, or a semiperiphery moving
to peripheral status) in relation to the dynamics of the capitalist world
economy.

   Moreover, aside from studying the peripheral and semiperipheral
states, world-systems analysis also highlights the unity and struggles
among the core states. For Wallerstein (1991a), the concept of "hegemony" refers to the situations in which one core power is so much more
powerful than other core powers (in all or most dimensions of power)

that it can get its way in the capitalist world economy with a minimal use of force and can be an exceptional locus of capital accumulation. Wallerstein argues that there have been only three hegemonic powers in the history of the world economy: the United Provinces in the mid-17th century, the United Kingdom in the mid-19th, and the United States in the mid-20th. Nevertheless, hegemonic domination cannot last for long. Very soon other core states are able to catch up and challenge the hegemonic state economically, culturally, and militarily. What happens after the decline of a hegemonic power, then, is the emergence of *rivalry* among the core states, a situation in which the power distribution within the core becomes much less lopsided, and consequently the intracore distribution of capital accumulation is much more even.

Furthermore, world-systems analysis contributes by examining the following five kinds of global dynamics that go beyond the confines of nation-state: incorporation, deepening, social construction, cyclical rhythms, and antisystemic movements. *Incorporation* refers to the expansion of the world economy's outer boundaries to other parts of the world. The process of incorporation started in the 17th century; by the late 19th century, there was no area on the globe that remained outside the operations of the interstate system. As such, the secular trends of the world economy turned from territorial expansion across the globe to the deepening of capitalist relations. *Deepening* refers to commodification and industrialization processes through which production in one zone of the world economy is geared into, dependent upon, and integrated with production in other zones of the world economy. During incorporation and deepening, Wallerstein (1991a) contends that not just the economy and the state, but also "peoplehood" (race, nation, ethnic group), gender, household, and even civilization are *socially constructed* and reconstructed by the dynamics of the world economy. The very construction of peoplehood and other social labels, then, becomes the key ideological battleground where opposing classes, status groups, and states settle their conflicts in the world economy. In this formulation, the working of the world economy is far from unproblematic. Instead, the world economy is constantly undergoing cyclical rhythms and challenged by antisystemic movements. For Wallerstein, the term *cyclical rhythms* refers to alternate patterns of expansion and stagnation as a result of the imbalance between global effective demand and global supply of goods in the world economy. As the accumulators of capital lose their ability to resolve the contradictions of the world economy, a worldwide family of *antisystemic movements* has emerged to transform the world economy in a more democratic, egalitarian direction. This includes labor movements, nationalistic movements, ethnic movements, women's movements, environmental movements, and the like.

To conclude, world-systems analysis, in its mature version, has gone beyond the problems of the dependency perspective to provide a methodological break with 19th-century social scientific inquiry. It offers a new mode of thinking that stresses large-scale, long-term, and holistic methodology. In addition, it has formulated many innovative concepts—such as incorporation, semiperiphery, regionalization, hegemony, rivalry, and antisystemic movements—to examine the changing development in the world economy. Although world-systems analysis has contributed to an original line of research on global dynamics (Arrighi, 1990; Bergesen, 1992; Chase-Dunn, 1989; Gereffi & Korzeniewicz, 1994; Martin, 1994; McMichael, 1992; Silver, 1992; Smith, Collins, Hopkins, & Muhammad, 1988), how useful is it in guiding researchers to examine the nations, states, and people of the East Asian region?

WORLD-SYSTEMS ANALYSIS AND EAST ASIAN DEVELOPMENT

The methodological and conceptual tools of world-systems analysis are helpful for East Asian studies, because they help researchers set up new research agendas and raise new research questions that go beyond the confines of the economic, cultural, statist, and dependency perspectives in the literature on development. For instance, echoing the call for large-scale, holistic analysis, Cumings (1987) points out that the industrial development in Japan, Korea, and Taiwan is a historically and regionally specific phenomenon in which a tripartite hierarchy of core, semiperiphery, and periphery was created in the first part of the 20th century and then slowly recreated after World War II.

In addition, many researchers who are close to the world-systems school have made a significant contribution by clarifying the impact of world-system and regional dynamics on East Asian development. At the political level, Cumings (1987) and Palat (1993) have shown that the rise of the United States as a global hegemonic power and the spread of Communism in East Asia in the late 1940s have profoundly shaped the path of development of socialist China, capitalist Japan, and postcolonial Taiwan and South Korea. On the other hand, the hegemonic decline of the United States and the rising economic power of Japan since the 1980s have both led to their growing rivalry and provided more opportunity for East Asian states to strive for upward mobility in the world economy (McMichael, 1987).

At the economic level, the rapid industrialization of East Asian states owed much to the transformation of the capitalist world economy from so-called "Fordism" to flexible accumulation (Palat, 1994). Confronted by volatile markets, intensifying competition, and falling rates of profit, major transnational corporations in the core since the late 1960s began to rationalize their manufacturing operations by subcontracting and relocating production facilities to new geographical arenas unaccustomed to Fordist standards of high wages and consumption. Studying this global relocation of production sites, Arrighi, Ikeda, and Irwan (1993) examined how Japan's multilayered subcontracting system has not only led to the further economic ascent of Japan, but also made a transborder expansion to Hong Kong, Korea, and Taiwan, resulting in the spread of the "Asian miracle" to select locations in East Asia. In a similar vein, Gereffi (1992) reported that the East Asian NIEs have been most successful in the areas of commercial subcontracting and component supply to transnational firms.

Summing up the pattern of post-World War II development in East Asia, Arrighi (1994b) argues that it resembles a three-stage rocket. In the first stage, the main agency of expansion was the U.S. government, whose strategies of geopolitics propelled the upgrading of the Japanese economy and created the political conditions of the subsequent transborder expansion of the Japanese multilayered subcontracting system. In the second stage, Japanese business itself became the main agency of expansion. As the catchment area of its subcontracting networks came to encompass the entire East Asian region, the Chinese capitalist diaspora was revitalized and the Chinese government was offered unique opportunities to mobilize this diaspora in the dual pursuit of economic advancement for mainland China and national reunification for greater

China. In the incipient third stage, it is precisely the Chinese government acting in concert with the Chinese capitalist diaspora that seems to be emerging as the leading agency of expansion.

What this book hopes to accomplish, then, is to further extend world-systems analysis in order to explain the unique pattern of East Asian development over the past 2 centuries. Although the above-mentioned world-systems studies have brought in global and regional dynamics as explanatory factors, this book wants to go one step further, to examine how these global and regional dynamics have actually emerged at the nation-state level and shaped national and local development. Though the above-mentioned studies tend to focus on 20th-century Asia, this book wants to adopt a longer time span, to trace how East Asia was historically incorporated into the world economy in the mid-19th century, and to see how this mode of incorporation has affected subsequent East Asian development. Finally, although the above-mentioned studies emphasize political and economic forces, this book wants to examine the interactions among political, economic, and cultural forces in order to explain such pertinent issues as Communism, industrialization, and national reunification in East Asia.

Through such undisciplinary, holistic world-systems analysis at the national level, this book argues, modern East Asia has passed through the following periodization in the past 2 centuries: incorporation, regionalization, ascent, and centrality.

Incorporation. Instead of focusing merely on post-World War II development, the long time-span orientation of world-systems analysis will call upon researchers to begin their research from the early 19th century—the period when East Asia was incorporating into the capitalist world economy. The concept of incorporation, for instance, will direct researchers to such questions as: What was East Asia like before its incorporation into the world economy? When, why, and through what historical processes and events did East Asia start incorporating into the world economy? What were the different forms of incorporating the East Asian states into the world economy? How did the people in East Asia react to the incorporation process? And how did the incorporation processes affect the subsequent development of East Asia? Chapters 2 and 3 will study the divergent patterns of incorporating China and Japan into the world economy, respectively.

Regionalization. Instead of focusing on what happened within any given nation-state boundary, the large-scale orientation of world-systems analysis will call upon researchers to extend their unit of analysis to the entire East Asian region. It will direct researchers to address new issues with regard to interstate dynamics in the East Asian region. For example, why did Japan, a semiperipheral state, immediately start a project of East Asian regionalization right after its incorporation into the world economy? How did this Japanese regionalization project shape the historical development of Taiwan, Korea, and even mainland China? And how did this East Asian regionalization project, in return, profoundly transform the Japanese economy, politics, and society in the first half of the 20th century? Chapter 4 will examine the efforts of Japan in trying to construct an East Asian empire in the early 20th century, and Chapter 5 will trace how Japan's regionalization project altered China's path of development.

Ascent. Instead of confining itself to the study of capitalist states in East Asia, the world-systems analysis concept of antisystemic movements will call upon researchers to examine the origins, development, and transformation of Communist regimes in the East Asian region. For example, it will direct researchers to raise such questions as: Why were antisystemic movements successful in mainland China and North Korea but not in other states in East Asia? How did the consolidation of American hegemony after World War II affect the path of socialist development in China? What explains the Chinese shift in strategy from attempting to transform the world economy in the 1960s to pursuing upward mobility within the world economy since 1978? And what impact did the Communist revolutions in East Asia have on the upward mobility strategies of Japan, Korea, Taiwan, and Hong Kong after World War II? Chapter 6 will study China's socialist path of ascent, and Chapters 7 and 8 will explain Japan's rise to the core and the NIEs' rise to the semiperiphery, respectively.

Centrality. By the 1980s, East Asia has become a new epicenter of capital accumulation in the world economy. Instead of assuming that underdevelopment is inevitable and the Asian "dragons" are in distress, the concepts of hegemony and rivalry in world-systems analysis will call upon researchers to examine how the "corization" of Japan and its economic dominance in East Asia in the last 2 decades of the 20th century have inevitably run into conflict with the United States, and how the reunification project among mainland China, Taiwan, and Hong Kong has created the possibility of a powerful Chinese nation-state in the next century. For example, to what extent is U.S. hegemony in the world economy threatened by the rise of East Asia as a new center of capital accumulation in the world economy? What are the political-economic bases for the newly increased Japan-bashing in the United States? How did the prospect for Chinese national reunification among mainland China, Taiwan, and Hong Kong transform East Asian politics and economy? Chapter 9 will look into the origins and development of United States-Japan hegemonic rivalry, and Chapter 10 will examine the intricate relationship in the Chinese triangle of mainland China, Taiwan, and Hong Kong.

In short, incorporation, regionalization, ascent, and centrality are some of the pertinent issues informed by a world-systems analysis on the historical development of modern East Asia. We will discuss these issues in more detail in the rest of this book.

PART II

Incorporation

Since the emergence of the capitalist world economy in the 16th century, there has been a constant expansion of its outer boundaries to other parts of the world. In world-systems analysis, incorporation was a result of the exhaustion of leading monopolies, which led to periodic stagnation in the world economy. The expansion of the boundaries of the world economy, therefore, was a mode of incorporating new low-cost labor in the peripheries, which in effect compensated for the increase of real wages in the core (in order to promote effective demand) and thereby kept the global average wage down.

Nevertheless, the process of incorporation was not unproblematic. As Wallerstein (1988) points out, people everywhere offered resistance, of varying efficacy, to the process of incorporation because it "was so unattractive a proposition in terms both of immediate material interests and the cultural values of those being incorporated."

Therefore, when capitalism started to develop in Western Europe in the 16th century, the East Asia states quickly adopted an exclusive policy to shut themselves off to foreigners. In Wallerstein's (1976) terminology, East Asia thus became "an external arena" of the capitalist world economy.

The core states in Western Europe had naturally made many attempts to incorporate East Asia into the capitalist world economy since the 16th century. The Portuguese were the first to send warships and trading boats to China to request the expansion of foreign trade. Then arrived the Spanish, the Dutch, the British, the French, and the Americans. However, it was not until the mid-19th century that East Asia began to be incorporated into the world economy.

This timing is crucial because it helps to explain the specific mode of incorporation of East Asia into the world economy. In the mid-19th century, the world economy was in an upward phase, marked by very rapid industrialization. Great Britain was the hegemon during this period, with a virtual monopoly in industrial production and military technology. This industrial and military strength fostered Great Britain's promoting the doctrine of free trade and market incorporation—the extending of British interests informally through a vast market network, rather than by direct colonial rule (Dixon, 1991).

China, in this respect, became a necessary component of British economic hegemony, because the Chinese market offered what appeared to be an outlet for the booming productivity of the British-led new manufacturing era. On the other hand, other states in East Asia (Japan and Korea) had received much less attention from Western core states as they were small in size, lacking in market potential, and situated outside the European trade routes. It is, therefore, of no historical coincidence that China was the first, Japan was the second, and Korea was the last to be incorporated into the world economy.

As such, the crucial research question that needs to be addressed is: How did such market mode and historical sequencing of incorporation into the capitalist world economy affect East Asian development? In Chapter 2, it will be argued that market incorporation and domestic resistance had not reduced China to a periphery, thus providing some political space for the Chinese officials and merchants to start a modest self-strengthening program in the second half of the 19th century. In Chapter 3, it is further argued that market incorporation and geopolitical factors had even enabled Japan to move quickly into a semiperipheral state in a few decades.

2. The Decline of the Chinese Empire

B efore East Asia was incorporated into the capitalist world economy, it was dominated by the Chinese empire. This chapter will first examine the historical process of incorporating the Chinese empire into the world economy in the mid-19th century. Then it will highlight the repercussions of incorporation on China's politics, economy, and culture in the late 19th century. The key argument of this chapter is that China in this period was closer to a declining empire than to a periphery. China was by no means a peripheral country, because it still possessed a considerable overseas tributary empire. But the cost of maintaining this empire also served as a critical weakness of the Chinese state.

PREINCORPORATED CHINA
IN THE EARLY 19TH CENTURY

The Chinese Empire in East Asia

Before its incorporation into the capitalist world economy, China was the Middle Kingdom, a world empire that dominated the East Asian region. The Chinese empire had developed a tributary system for foreigners and foreign trade.

In this tributary system, foreigners were granted permission to establish trade with China on the condition that their ruler or the ruler's emissaries demonstrate subservience to the Chinese emperor by personally bearing him tribute. On presenting the tribute, usually a largely token offering of native products, the foreigners also had to perform *ke tou* (kowtow), which consisted of three kneelings and nine bows of the head to the floor in the presence of the emperor. In return, the Chinese emperor formally invested the foreign power with the nominal status of a vassal, provided it with an imperial letter of patent, and allowed it to establish trade and contact with China (Higgins, 1992, p. 30).

Through this tributary system, Chinese languages, culture, and ideology spread to Korea, Vietnam, areas of Inner Asia, and Japan, making these countries look to Confucian China as the source of civilization. In this respect, the system of political relations in preincorporated East Asia was a hierarchical one—with the Chinese empire at the top, surrounded by its vassal neighbors (Liu, 1980).

From the perspective of tributary relations, the Chinese imperial bureaucrats perceived the Westerners as no different from their East Asian neighbors. The Westerners, too, were "barbarians" who should observe the rules of the tributary system and fit themselves into the civilized Sinocentric world order in their pursuit of foreign trade. Therefore, although the Chinese empire had been closely linked to other regions of the world through long trading networks for many centuries (Abu-Lughod, 1989; Jones, Frost, & White, 1993), this long-distance trade was always under the close supervision of the Chinese imperial state.

Particularly since the 7th century, an exclusive policy had been adopted by the Chinese state toward trade with the capitalist world economy. In 1836, 307 foreigners were confined to 13 groups of buildings called "factories," in a total space of 1,100 feet by 700 feet. These buildings were the property of Chinese Hang merchants and were leased to the foreigners, who were forbidden to trade outside these 13 factories and were not allowed to enter the city of Canton (Guangzhou). They could not even reside permanently in these buildings, as they had to leave South China at the end of the trading season (Banister, 1931, p. 99).

In addition, the foreigners had to contend with the *gong hang* monopoly. As See (1919) points out:

> The main concern of the foreign trader was to sell his import cargo, and if he did, he must sell it to his security merchant only, and to none other. . . . Furthermore, it was only through his security merchant that he could buy his export cargo. (pp. 66-67)

Furthermore, Chinese foreign trade was only a trade of luxury goods. It consisted mostly of tea and silk, with very little in the way of bulk goods or necessities. As a result, China's foreign trade made very little headway from the 16th century to the turn of the 19th century.

Finally, foreign trade was a one-way enterprise, with China exporting large quantities of tea and silk but importing only moderate quantities of cotton and wool in return. These favorable terms of trade meant a net flow of silver coins from the West to China.

In short, China's trade with the West exhibited the following characteristics: geographical restriction to Canton, *gong hang* monopoly, luxury goods, and inflow of silver. According to Wallerstein (1989, pp. 131-136), these are typical characteristics of trading between the capitalist world economy and an external arena.

What then explains China's capacity to remain an external arena up to the early 19th century? Answering this question will require our examining the remarkable state and class structure of China before it was incorporated into the world economy.

State and Class Structure

Unlike the European feudal system, where state capacity was restrained by parcelled sovereignty, the Chinese imperial state was a centralized bureaucracy with the capacity to unite China into one society. The Chinese state under the Qing dynasty was staffed by approximately 40,000 officials, who were literati degree-holders who had passed government-sponsored examinations on Confucian classics. Because only the landed upper class had the security and resources to devote itself to the leisurely life of Confucian literati, the examination system served as a vital political channel, binding the landed upper class with the state (Moore, 1966, pp. 162-174; Skocpol, 1979, pp. 69-72).

The landed upper class was significantly strengthened by its links to the state. Passing the imperial examinations and becoming state officials had greatly enhanced the upper class's status, turning its members into respectable gentry responsible for running local community affairs. Moreover, office holding, accompanied by corruption and "squeezes," was a very important source of revenue in the Qing dynasty for consolidating or even expanding land ownership (Chang, 1955, 1962).

The Chinese state, though, was highly wary of the usurpation of local power by the landed upper class. As a result, the state tried hard to enforce the loyalty of officials. First, in accordance with a "rule of avoidance," landed upper-class members appointed as governors and magistrates had to supervise provinces other than those in which they were born and raised. They were also not allowed to employ family members without official permission. Second, there was a "rule of circulation of office," in which the officials were frequently transferred and scrambled in different mixes in order to avoid the development of permanent cliques or alliances between officials and the local upper class. Finally, duplicate jurisdictions and functions were deliberately built into the provincial administrative structures, so that the central state would have overlapping lines of surveillance and command (Michael, 1964, p. 58; Skocpol, 1979, p. 71).

As a whole, this political alliance between the landed upper class and the state worked very well in preventing other social classes from challenging the existing political order. The peasantry, for instance, was absorbed into local lineages or village associations of the landed upper class. Therefore, although hunger and poverty often existed in the countryside, the Chinese peasantry could not form an independent class organization to protect its class interest (So, 1986b, pp. 37-45). The merchants, too, were either attracted to the high status of the landed upper class or intimidated by the stringent state controls over trade. Thus they hired the best literati to educate their children, hoping that they would pass the examinations, become bureaucrats, and use government offices to assure patronage of their parents' commercial pursuits (Fairbank, 1958, pp. 42-47). As a result, despite the existence of robust trading in standard market towns, long-distance trade between the countryside and the cities, and many profitable industrial and commercial activities, these sprouts of capitalism lacked the dynamic of ceaseless capital accumulation to blossom into full-fledged capitalism (Perkins, 1969; Skinner, 1964).

However, by the end of the 18th century, there were signs that imperial political and economic order had begun to break down. First, there was phenomenal population growth from around 80 million in 1400 A.D. to around 400 million by the mid-19th century. Clearly the traditional economy was reaching the limits of its possible expansion. Then there were growing bureaucratic inefficiency, luxury consumption by the landed upper class, and increasing official corruption—all exerting more and more pressure on the overburdened and land-hungry peasantry. Consequently, the White Lotus Rebellion of 1795-1804 resulted, signaling the decline of one dynasty and the advent of its replacement (Elvin, 1973; Skocpol, 1979, pp. 74-75). These traditional forces undermining the Qing dynasty were now joined by Western imperialist intrusions in the early 19th century.

Using the excuse that the Chinese state burned several thousand chests of British property (opium), the British sent an expedition to conquer China in 1839. This was the beginning of the Opium War and attempts to incorporate China into the capitalist world economy.

INCORPORATION ATTEMPTS
AND ANTISYSTEMIC MOVEMENTS

The Opium War

The Opium War has been labeled an "accident of history." It is argued that the real intent of the Western states was not to force China to import opium, but to develop "diplomatic equality and commercial opportunity." It just happened that "Britain represented all the Western states, which would sooner or later have demanded the same things if Britain had not" (Fairbank, Reischauer, & Craig, 1978, p. 454).

Although the above argument has the merit of highlighting the quest for free trade during market incorporation in the mid-19th century, it does evade many crucial research questions that should be addressed: Why did Britain start the conquering instead of other nations? Why was opium involved rather than tea or silk? And why did the incident take place in the late 1830s but not earlier?

From a world-systems perspective, Britain was the natural candidate to start the opening of China. In the early 19th century, Britain was, to use a modern term, the superpower of the world. With the Industrial Revolution gathering force in Manchester, Britain's global economic presence surpassed that of any other Western state, and there was a strong urge to find foreign markets for British products. Furthermore, its military victories over France placed Britain at an increasing advantage in the expansion of its commerce with China. In fact, Britain was sending twice as many ships to China as all other nations combined (Borthwick, 1992, p. 89). Subsequently, Britain's policy toward China served to set the tone for other Western states.

Nevertheless, it was only after successfully transforming the political economy of its Indian colony and developing the India-China-Britain triangular trade that Britain began to have a strong interest in opening China. The British encouraged the cultivation of opium in India, shipped it to China, and used it to pay for tea and silk. In the beginning, the amount of Indian opium imported into China was fairly small, about 200 chests in 1760 and about 4,000 chests in 1800. But opium importation rose drastically in the early 19th century, jumping to 20,000 chests in the 1820s and 30,000 chests in the 1830s (Hsiao, 1967, p. 411; Wong, 1976, p. 23). As opium production expanded, it soon came to provide one seventh of the annual revenue of the British government in India, and it played an important role in the India-Great Britain balance of payments. In addition, it also started the outflow of silver from China to Britain, because China had became the major market for staple goods produced in British India (Moulder, 1977, pp. 101-102).

Thus, the involvement of opium was no mere accident. Still, Anglo-Sino conflict would not begin until the deregulation of British trade in Canton. As Wallerstein (1989, p. 167) points out, "the triangular trade was an invention of the East India Company," which monopolized the growing of opium in India and exports to China. As long as the East India Company traders maintained the monopoly of foreign trade to China and were able to reap rapid fortunes, they were quite satisfied with the restricted trading conditions in Canton. But the deregulation of British trade in the late 1830s had led to a flood of new British merchants attempting to enter the lucrative business. When British free country traders began to enter China on an increasing scale in the 1840s, they found the old Cantonese trading system intolerable—they had no access to markets; they could not even walk down a street of shops; and they could not send agents out to inquire about prices, but in all cases had to accept without objections the prices offered by the Hang merchants. It was under such restricted trading conditions that these country traders used the ideology of free trade to justify the British military expedition in the 1840s.

In the spring of 1841, British troops were ambushed as they marched through San Yuan Li on their way to attack Canton; a dozen British soldiers were killed (siao, 1967, p. 492). This was the legendary San Yuan Li Incident, the first antisystemic movement that emerged in resistence to China's incorporation into the capitalist world economy.

The San Yuan Li Movement

Most sociological studies that deal with the Opium War have neglected this crucial San Yuan Li Incident (Moore, 1966; Moulder, 1977; Skocpol, 1979). They simply assume that the incorporation process was unproblematic, that the Western states were so strong that they could easily incorporate China into the capitalist world economy. Skocpol (1979, p. 73), for instance, asserts: "Britain could back the aspirations of its citizens for expanded 'free trade' in all of China with the military organization and technology born of industrialization. After inflicting decisive naval defeats on Chinese forces in the Opium War of 1839-42, Britain achieved expanded trading rights."

However, the incorporation process was far from unproblematic. The threat of foreign conquest led to local militarization in South China. At the peak of the antiforeign movement in the 1840s, the local militia was the organization that recruited men and raised money for regional defense. Led by the landed upper class, the local militia received popular support in South China. This was because the importation of opium and the draining of silver out of China had given the landed upper class an ideological basis for uniting the peasantry to fight against foreign intrusion (So, 1984, pp. 96-99). Thus, during the San Yuan Li Incident, "upon the sound of the gong, people from 103 villages gathered, men and women numbering several thousand" (Hsiao, 1967, p. 493).

The historical significance of San Yuan Li is that it became a legend in the antiforeign movement. Temples were built to glorify the defeat of the British, and participants in the incident were treated as heroes (NHHC, 1873, *chuan* 5:5). It was unimportant that only a dozen British soldiers were actually killed in the incident; what was important was the belief that the landed upper class and the peasantry in South China had defeated the British. According to Wakeman (1966, p. 53), "this belief was probably the most important single motive of the later anti-foreign movement."

Faced with such strong local opposition in South China, the British expedition changed its strategy. It moved north, attacking Nanking [Nanjing], and won the Opium War. What followed was the signing of the Treaty of Nanking, the opening of treaty ports to foreign trade, the ceding of Hong Kong, and the payment of indemnities to the British. This quickening of the incorporation process, incidentally, also led to the Taiping Rebellion.

The Taiping Rebellion

After the signing of the peace treaty, the antiforeign movement in South China not only failed to subside, but had actually intensified. Facing a spectacular rise of illegal activities (such as smuggling, the export of indentured labor, dealing in arms and other contraband), the people of South China were determined to keep the "barbarian" out of their local communities. The 1840s, therefore, witnessed what Engels (1972, p. 124) described as the Chinese popular war against foreign intrusion. As recorded in Britain's *The Chinese Repository*: In 1842, "the British flagstaff was set on fire . . . the British factory was set on fire, and the veranda, chapel-belfry and skylight were soon burning furiously." Although the Treaty of Nanking allowed foreigners to move their residences from the congested *gong hang* to the city of Canton, they were still denied this privilege because the Chinese "declared the impossibility of living under the same heavens with the English devils, and swore to destroy them." When the foreigners pushed for their treaty rights in 1846, riots occurred. "Shat fan-kuei, ta fan-kwei (kill the foreign devils, beat the foreign devils) raged and echoed through all the streets in the vicinity of the foreign factories. Hundreds of the basest of men were already collected and many hundreds more were hastening to the scene of riot" (*Chinese Repository*, 1842, vol. 11, p. 687; 1846, vol. 15, p. 365).

Because the foreigners had already won the Opium War, they now had few reasons to stay in Canton in the face of such strong local opposition. Accordingly, the foreigners deserted Canton and started their business enterprises anew in Shanghai, which supplanted the former as the chief center of foreign trade (*Consular Report*, 1889, p. 382). In Shanghai, the foreigners found scope and opportunity for the full exercise of their new facilities and privileges, and trading methods there were more enterprising than they had been under the domination of the old *gong hang* system in Canton.

After the Opium War, Canton was no longer a national center of general distribution, but only a distributor to the southern provinces; its foreign trade subsequently dropped drastically. British import trade to Canton dropped from $15.5 million in 1844 to $6.5 million in 1848; and British export trade dropped from $18 million to $8.6 million in the same period. This decrease in foreign trade had affected South China in the following ways: First, it meant a loss of customs revenue for Canton, dropping from 19.5 million taels in 1846 to 14 million taels in 1848. Because the Opium War had dried up the treasury of Guangdong province, a further decrease in tax revenue from customs could only be compensated for by increasing taxation on the peasantry. Second, the decrease of foreign trade had resulted in massive unemployment of transportation workers located at trade routes, putting as many as 100,000 porters and 10,000 boatmen out of work. Third, the dislocation of the regional economy led to the mushrooming of secret societies and bandit gangs, whose membership was drawn from the affected porters, boatmen, and discharged soldiers (Wakeman, 1966, pp. 98-100; Wong, 1976, p. 136).

Finally, the South China secret societies raised the banner of dynastic revolt and transformed themselves into the Taiping Rebellion in 1851. In 1852 more than 10,000 Taiping rebels marched north toward the Yangtze provinces, gathering tens of thousands more supporters along the way. The Taipings defeated all the imperial armies that the state sent against them. In 1853, with an army of more than half a million men, the Taipings established their capital in Nanjing. The leader of the rebellion, Hong Xiuquan, claimed that he was the younger son of Jesus Christ and prepared religious tracts based on Protestant pamphlets and Utopian Communism. In his Heavenly Kingdom, landlordism was to be abolished and the land divided equally among the peasants. Surplus beyond individual needs was to be gathered in public storehouses and allocated in accordance with community goals. Equality between the sexes was to be established. Opium smoking, as well as drinking and gambling, were to be forbidden (Moulder, 1977, pp. 155-156).

Fighting for its survival, the Qing government made two strategic moves to deal with the Taipings. First, it lifted its "rule of avoidance" and "rule of circulation of offices." Officials were urged to go back to their native provinces, utilize their kinship networks and resources, and expand local militia into provincial armies. In the turmoil of war, locals were frequently appointed as provincial governors and were allowed to use provincial taxes and the new *likin* tax on goods in transit to finance the armies. Another strategic move by the Qing government was to seek help from Westerners. At first, Westerners were sympathetic to the Taipings because of the movement's links to Christianity. But Westerners changed their views after the Taipings prohibited opium smoking, after trade became increasingly disrupted as the conflict dragged on, and after Taiping armies attacked Shanghai. At this point, the West began giving military support to the Qing imperial government and the regional armies. British and American officers also trained and led Chinese soldiers and foreign mercenaries to defend Shanghai and other cities. These two strategies of the Qing government proved to work very well. Provincial armies were highly effective in containing the Taiping rebels, and foreign weapons helped hasten the disintegration of the Taiping Kingdom in 1864 (Cohen, 1970, pp. 32-38; Moulder, 1977, pp. 157-159).

Nevertheless, the Taiping Rebellion had exerted a profound impact on the Chinese state. First, the long period of the Taiping Rebellion (1851-1864), the sheer magnitude of the problems created in its aftermath, and the spread of the rebellion to other regions had monopolized the Qing government's energies in handling these domestic crises. As a result, the Qing government had little time to respond to Western invasions during the 1850s. Therefore, almost 2 decades had lapsed before the Qing government was able to formulate any coherent policy to deal with China's incorporation into the capitalist world economy. In addition, the Taiping Rebellion had considerably weakened the Qing government. Drained by the decade-long war with the rebels, by lifting the crucial "rule of avoidance and office circulation," and by allowing the provinces to control and collect taxation, the central Qing government could no longer control the provinces in the same way it had before. Thus emerged the trend of regional power and militarism in the late 19th century.

Beginning in the 1840s, therefore, the Chinese empire was under considerable stress; many students of modern Chinese history are quick to point to the harmful impact of imperialism and core domination in tearing the Chinese empire apart.

THE DECLINE OF THE CHINESE EMPIRE

Core Domination

The Qing government waged a number of wars against the Western core states in the mid- and late 19th century. After losing all these wars, it was forced to sign "unequal treaties," which constituted a significant encroachment on China's sovereignty. The 1842 Treaty of Nanking and the 1860 Convention of Peking [Beijing], for instance, included the following features (Moulder, 1977, pp. 106-110):

- The opening of more Chinese seaports (called treaty ports) for trade. Western imports could now pass into the interior of China duty-free, after payment of import duties at the port plus a small extra charge.
- The ceding of Hong Kong and the adjacent Kowloon peninsula to Britain.
- The establishment of extraterritoriality. The Qing government lost the right of jurisdiction over foreigners in China.
- The abolition of tariff autonomy. China's tariffs were reduced to about 5% ad valorem.
- The payment of indemnities to the British, for example, 21 million taels after the Opium War and 16 million taels after the Second Opium War. This was secured by the Chinese customs revenues, which, in the meantime, had come under the control of Western states.
- Permitting Western merchants, missionaries, politicians, and so on to travel outside the treaty ports and into the interior for trading, proselytizing, and the like, upon acquisition of passports from their consuls in the ports.
- Permitting Western warships to anchor at the treaty ports to protect commerce. Each nation was granted most-favored-nation status, whereby any subsequent privileges granted to one nation would automatically accrue to others.

In addition to the above political encroachment, there was economic encroachment. First, there was Western dominance in shipping, in shipbuilding and repairs. Throughout the 19th century, China's foreign commerce was carried largely on Western-owned ships, and Western firms constructed large shipyards in the treaty ports as early as the 1860s. Second, Western firms were involved in manufacturing for the Chinese domestic markets. By the 1880s Western firms were producing paper, matches, soap, cotton textiles, and cigarettes in China. The influx of these Western products destroyed rural handicraft industries in the villages, causing unemployment and hardship for the Chinese peasantry. Third, the importation of opium continued to increase after the Opium War. It was only 40,000 chests in 1838, but rose to a peak of 87,000 in 1879. Opium and foreign imports led to an outflow of specie to Western states (Moulder, 1977, pp. 102, 111-114). Thomas (1984) estimates that

> the largest single loss caused by foreign intervention was the 817 million taels of opium that China was forced to allow to be imported from 1870 to 1897. Opium purchases soaked up about 29 million tael per year or the equivalent of about one-third of the annual revenue of the Chi'ng [Qing] central government. The outlay of China's cash for opium was greater than its land taxes, the largest single source of government revenue. (p. 65)

Finally, accompanying the political-economic encroachment was cultural encroachment. The Convention of Peking opened China to missionary activities, granting French missionaries the right to buy or rent land and to erect buildings in the interior of China, outside the treaty ports. With the blessings of the unequal treaties, missionaries proceeded to penetrate China. In the 1870s there were more than 13,000 Protestants and 300,000 Catholics; by the 1890s, the number had risen rapidly— 80,000 Protestants and more than a half million Catholics (Moulder, 1977, p. 125). According to Cohen (1970, pp. 53-55), the missionaries directly undermined the cultural hegemony of the Chinese landed upper class; missionary attacks on ancestor worship and "idolatrous" folk festivals offended all Chinese, not merely the elites. In addition, the missionaries' exploitation of their privileged legal status (such as intervening in lawsuits to aid their parishioners) served to challenge the authority of the Qing officials.

Nevertheless, despite this political, economic, and cultural encroachment, China had not yet degenerated from an empire to a periphery in the late 19th century. This is an important argument because it differs from those offered in the China field.

In the literature, students of the modernization school argue that the foreigners were just "the outsiders" in the Chinese political economy, and their impact on China was small. Had foreigners played a more significant role, they would have brought more positive benefits to enhance China's modernization. The roots of China's backwardness, then, were such negative factors associated with Confucianism—conservative traditions, corruption, the dearth of innovative ideas, and a lack of risk-taking entrepreneurs (Dernberger, 1975; Fairbank, 1958; Murphey, 1977; Rawski, 1978).

On the other hand, students sympathetic to the radical dependency school charge:

> Imperialism came to China as an unwelcome intruder: pushing opium, Christianity and cotton yarn. The opium enhanced political corruption and moral decay; Christianity threatened the values and the status of the gentry; and the yarn deprived handicraft spinners of their livelihood. . . . Imperialism produced economic, social and political disruptions, distortions, and instability of such a nature as to make successful modernization of any bourgeoisie-democratic variety impossible. (Esherick, 1972, p. 10, 14; see also Lasek, 1983; Wright, 1986)

In spite of both schools' different interpretations of the deterrents to China's development, they basically share the basic assumption that China in the late 19th century had become a backward periphery, either unable to promote modernization or unable to resist imperialist encroachment. In other words, both schools' literature assumes that "if China was not an empire, then it must have fallen into a periphery." Examining the political, economic, and cultural development of China in the late 19th century, however, shows that China was closer to a declining empire than to a periphery.

Declining Empire, Not Periphery

At the political level, China was still an empire in the following three aspects: (a) It continued to dominate its vassal states; (b) it promoted diplomatic equality in the interstate systems; and (c) it still possessed a state to protect its interests.

First of all, the Chinese state maintained its influence over its vassal states, as it protected Korea from Western imperialist dominations. Thus Liu (1980, p. xviii) remarks: "In the early 1880s China was clearly not entirely devoid of military capacity. Nor were the Chinese completely ineffective in their use of Western military equipment—warships to display in Korean harbors and telegraph lines to communicate between Tianjin [Tientsin] and Shanghai, the principal shipping center."

Second, although the new treaty system shook the foundation of the tributary system of the Chinese empire, it merely affirmed the principle of diplomatic equality between China and its Western treaty partners. Thus, the Qing government set up the Zongli Yamen (a proto-foreign office) to handle diplomatic relations with the West arising from various treaty obligations. The 1860s saw some of the Qing officials, such as Prince Gong, formulate the so-called cooperative policy. This policy argued that there was no better way for China to protect itself from foreign imperialism than to abide by the provisions of the Sino-Western treaties, which could at least restrain Western intrusion to some extent (Liu, 1980, p. xv). Of course, the Western core states in the world economy were senior partners who often took advantage of the Qing government, but the Chinese state had not yet been fully deprived of its autonomy, nor become a colony or semicolony totally subservient to foreign rule.

Third, as a result, China still possessed a fairly strong state to safeguard its own interests. Up to the last decade of the 19th century, the Chinese government prevented foreign participation in public utilities, such as telephone and telegraph services. China also was able to avoid significant borrowing of foreign capital, because of the fear of foreign control. The sums that the Qing government borrowed were small, only about 13 million pounds from the West, up to 1894 (Moulder, 1977, p. 114, 116).

In sum, although China was inserted into the interstate system of the capitalist world economy under Western domination, these core controls through the unequal treaties had not kept China from maintaining control over its vassal states, or from striving for diplomatic equality, or from protecting its domestic interests.

At the economic level, China was not a periphery because it maintained control over its production processes. Although export-oriented cash crop regions such as the South China silk district began to develop, although foreign imports increased, and although the foreigners exercised monopolies in such industries as shipping, the foreigners had failed to extend their control into rural China and restructure its production processes. Thus, although the Chinese economy had been, to a certain extent, incorporated into the capitalist world economy by the late 19th century, China's economy was still mostly owned and managed by Chinese merchants and industrialists.

Take the silk industry, for example. Jardine, Matheson and Company had set up a modern silk-reeling filature in Shanghai in 1861, but Chinese merchants refused to supply them with the needed high-quality cocoons, forcing Jardine to close its modern filature. Jardine lost HK$276,000 during the dozen years of its existence (Brown, 1979; Eng, 1986, p. 38). In South China, where local opposition to foreign domination remained strong, no foreigner had ever owned a silk factory. As one British consul in Canton remarked: "Foreigners had little left to them other than the export trade" (quoted by Allen & Donnithorne, 1954, p. 41). But even within the scope of the export business, foreign firms seldom had any direct contact with Chinese manufacturers. The native Chinese compradors of the foreign firms conducted the whole export transaction; they contacted the merchants of the Chinese silk commission house, determined how much to buy, settled the price, and tested the silk quality. Because the foreigners failed to exercise any control over the production and marketing processes, they were unable to negotiate prices in their favor. An American consul in Canton thus complained:

> Foreign merchants in China, with millions of dollars of capital at their command and fleets of ships in waiting . . . have never yet been able to fix the price of these Chinese products, but have always been compelled to submit to the prices and terms of the silk-guilds, and do their business in China through native compradors, and comply with Chinese arrangement generally, and all because of the inability of foreign merchants and capitalists to cope with or override or break down the influence of the trade of China. (*Consular Report*, 1886, pp. 265-266)

While avoiding foreign domination, the South China silk industry developed rapidly. In the 1880s, there were only 6 modern filatures, employing 2,970 workers, and exporting 2,516 piculs of steam-reeled raw silk annually. By the 1890s, the number of modern filatures jumped to 63, employing 31,185 workers, and exporting 26,847 piculs of steam-reeled raw silk annually. This started the rise of the Chinese bourgeoisie and the big push toward rural industrialization around Canton (So, 1986b, pp. 103-116).

At the cultural level, China was not a periphery in the sense that its Confucianism—the ideology of the state and the landed upper class—

was still in full force, preserving the existing political and social order. Despite the assault by Western missionaries on Chinese Confucianism and superstition, these efforts had not been successful because of China's domestic strong antimissionary movement in the late 19th century. Cohen's (1963) work on missionaries during the 1860s lists 34 major incidents in 12 different provinces during that decade that involved personal injury and/or property damage, and in which 24 foreigners and 130 Chinese Christians were killed. The threat to the culture and power of the landed upper class prompted them to organize antimissionary riots and attacks on Christian church property. Even the imperial government was incapable of stopping the outbreaks, no matter how much foreign consuls urged it to do so.

What then explains China's ability to avoid political, economic, and cultural peripheralization up to the last decade of the 19th century? First of all, although the Qing state had been weakened by external intrusion and internal rebellion, the Chinese landed upper class emerged from these processes strengthened. Members of this class gained control over the provincial tax base; they were allowed to serve in their native provinces and organize local militia. Their influence over local villages also remained intact. Therefore, it was this strong landed upper class, together with its popular antiforeign movement, that halted China from the degeneration into a periphery. For example, no sooner had the British and French successfully occupied Canton in 1858 than the landed upper class in South China expanded the local militia into the Guangdong Central Militia Bureau to fight the foreigners. In Wakeman's (1966) account:

> The rural militia terrorized the city during the first month of 1858. Policemen and soldiers were seized whenever they wandered near the gates. . . . Incendiary rockets and arsonists fired on buildings every night. The wealthier classes fled the city. The suburbs, depopulated and ruined, gave cover to predatory bands. The foreigners, whether in the provincial capital or in Hong Kong, even found it difficult to buy food or hire help: the district magistrates ordered shopkeepers to leave Canton, and twenty thousand laborers returned to their homes from Victoria. (p. 168)

What was a foreign army to do against South China residents who took such a fanatical part in the struggle against the foreigners? Where—and how far—could a foreign army penetrate into the enemy's country, and how would it maintain itself there? Canton might be totally destroyed and the coasts nibbled at all possible points, but all the forces the British could bring together would not suffice to conquer and hold the two provinces of South China. What, then, could the British forces do further?

In addition, there was the factor of rivalry among Western core states. For instance, other foreign merchants were highly dissatisfied with the British and the French occupation of Canton in 1858. The American consul asserted that the British officers disregarded the safety of foreign trade and urged that neutral trade should not be allowed to suffer because of the problems between the British and the Chinese (Griffin, 1938, p. 243). As in the case of imperialism in other regions, there was always the problem of imperialist rivalry in China: how to divide the fruits of victory, who gets what, and how much? The occupation of Canton in 1858 presented so many complications for the British and the French that it kept them inactive in South China for 4 years. After Britain and France returned Canton to the Qing government in the early 1860s, there was no more direct foreign aggression on China proper until the 1890s.

This breathing space from the 1860s to the 1890s, then, provided a golden opportunity for the Chinese empire to rebuild itself after facing challenges from the capitalist world economy.

REBUILDING THE CHINESE EMPIRE

The Self-Strengthening Movement

After defeating the Taipings and holding the foreigners at bay in the 1860s, China's powerful provincial governors at first called for the Qing government to develop new military projects. Thus, Li Hongzhang set up several gun factories, two major arsenals, and a machine factory; Zuo Zongtang, another regional ruler, set up the large Foochow dockyard and a school for navigation and shipbuilding (Moulder, 1977, p. 189). The rationale for these military adventures, as Li explained to the court, was "that the foreigners' domination of China was based on the superiority of their weapons . . . in order to strengthen herself China must learn to use Western machinery, which implied the training of Chinese personnel" (quoted in Fairbank, 1958, p. 144).

In the 1870s the provincial governors further called for the development of nonmilitary projects. These proposed projects had two major goals: to strengthen China's ability to resist foreign domination, and to achieve financial success and profitability. For the first goal, Chinese officials developed an alliance between the state and merchant capital. Under the so-called Guan Du Shang Ban system (better translated as "government-supervised merchant undertakings"), the state would provide loans and other support, and selected merchants (usually chosen from those who had experience with foreign business) would provide management and investment capital. Foreigners were totally excluded from these enterprises, because Chinese officials believed that Chinese ownership was the only way to retain the benefits of industrialization. For the second profitability goal, advanced foreign technology would be imported and foreign technicians would be hired in order to maximize productivity. In addition, the proposed enterprises would be set up in core economic sectors that could gain maximum advantage from forward and backward linkages (Thomas, 1984, p. 64).

The first proposed industrial enterprise was the modern Chinese shipping company, called China Merchants' Steam Navigation Company. Established in 1872, it was designed to regain control of China's internal shipping, to counter foreign control of this strategic area, and to gain some of the income lost to foreign companies. By the early 1890s, China was reported to have a total of 76 modern manufacturing enterprises and 33 coal and metal mines. Some of the key government-supervised merchant undertakings included: the Kaiping Coal Mines, the Imperial Telegraph Administration, the Imperial Chinese Railway Administration, the Shanghai Cotton Cloth Mills, and the Heng Yang Ironworks (Feuerwerker, 1969, p. 36; Thomas, 1984, pp. 17, 81). Was the Self-Strengthening Movement working?

Economic Success, Political-Military Failure

In the literature, the Self-Strengthening Movement is usually portrayed as a failure. For many historians in China, this economic effort was flawed from its inception, because China was already overwhelmed by foreign domination from the 1860s, and because the leaders of these projects acted only in self-interest or in the interest of the foreigners (Feuerwerker, 1968a). For many historians in the United States, this late-19th-century industrialization also proved to be generally abortive because of the traditional obstacles to modernization. Thus, it is pointed out that conservative officials objected to the proposed projects; that the enterprises were hamstrung by bureaucracy; that the approved projects were underfunded; that few Chinese officials and merchants were familiar with foreign technology or business methods; and that corrupt officials and greedy merchants milked the enterprises' current profits instead of reinvesting them (Fairbank, 1958, pp. 142-146).

However, a study by Thomas (1984) on the economic projects of the Self-Strengthening Movement has challenged the above interpretations. With regard to foreign domination, Thomas agrees that foreign domination had obstructed Chinese industrialization. For one thing, Chinese entrepreneurs had to operate within a domestic environment in which foreign merchants enjoyed special economic privileges: Foreign indemnities and opium imports drained China's capital market; foreign diplomats occasionally used superior military power to expand the competitive edge of foreign merchants. Using extraterritoriality, or freedom from Chinese laws, foreign merchants were able to avoid the Chinese state's legal power over fraud, deception, financial manipulation, and nonpayment of debts.

Nevertheless, Thomas argues that, in spite of the combined burdens of foreign domination and domestic obstacles, some Chinese officials were still able to create a nurturing environment for domestic industrialization. After examining five key self-strengthening enterprises, Thomas documented that Chinese merchants were able to combine national-level resources with their managerial expertise. The enterprises they developed were successful in maintaining Chinese control and were economically profitable. China's pre-1894 record of economic success compares favorably with Japan's poor record from 1868 to 1880. Feuerwerker (1958, p. 53) further points out that before "the Sino-Japanese War the disparity between the degree of modern economic development in the two countries was not yet flagrant."

Why were most Chinese self-strengthening enterprises successful? For Thomas (1984, pp. 102-105), the explanation lies in the following factors. With regard to foreign domination, Thomas stresses that before 1894, the Qing government still retained sufficient sovereignty to ex-

clude foreigners from most core areas of economic development. With
regard to China's so-called lack of entrepreneurship, Thomas points out
that Chinese compradors adapted quickly to Western ways, including the
use of foreign technology and the joint-stock company, and soon became
capable managers. Talented compradors also left foreign firms to
manage Chinese self-strengthening enterprises. According to Thomas,
the cooperation between the merchants and the Chinese state was most
critical in protecting such enterprises during periods of foreign domination and domestic constraints.

With regard to the charge of Chinese corruption, Thomas reveals that
although the Qing officials were famous for corruption, they had successfully resisted most foreign bribes and pressures, such as offers of
personal loans from representatives of Jardines. Finally, with regard
to the so-called Confucian-based conservative opposition to the Self-
Strengthening Movement, it is worth noting that the provincial governors had proposed an innovative way of reinterpreting Confucianism to
endorse the self-strengthening projects. The best-known illustration is
the phrase *Zhong Xue Wei Ti, Xi Xue Wei Yong* ("Chinese learning for
the essential principles, Western learning for the practical applications").
Because Western guns, ships, and machinery were seen as merely practical applications to bring wealth and power to China, and because
Western practices were seen as nonthreatening to the dominant Confucian values, this pragmatic interpretation of Confucianism greatly
helped to legitimize the adoption of Western technology and military in
the early 1870s. Thomas argues further that as each new enterprise
succeeded, support for industrialization grew. So, by the early 1890s,
even the most conservative officials agreed to the need for industrialization in China. There was official support for almost all industrial projects, so long as they remained under Chinese control.

As such, by the early 1890s, with its own shipping company, telegraph
administration, coal mine, cotton mill complex, and ironworks, it could
be argued that the Chinese empire was at that time able to avoid the fate
of falling into a periphery. Thomas (1984) envisions an optimistic scenario that, as industrialization progressed,

> central government opposition to industrialization fell away, and Li, the
> major government promoter of economic self-strengthening, had become
> one of China's most powerful officials. China was also developing a coterie

of highly trained merchant-managers able to initiate and manage foreign-style industrial enterprises. They often capitalized new industries from earnings of previous successful enterprises. (p. 104)

The weakness of the Self-Strengthening Movement, therefore, was not in its economic failure. Rather, its fatal error was its inattention toward conducting political reforms and its failure to build up a strong military. Politically, the self-strengthening reform programs actually represented an onset of a decentralizing process in the polity. The participation of the local gentry in the antiforeign movement, the relaxation of controls over local officials, and the development of locally based military forces all signaled the decline of the central government over local forces. One symptom was the haphazard and uncoordinated nature of the various economic reform programs. Most of the modern ventures were the result of local initiatives, often induced by competition between provincial governors. The establishment of the *likin* system also strengthened local financial capacities at the expense of the central state treasury, leading to the fragmentation of the national market. Consequently, the Self-Strengthening Movement had proposed no political reforms to recentralize the state so that it could become an effective machinery to mobilize societal resources for capitalist industrialization.

In addition, the Self-Strengthening Movement had failed to achieve its primary objective of building up the military in order to defend China from future foreign aggression. This failure ultimately proved fatal for the Chinese empire. Although the emergence of local militia during the Taiping saved the Qing state from Chinese peasant rebels, they were ill-suited for the defense of China against foreign intrusion. For one thing, local militia were put under the control of provincial officials, not the centralized command of the central government. When one provincial governor was fighting foreigners, the other local armies were not necessarily forthcoming in sending reinforcements. Furthermore, as China was under the threat of maritime powers, the building of a modern fleet was critical for the integrity of the Chinese empire. The Qing state did manage to assemble a fleet, but it was plagued by the same decentralizing forces and rivalries among provincial officials. Shortages of funds continued to hinder the procurement of a modern fleet, and a professional naval command system and a well-trained and competent corps of naval officers were also conspicuously absent (Rawlinson, 1967).

The failure to consolidate central state power and to develop strong modern military forces, therefore, sealed the doom of the Self-Strengthening Movement when China proved unable to wage a concerted military and diplomatic campaign against Japan during the first Sino-Japanese War.

CONCLUSION

This chapter examines the historical process of China's incorporation into the capitalist world economy. At the turn of the 19th century, China was an East Asian empire with a centralized bureaucracy and a strong landed upper class. Foreign trade at Canton was tightly controlled, because the Chinese state perceived trade as a favor granted to vassal states. It took Britain's waging the Opium War in 1839 to open up China for trade and diplomacy. Britain took the lead because it was the hegemonic power during this period, and because it developed a highly profitable opium trade between China and its colonies in India. Nevertheless, there was a robust antisystemic movement in South China against foreign intrusion, enabling Britain to move its economic base from Canton to Shanghai in Central China. This sudden shift of foreign trade in the 1840s caused the loss of customs revenue and unemployment in South China, leading to the Taiping Rebellion in the 1850s. Facing foreign domination and internal unrest, the Chinese empire began to decline in the mid-19th century. However, China was able to avoid full-scale peripheralization in the late 19th century, because its strong landed upper class and the popular antisystemic movement, as well as imperialist rivalries among Western core states, prevented foreign intrusions into rural China. Therefore, China was still able to keep its vassal states, maintain a fairly autonomous state to protect its interests, and strive for diplomatic equality in the interstate system. Foreigners failed to own or control China's production process, nor were they successful in uprooting the Confucian cultural system. As a result, provincial Chinese officials and merchants were given political space to start a self-strengthening industrial program in the late 19th century. Judging from the economic performance of the key industrial enterprises, this self-strengthening effort worked quite well and had the potential for keeping the Chinese empire from falling apart. Nevertheless, this empire-rebuilding effort eventually collapsed, because the Self-Strengthening Movement was unable to consolidate central state power and develop a strong military force against foreign invasion.

Why is putting China in the category of *declining empire* rather than *periphery* so important? This is because the label of declining empire sensitizes researchers to better understand China's dilemma after the mid-19th century. China was by no means a peripheral country, because it still possessed a considerable overseas tributary empire. But the cost of maintaining this empire also served as a critical weakness for the Chinese state. For example, in order to protect its vassals, the Qing state was forced to engage in a war with France in the 1880s, and in another war with Japan in the 1890s. Successive defeats in these wars further weakened the central authority of the Qing state and drained resources away from investment in the Self-Strengthening Movement's projects. In this respect, there may be some similarities between 19th-century China and late-20th-century United States in that they both shared the "declining giant" syndrome. In both cases, the maintenance of an empire incurred such high economic costs that it accelerated national decline.

In addition, conceptualizing China as a declining empire sensitizes researchers to the important fact that although the Qing bureaucracy was not strong enough to totally hold off foreign encroachment, it was strong enough to suppress domestic challenges. After the imperial state held on to its power and endured the challenges of antisystemic movements, the seeds of revolutionary change from below were defeated. Subsequently, the Qing state was more interested in promoting a conservative Self-Strengthening Movement to invigorate itself than in undergoing structural transformation in the late 19th century to respond to the trauma of incorporation into the world economy.

The above discussion on Chinese incorporation illustrates very well that the process of incorporation into the world economy was never unproblematic. As Wallerstein (1988) points out, people everywhere offered resistance, of varying efficacy, to the process of incorporation, because it was so unattractive a proposition in terms of both immediate material interests and the cultural values of those being incorporated. If the resistance was successful, people in an external arena could negotiate more advantageous terms of incorporation with the core states.

In this respect, the discussion on Japanese incorporation in the next chapter will demonstrate under what special historical conditions an external arena could avoid entering the world economy as a periphery.

3. The Great Escape of Japan

Following China, Japan also became part of the capitalist world economy by the mid-19th century. However, when Japan was confronted with the threat of market incorporation from Western core states, the Meiji elites quickly centralized the government, promoted dynamic economic transformations, and embarked on overseas imperialist ventures. The aim of this chapter is to explain why Japan was able to escape the fate of peripheralization during its incorporation into the capitalist world economy.

PREINCORPORATED JAPAN
IN THE MID-19TH CENTURY

From Cultural Borrowing to Tokugawa Isolation

Because it was situated close to China, Japan's historical development was strongly influenced by the Chinese empire. In the 7th century, during the Taika Reforms, the Japanese turned to the Chinese empire for cultural and institutional innovations and sent a 600-member mission to China. After the mission returned to Japan, the Japanese state adopted key elements of governance from the Chinese model, particularly the system of a centralized state headed by an absolute sovereign (Borthwick, 1992, p. 48).

Later, in the 16th century, Toyotomi Hideyoshi (1536-1598)—a powerful shogun in Japan—believed that the time was ripe for the conquest of China to set up a great Japanese empire in East Asia. Hideyoshi's natural avenue of conquest lay through the Korean peninsula. His wars with Korea and China seriously weakened both the Yi and Ming dynasties, respectively. Japan, on the other hand, benefited culturally. The continental invasion broadened the exposure of the Japanese to the Neo-Confucianism of Zhuxi, led them to acquire the technology of movable-type printing, and enriched the Japanese ceramic industry with porcelain ware (Borthwick, 1992, p. 48).

Hideyoshi, however, died during his continental expedition in 1598. His successor was Shogun Tokugawa Ieyasu (1542-1616), who, initially, actively sought foreign commerce with China and the few European ships that were beginning to appear on his shores. For a short time, the Dutch and the English were permitted to establish trading posts, and Spanish Franciscan monks were allowed to proselytize in Japan. But Ieyasu soon grew suspicious of the "subversive" activities of the Europeans, such as converting the Japanese to Christianity and instigating peasant rebellion. In response, Shogun Ieyasu, and later Shogun Hidetada and Shogun Iemitsu, decided to close off Japan from outside influence: The missionaries were expelled; the construction of large ocean-going ships was forbidden; the number of Europeans in Japan was reduced to a tiny group of Dutch who were allowed to trade only on the island of Deshima in Nagasaki harbor; all other foreign trade was banned, as was the return of Japanese people from abroad, on the grounds that they would bring with them the corruption of foreign ideas (Borthwick, 1992, p. 50).

Virtually cut off from trade with the West, Japan existed as an external arena of the capitalist world economy until the mid-19th century. Still, Japan maintained some cultural contact with the West through the small Dutch outpost in Nagasaki harbor. In the early 18th century, Shogun Yoshimune had several books translated from the Dutch that were of strictly utilitarian value; and independent Japanese scholars were permitted to pursue so-called Dutch learning (*Rangaku*) by acquiring foreign books on medicine, science, and military technology. These scholars would later be a vital element in Japan's burst of activity to catch up with the industrializing world in the late 19th century (Borthwick, 1992, p. 50).

Along with isolationism, the Tokugawa shogun also set up policies to preserve the political and economic stability in Japan.

State and Class Structure

Unlike the Chinese centralized imperial bureaucracy, the Japanese state was generally characterized as *feudal*. For instance, Japan under the Tokugawa regime was divided into more than 250 fiefs of different sizes. The Tokugawa family administered a domain that covered almost one quarter of the country, including the great trade centers of Edo (the seat of government), Sakai (close to Osaka), and Kyoto (where the imperial court was situated). As the largest and the most powerful feudal lord, Tokugawa Ieyasu became the shogun of Japan and exercised the actual power of government. Although the emperor of Japan was relegated to the austere obscurity of the Kyoto Palace under this political arrangement, the emperor remained, in theory, the source of all power; in principle, it was the emperor who delegated temporal power to his generalissimo (Kitagawa, 1966).

The remaining three quarters of Japan was divided up among daimyo, or great feudal lords. Those daimyo who had been loyal to Tokugawa, the *fudai* (inside lords), were rewarded as favored vassals. The lords who had initially opposed Ieyasu before he became shogun were called *tozama* (outside lords), and included the lords of distant provinces in Choshu, Satsuma, and Saga. The *tozama* were excluded from any share in government responsibility.

The *bakufu*, or shogunate government, maintained itself through a skillful system of checks and balances, achieved through the geographical distribution of inside and outside lords. It also set up a *sankin-kotai* (hostage system), which required all daimyo to reside alternately in their own domains and in Edo, leaving their wives and families behind in the capital as hostages when they returned to their own fiefs. The daimyo had to bear the heavy expenses of moving and maintaining their households in their fiefs and Edo. In addition, the daimyo were forbidden to have direct contact with the imperial court in Kyoto. Finally, financial burdens were imposed on the daimyo, to keep their treasuries empty. Very often, the Tokugawa government would ask a daimyo to undertake a large project that would strain his finances to the utmost (Norman, 1975, pp. 121-122).

With respect to class structure, the Tokugawa regime attempted to freeze Japanese society into a rigid hierarchical mold. The four classes in Tokugawa society—samurai (warriors), peasants, artisans, and merchants—each had regulations covering all the minutiae of clothing, ceremony, and behavior, and these had to be strictly observed. For instance, samurai had the right to slay any commoner who dared to be disrespectful. In such a class structure, social mobility was constrained by the hereditary nature of class categories.

Samurai were placed at the top of the class structure, because they were the only class allowed to bear weapons, and because their martial values (bushido) provided guidance for exemplary conduct that included rectitude, benevolence, and politeness, along with courage and honor. Divorced from any productive function, a samurai drew a rice stipend in return for fighting at his lord's command. Peasants were placed second on the social scale because small-scale agriculture was the economic basis of the shogunate and the feudal lords. But peasants had low living standards and had to pay at least 40% of the harvest to their lords. The merchant class was placed last on the social scale because they were regarded as an unproductive, shifty class that would stoop to any method to make money (Borthwick, 1992, p. 49; Norman, 1975, pp. 123-128).

By the early 19th century, however, this rigid class structure and feudal economy began to disintegrate. Agricultural revolution, commercialization and merchant affluence, the impoverishment of the daimyo, the bureaucratization of samurai, new cultural values, and the increasing misery of the peasants were all factors in this disintegration.

Social Changes in Late Tokugawa

First, as Yamamura (1980) has shown, the period from 1550 to 1650 witnessed an agricultural revolution. The large rise in agricultural productivity during this century was made possible by several proximate conditions: increasing effectiveness of water use, development and dissemination of higher-yielding varieties of rice, availability of inexpensive hoes, and increasing use of fertilizers.

Second, during the long period of Tokugawa peace and increased agricultural productivity, a new money economy was gradually supplanting the old natural rice economy. In addition, the *sankin-kotai* system greatly facilitated commodity circulation, extended the market, and promoted the growth of Osaka and Edo (Tokyo) into prosperous urban centers. The result was that the merchant class became wealthy amid a thriving commerce between cities and districts (Sheldon, 1958; Storry, 1961).

Third, while the merchants grew steadily wealthier as suppliers of goods and services to the daimyo, many daimyo themselves fell into debt. The heavy expenses of moving between their fiefs and Edo, under the *sankin-kotai* system, and the large sums spent in undertaking public works in their domains served to keep the daimyo in a weakened financial position. Many daimyo became dependent on the merchants to maintain their lavish expenditures. Although the daimyo could use their social position to cancel debts to merchants, this was not an effective long-range solution to their growing impoverishment (Livingston, Moore, & Oldfather, 1973; Sanderson, 1994).

Fourth, the long period of Tokugawa peace turned the samurai into civilian administrators, paid in stipends of rice. No longer needed to follow their lords into battle or to defend their lords' castles, the samurai were assigned such administrative duties as formulation of financial policy for the government of a rural district. Many samurai, following the plight of their feudal lords, were in a state of chronic debt. This was because although samurai received their incomes in rice, their living expenses in urban Edo and Osaka, under the *sankin-kotai* system, had to be paid for in cash. Thus, to make ends meet, samurai also needed to turn to the merchants for money (Beasley, 1963).

Many samurai were cut off from their rice stipends and released from their allegiance when their impoverished daimyo could not find enough bureaucratic offices in which to place them. These lordless samurai became *ronin* (literally, wandering men), owing no fealty and professing no fixed occupation. The emergence of a large number of rootless *ronin* in the early 19th century was one of the key factors responsible for the dissolution of the Tokugawa regime (Norman, 1975).

Fifth, the decay of the feudal order could also be seen in the cultural realm. The increasing affluence of the merchants in urban centers led to the full flowering of a carefree, far less puritanical culture than the original austere samurai-centered culture. The "floating world" of Edo, as Beasley (1963, p. 15) described it, was a world "of fugitive pleasures, of theaters and restaurants, wrestling-booths and houses of assignation, with their permanent population of actors, dancers, singers, story-tellers, jesters, bath-girls and itinerant purveyors." This nascent pleasure culture of the merchants was in sharp contrast to the samurai ideal of restraint, diligence, and economy.

Another trend was the revival of *kokugaku* (national studies) school, which promulgated the ideology of the existence of a unique Japanese culture. This school developed a supposed mystique about the divine blessings bestowed upon Japan, and a focus on the emperor as the symbol of all that was Japanese (Borthwick, 1992). By elevating the emperor to such a preeminent status, imbuing him with divine origins and supreme authority even over the Tokugawa government, this emperor cult was quickly embraced by those who blamed the government for their impoverishment.

Finally, the feudal Tokugawa order was shaken by the increasing misery of the peasants and by peasant rebellions (Smith, 1959). With the penetration of the money economy into the countryside, peasants could no longer obtain everything they needed through barter. Because of fluctuations in market demands and prices, peasants had to turn in desperation to usurers for aid in buying fertilizer and daily necessities, offering their land as surety. Then, many peasants were reduced to tenants when they were unable to pay back the loans on time. Thus, in addition to the customary feudal overlord, the peasants were now burdened by the demands of a new landowning-usurer class, which cost them 50% to 70% of their harvests. In times of extreme distress, the peasants rose up in large-scale riots and violent disorders. Borton (1938, p. 49) points out that, in the early 19th century, there was an average of more than six peasant uprisings a year against the rich merchants, landlords, and corrupt administrators.

In sum, the feudal order of the late Tokugawa regime was under severe stress. This was the feudal order that foreigners confronted when they tried to incorporate Japan into the capitalist world economy in the mid-nineteenth century. Although the dominant view on Japanese commercial development emphasizes the early construction of the national market and its continuity, Lie's (1992a) revisionist account points to discontinuities in the economic history of Japan from the Tokugawa to the Meiji period, after Japan was incorporated into the world economy.

INCORPORATION ATTEMPTS
AND ANTISYSTEMIC MOVEMENTS

Commodore Perry Arrives

In 1853 the two steamships of Commodore Matthew Perry's squadron dropped their anchors at the entrance to Tokyo Bay. Perry demanded that ports be opened where American ships might be provisioned, that arrangements be made for the humanitarian treatment and return of shipwrecked foreign sailors, and that commerce between Japan and the United States be permitted. Predictably, the shogun's representatives dragged their feet on the negotiations. Perry had to return in 1854, this time with an eight-ship squadron, roughly one fourth of the U.S. navy, before the Treaty of Kanagawa was signed. However, this treaty was not much more than a "shipwreck convention."

Thereafter, it took Townsend Harris, the first resident diplomat in Japan, 4 years of negotiation to convince the shogun to sign another commercial treaty with the United States, in 1858. Shortly afterward, similar treaties were signed with other European states—Britain, France, Russia, and the Netherlands. These treaties were patterned after the Chinese treaties of Nanking and Tianjin; thus, they included the opening of treaty ports to Western trade and residence, extraterritoriality, most-favored-nation clauses, and tariffs fixed at 5% ad valorem (Gibney, 1992, pp. 119-122; Moulder, 1977, pp. 132-133).

Why did the United States take the lead in incorporating Japan into the capitalist world economy? Why did this event take place in the mid-1850s? Why did the opening of Japan occur so peacefully, without much bloodshed and violence?

As Norman (1975, p. 142) notes, geopolitics played an important role in explaining why the United States took the lead in opening Japan. Of all Asian countries, Japan was the farthest removed from the reach of the great European naval powers. Japan also was shielded from the land power of the Russian Empire by the vast, half-explored steppes of Siberia. Moreover, the Western powers were preoccupied with other areas of Asia, such as Indonesia, India, and China, where significant trade and investments had already been established. These areas had become a buffer, shielding Japan from the West. Furthermore, it was widely believed that efforts to open Japan would not be worth the cost, because Japan had little of interest to trade with the West and little demand for Western manufactures. This left the United States as the only candidate that might be interested in Japan. Eng (1986, p. 164) argues that Japan was seen as a logical stopover for the replenishment of fuel and supplies for American ships crossing the Pacific.

But why did the opening of Japan not take place right after the 1839 Opium War? Why did it not occur until the mid-1850s? Before the development of California, the United States was even farther from East Asia than was Europe. So Perry's expedition had to wait until such events as the annexation of California, in the late 1840s, and the development of California clippers ships' route through New York, San Francisco, Canton, or other ports over the Pacific stretch, in 1850. Flushed with the recent easy victory over Mexico, the Americans were anxious to sail the waters beyond the newly settled Pacific shore. Also, whaling had become a big industry, and trans-Pacific whalers desperately needed friendly ports for water, coal, and food supplies. Before 1854, shipwrecked American sailors had encountered bad experiences when cast upon the shore of Japan (Gibney, 1992, p. 119).

There are other reasons why the mid-1850s proved to be the right time for the U.S. opening of Japan. France, Britain, and Russia were engrossed in the Turkish question, leading to the Crimean War of 1854-1856. Britain and France also were most active in promoting the further invasion of China in the Second Opium War. Thus, the United States was left alone to pursue its interest in Japan. As Commodore Perry wrote before his Japan expedition: "Fortunately the Japanese and many other islands of the Pacific are still left untouched by this unconscionable government [i.e., Britain]; and some of the them lay in the route of a great commerce which is destined to become of great importance to the United States."

Finally, why did the United States not use force to open Japan? For one thing, the United States was still far from a superpower in terms of military strength. Commodore Perry needed to return in 1854, 1 year after his arrival in Tokyo Bay, with more steamships in order to press Japan to accept even the "shipwreck convention." On the other hand, U.S. force and violence were unnecessary in this pursuit. Townsend Harris was able to persuade shogunate officials that a treaty signed quickly with the United States (which had no territorial designs on

Japan) would forestall the appearance of European warships, which might repeat the sort of hostilities that had occurred in China. In fact, the shogun signed the treaty with the United States right after the Anglo-French fleet had attacked, burned, and captured Canton in 1857, during the Second Opium War.

The yield to foreign influence by the shogun realigned political forces in the late Tokugawa regime.

Antisystemic Movements and Political Changes

Like the Chinese, the Japanese attempted to resist entry into the world economy. The resistance took place at three different levels: at the political center, at treaty ports, and at outer feudal domains.

First, the conservative Tokugawa coalition, which disapproved of the treaty with Harris, seized the opportunity to bargain with the shogun. They tried to tie their proposed reform of the shogunate government with approval of the Harris Treaty. The proposed reforms included changes in succession procedures to ensure the choice of a mature and able shogun—startling evidence, as Jansen (1970, p. 98) points out, of "the way the outside threat had produced reverberations in the center of what had always been the private concerns of Tokugawa house policy." In addition, the emperor also refused to ratify the treaty and called upon the shogun to repudiate the treaty and take immediate steps to drive the Western "barbarians" from Japan. In response, Ii Naosuke, chief administrator of the shogun government, acted firmly to purge the dissenters; he also made vague a promise to the emperor to expel the foreigners by 1863. In February 1859 the Imperial Court finally and reluctantly approved the Harris Treaty (Gibney, 1992, p. 121).

In the early 1860s there was a variety of incidents involving foreigners in the treaty ports, with bands of hostile samurai attacking them. As Gibney (1992, p. 125) reveals, Henry Heusken, Townsend Harris's own interpreter, was cut down on the streets of Edo in 1861. British diplomats were attacked in their embassy, and the British embassy in Edo was burned down by hostile samurai in 1863.

There was an economic foundation to the antiforeign feeling of these lower samurai and *ronin*. After the signing of the Harris Treaty, foreign products were allowed to enter Japan, and Japanese foreign trade took a sudden leap. Since import tariffs were limited by treaty provisions, foreign manufactured goods began to flood the country; imports into Japan rose from 4.4 million yen in 1863 to 6.0 million yen in 1865. Foreign imports not only drove domestic articles off the market, but also forced up prices. In addition, the outflow of gold after the opening of Japan induced the Tokugawa government to debase the coinage (reducing the gold content of coins by more than 85%), which further drove up commodity prices. Rampant inflation heightened the economic distress of samurai, whose income in rice was fixed but, when translated into money, actually shrank in value as commodity prices rose. Norman (1975) points out:

> The economic distress of the lower samurai, sharpened by the meteoric rise in prices, threw them into a truly wretched state of penury, deepened their hatred of the Tokugawa government and its foreign policy, and induced them to fasten the responsibility for their troubles on foreign barbarians and their trading operations. (p. 149)

Resentment against the shogunate also grew, resulting in attempts to assassinate leading Tokugawa government officials; Ii Naosuke—the shogunate official who pressed for the 1858 Harris Treaty—was cut down by a small party of samurai in 1860.

Finally, there were intense antiforeign sentiments at the outer feudal domains. Satsuma and Choshu, two of the domains farthest removed from the direct influence of the shogunate at Edo, were both large and sufficiently independent-minded enough to serve as centers of new resistance. Here, the Tokugawa government was strongly criticized for its failure to throw out the Westerners. At the same time, the feudal lords of Satsuma and Choshu were able to enhance their military capacities, because they could more easily purchase Western arms, ships, and military advisers (Craig, 1961). In the so-called Namamugi Incident of 1862, a party of English men and women was set on by Satsuma samurai when they misunderstood signals and did not make a place quickly enough for a procession escorting the daimyo. An Englishman named Richardson was killed in this affair. In June 1863 the Choshu daimyo ordered shore batteries at Shimonoseki to fire on foreign ships, as June 25 was the date that the shogun had formally set for the expulsion of foreigners from Japan in an earlier memorial to the emperor. In retaliation for the Satsuma attack, a British squadron sailed into the harbor of Kagoshima in Satsuma in 1863, set the town on fire, and destroyed most of the shore batteries. In retaliation for the Choshu attack, a mixed British, French, and American fleet destroyed most of the shore batteries and caused considerable damage in Shimonoseki in Choshu in 1864 (Gibney, 1992, p. 125).

These foreign attacks at Kagoshima and Shimonoseki were sufficient to convince the Satsuma and Choshu leadership that it was time to come to terms with the capitalist world economy. It was amazing that the most virulent antiforeign elements in Satsuma and Choshu sharply changed course after these events, setting out on a totally new policy of making friends with the foreigners and learning as much as possible from them. In response, the West began to perceive the antiforeignism of Satsuma and Choshu as more a "club to beat the Tokugawa government" than a sincere indication of anti-Western sentiment. Thereafter, the British (and others) began to be more sympathetic to Satsuma and Choshu, and began withdrawing their relatively unqualified support for the Tokugawa government (Moulder, 1977, p. 168).

In 1866 Satsuma and Choshu formed a secret alliance. They openly worked against the shogun government, and utilized the emperor cult to sanctify their pursuits. In order to avoid a full-scale armed confrontation between the shogun and the outer domains, the daimyo of Tosa proposed a compromise: The shogun would resign his powers and agree to stand as but one, though still the greatest, feudal lord in a new national structure headed by the emperor. The proposal was agreed to by the shogun, and the Imperial Court in January 1868 issued a script that "the Shogun Tokugawa Keiki has abdicated his administrative power. Henceforth all administration will be carried out under Our direct control, and all public affairs will be executed under the name of emperor" (Jansen, 1970, pp. 95, 101). In October the young emperor Mutsuhito chose Meiji (bright rule) as the name for his reign. Thus began the famous Meiji Restoration in 1868.

The Meiji Restoration

Although there are several excellent historical accounts of the Meiji Restoration (Gibney, 1992; Jansen, 1970; Norman, 1975), there are still many interesting research questions to be answered. Why did the antiforeign movement suddenly stop in the mid-1860s? Which political groups supported the Meiji Restoration? What values did these groups share, and why were they able to promote a national movement to challenge the shogun? And why did the foreigners fail to stop the Meiji Restoration?

First, Japan had the advantage of late entry into the capitalist world economy. It was able to observe what the foreigners had done to neighboring China. Takasugi Shinsaku, a Choshu samurai who visited Shanghai in the early 1860s, was appalled by Chinese subservience to the foreigners:

> Here most of the Chinese have become the servants of foreigners. When English and French people come walking, the Chinese give way to them stealthily. Although the main power here is Chinese, it really is nothing but a colony of England and France. . . . Thinking of the case of Japan, we'll have been forewarned—who can be sure the same fate will not visit our country in the future? (Livingston et al., 1973, p. 84)

In this respect, after the foreigners' shelling of Kagoshima and Shimonoseki, the Satsuma and Choshu samurai must have realized that it was futile to provoke the foreigners further. If the Chinese empire could not defend itself from foreign invasion, how could Japan avoid such a fate? The effects of imperialism in China made a lasting impression on the best minds in Japan, whose writings sounded a clarion call for national defense and even the adoption of Western industry and military science (Norman, 1975, p. 145).

Second, in response to the threat of foreign domination and colonialism, there emerged a new generation of young *shishi* (men of spirit). Many of these *shishi* were *ronin* who had left their original domain and moved across Japan like high-level drifters, alternately studying and fighting as they went from teacher to teacher. There were also young samurai in positions of power. Over the years, daimyo had delegated more and more of their governing to younger men. These *shishi* quickly embraced the thinking of Yoshida Shoin, the founder of the famous Shoka Sonjuku (the "village school under the pine tree" at which many key figures in the Meiji Restoration studied). Shoin once wrote: "The barbarians' artillery and shipbuilding, their knowledge of medicine and the physical science can all be of use to us—these should be properly adopted" (Gibney, 1992, p. 123). On the other hand, Shoin was dead set against the way in which the shogunate had opened the country for Commodore Perry and others. The message of these young *shishi* was: Revere the emperor, work against the shogun, and select people of talent for important posts, irrespective of their social origins.

Third, what the *shishi* cultivated was a higher national loyalty through the cult of the emperor. Before the *shishi* era, most Japanese were socialized to think of themselves as residents of a particular domain and not as citizens of a nation called Japan. Thus, the Tokugawa society endorsed the value of loyalty to one's lord, and the emperor was relegated to the austere obscurity of the Kyoto palace. In the mid-1860s, however, the mystique of the emperor as a Japanese national symbol was resurrected, and the young *shishi* activists were asked to put the national purpose ahead of traditional feudal claims (Jansen, 1970, pp. 100-102).

Fourth, what brought the *shishi* together was their rage during the Meiji Restoration. Sometimes called the "angry young men," they expressed "rage at the coming of the foreigners; rage at the monumental incompetence of the shogunate, carefully concealed until it was exposed by the opening of the country; rage at the prospects of continuing incompetence and national deterioration" (Gibney, 1992, p. 127). It was this rage of the young *shishi* generation that provided energy for such a profound historical event as the Meiji Restoration.

Fifth, after signing the Harris Treaty, the shogun could no longer mobilize the support of the *shishi*. Instead, he had very limited options for dealing with the charge that the treaty had resulted in national humiliation and internal chaos. So, after the defeat of Tokugawa royalists, the shogun was forced to step down when the daimyo of Tosa lamented that "the present disunity was a great disaster to us and of great happiness to the foreigners. This is exactly what they have been hoping for." What was needed was a government "for which no shame need be felt before future generations of foreign countries" (quoted in Jansen, 1970, p. 101).

Finally, the Meiji Restoration benefited from the fortuitous international context of the mid-1860s. The American Civil War guaranteed that no U.S. military successor to the persistent Perry would invade Japan for some years to come. The outbreak of the Anglo-Prussian War, and the absorption of Britain in the Chinese Taiping Rebellion, gave Japan what Norman (1975, p. 153) calls, a "vitally necessary breathing-space" in which to dismantle the old feudal order of the Tokugawa regime and rapidly build a modern, strong nation.

The threat of colonialism, the sense of urgency to save the nation, the rage of the *shishi*, the calling of the emperor cult, and the breathing space provided by the foreigners set the stage for the quick transition of the Meiji Revolution.

THE MEIJI REVOLUTION

In 1868 the Meiji Restoration had not gone beyond a coup within the ruling class. However, within the short time span of the next 3 decades, the new officials of the Meiji regime quickly put forward far-ranging, radical policies in the political, economic, and cultural spheres which had profound impact on Japanese society. In this respect, the restoration had been transformed into a bloodless revolution to propel Japan from a feudal society to a modern capitalist society.

Political Reforms

The slogan of the Meiji period was *fukoku kyohei* (rich country, strong army). Meiji officials instituted such reforms as state building, dissolving feudal classes, moral education, universal conscription, and the democracy project.

The immediate task confronting Meiji officials was state building, that is, to centralize political power and build a strong military establishment, to withstand foreign aggression. For this goal to be accomplished, Meiji officials needed to dismantle the daimyo class. In 1868 Meiji officials took over administrative control of the Tokugawa domain, nearly one quarter of Japan's total area. In 1869 the samurai leaders of pro-Meiji domains persuaded their daimyo to return their territories and people to the Imperial Court. Some other daimyo followed suit. In return, all daimyo were appointed as governors of their domains, but the daimyo now served as officials of the Tokyo government. After the Meiji government was strengthened by the formation of the Imperial Guard of 10,000 fighting men, it was bold enough to abolish feudal domains altogether. In 1871 the Meiji officials told the daimyo that they were no longer governors and that their domains would become prefectures. For compensation, the daimyo were given stipends equivalent to one tenth of the revenues of their former domains. Samurai were appointed to prefecture posts in the place of the daimyo-governors because they had, in fact, been practiced administrators (Akita, 1992, p. 129).

Then the Meiji government moved against the samurai. It divided this class into two groups: The lower samurai were made commoners by fiat; the government assumed responsibility for the stipends of the upper samurai. In 1873 a voluntary commutation of samurai stipends to government bonds was announced, and in 1876 the voluntary commutation was made compulsory. The interest-bearing bonds were capitalized at between 5 and 14 years of income, depending on the size of the samurai stipend. Thereafter, the Meiji government no longer needed to face the prospects of continuous payment for the samurai. In addition, the Meiji government abolished many samurai privileges. It lifted the ban on interclass marriage, lifted the prohibition on wearing swords, and eliminated the special samurai status under the law. The goal of the Meiji officials was to select people of talent for important posts—whatever social classes they came from (Moulder, 1977, p. 171). Thus the samurai now had to compete in school and for governmental posts with the sons of merchants and peasants. Why did some 300,000 upper samurai permit the Meiji government to take their privileges away? According to Akita (1992) and Smith (1961), this happened because the samurai had long been removed from the land, stripped of seignorial rights, and transformed into administrators. Had the upper samurai had a proprietary interest in the land—which served as the base of their power and the source of their pride—their reaction to Meiji reforms would have been different. Moreover, the samurai were subject to the higher national loyalty to the Meiji emperor instead of to their former feudal domains.

After dismantling the feudal daimyo and samurai classes, Meiji officials proceeded to build a strong military establishment to prepare Japan against domestic disorder and external foreign invasion. Even in the late 1860s, the Mejii government possessed no national army. The troops available to the government totaled just 9,000, essentially a collection of samurai whose primary loyalty was to their feudal domains. Consequently, General Yamagata, after an intensive survey of the military systems in Europe in 1870, proposed a conscription scheme through which participation by commoners in the nation's armed forces would be regular and universal. Moreover, the recruitment of army officers was geared to "men of talent," regardless of former social class, and opened to all citizens. As a result, the samurai no longer monopolized control over the means of coercion (Crowley, 1966).

The urgent need to achieve national security had also greatly influenced Meiji reforms on education. General Yamagata proposed the establishment of a public school system, which would include the rudiments of military training (drills) in the course of study. Another Meiji official argued that the way to elevate Japan to the leading position in the world was to lay the foundations of elementary education (Jansen, 1970). In addition to universal compulsory public education, the Meiji government stressed moral education. In 1890 the Imperial Rescript on Education declared: "loyalty and filial piety . . . [to be] the glory of the fundamental character of Our Empire, and . . . the source of Our education" (Akita, 1992, p. 132). Thus, education was aimed at the indoctrination of children into total loyalty to the emperor and was used as a means for social control and propaganda for the state.

Finally, Meiji officials had to deal with the emergent forces of democratization. In 1874 a group of samurai (led by Itagaki Taisuke), who resented Satsuma and Choshu's monopoly of political power, petitioned the government for a democratic, elected legislative assembly. This started the *jiyuminken undo* (popular rights movement), which was supported by rich peasants, landlord-entrepreneurs, government officials, and journalists. In 1877, with the aid of public rallies and press campaigns, the activists filed 55 petitions to the government, calling for a representative assembly and a constitution. The movement culminated in the formation of the Jiyuto (Liberal Party) by Itagaki in 1881, and the establishment of the opposing Kaishinto (Progressive Party) in 1882 (Bowen, 1980).

Meiji officials were now faced with a dilemma. On one hand, the Meiji government realized that it had to conform to the Western democratic model in order to be recognized as a member of the family of Western constitutional states. Thus, the Meiji government pressed forward with a constitution project. On the other, the Meiji government was skeptical about Western individualism, theories of human rights, and divisive multiparty politics, believing these would threaten national unity and weaken the state. Ultimately, in 1890, Meiji officials adopted a Western, but Prussian-style, constitution. The new constitution was clearly autocratic and highly centralized. Effective power lay with the executive, and the Diet was relegated to a secondary role. The imperial institution was resurrected, and the emperor was made the chief symbol of the state's authority. Thus, the emperor became sacred and inviolable; he commanded the armed services; he made war and peace; and he dissolved the Lower House at will (Ike, 1969). As designed by Meiji leaders, this emperor system would channel the forces of patriotism and loyalty into the development of Japanese society.

Economic Reforms

The economic problems confronting the nascent Meiji regime were as follows: Given the agrarian-based Tokugawa economy, how was Japan to extract sufficient resources to promote development? Given the urgency of developing the military for national security, how could Japan channel economic resources for this purpose? Given the need to industrialize as soon as possible, how could Japan enhance the investment climate to overcome merchants' initial reluctance to invest in pioneer industries? Given Japan's primitive techniques and ignorance in foreign trade, where would it find the expertise to run these modern enterprises? And given the loss of tariff control, how could Japan protect its domestic market from foreign imports?

First, in order to increase state revenues, Meiji officials quickly instituted a land tax reform. The aim was to eradicate the cumbersome and inequitable Tokugawa tax system of payment in kind. After carrying out a national land survey, Meiji officials ordered peasants to pay taxes equivalent to 3% of the land's assessed value. The taxes were to be paid in cash rather than in kind, and they were not adjusted in accord with the conditions of harvest. The result was an increase in annual revenues from the land tax, from about 36 million yen prior to the reform to an average of 43 million yen from 1881 to 1885. In addition, the entire land tax yield was now controlled by the central Meiji government, and its predictability increased the capacity for state planning. Thus, in all, the peasantry bore the brunt of Meiji modernization. The land tax provided the central government with 70% to 80% of its revenues during the late 19th century, but it also led to the growth of tenancy and peasant uprisings (Moulder, 1977, p. 172).

With greater resources, Meiji officials undertook a state-led industrialization program. From the start, strategic military industries were favored by the government; technologically, they were soon on a level with those of most advanced Western countries. Norman (1975) notes that

> it was the Meiji policy to bring under government control the arsenals, foundries, shipyards, and mines formerly scattered among various han [fief] or bakufu domains, then to centralize and develop them until they reached a high level of technical efficiency, while at the same time initiating other strategic enterprises such as chemical industries. . . . During the Meiji era, the control over the most vitally strategic enterprises, such as arsenals, shipyards, and some sectors of mining, was kept in government hands. (p. 234)

Next, after developing the strategic industries, Meiji officials set up pilot projects in nonstrategic industries. In the beginning, private investment appeared highly risky because of the backwardness of industrial technology, because of the conservative merchant outlook, and because such investment required large accumulations of capital (Smith, 1955). Hence, the Meiji government had to take the lead in stimulating a profitable investment climate for industrialists. In the 1870s Meiji officials promoted infrastructure projects such as railway construction and became involved in pilot factories in the textile and silk-reeling industries. After 1880 most government pilot projects were sold to private companies at extremely low prices. For example, government investment in the Shinagawa Glass Factory was about 350,000 yen, but the factory was sold for about 80,000 yen, payable over a 55-year period that began 10 years after the sale (Moulder, 1977, p. 180). As Hirschmeier (1964, p. 151) points out, "with so much done by the government in technical experiments and machinery investments, the purchasers of the enterprises, with some additional investments, could overcome the critical stage rather quickly and make these factories and mines the foundations of their own industrial enterprises."

In this way, the state had subsidized business by engaging in risky, primitive capital accumulation. Meiji officials could no longer afford to wait for a industrial bourgeois class to mature, for this might take decades or even centuries to develop. Instead, Meiji officials actively "manufactured" the Japanese bourgeois class through these subsidized pilot projects (So, 1990a). This active state promotion also helps to explain why Japan was able to skip the phase of competitive capitalism and jump right into monopoly capitalism. Big business in Japan had its origins not in small industries but in state-subsidized projects. The Japanese merchant houses simply took over profitable, large-scale state enterprises and formed the *zaibatsu* (economic conglomerates). In this respect, Japanese big business developed a cordial relationship with the state from the very beginning (Lockwood, 1954).

Given Japan's inexperience in foreign trade and technology, Meiji officials also actively promoted an expatriate policy. Norman (1975) records that

> the arsenals in Nagasaki were originally under Dutch supervision, the Yokosuka shipyard arsenal and iron works under French, and other shipyards under English care. These foreign technicians trained the Japanese so that in time native workers were technically as literate as their foreign tutors. In the textile industries foreign managers and assistants were also employed: English in the Kagoshima spinning mill, French in Tomioka and Fukuoka, Swiss or Italian in the Maebashi filatures. (p. 233)

In addition, the best Japanese students were sent abroad to master the most up-to-date techniques, and they replaced foreign advisers upon their return to Japan.

Finally, given the loss of tariff controls, Meiji officials developed the following policies to protect the domestic market (Moulder, 1977, pp. 184-186): First, government purchase policies favored national industries over Western ones whenever possible. Thus the government subsidized private industry by becoming its chief customer; it was purchases by the army and navy, for instance, that permitted the establishment of modern leather and woolen manufacturing in Japan. Second, the government enacted laws to encourage Japanese citizens to purchase the products and services of native Japanese industries. For example, the government in 1876 established regulations that restricted Japanese citizens' use of foreign ships. With the help of such regulations, the Mitsubishi firm was able to buy out a major British shipping firm in Japan. Third, the government discouraged foreigners from investing in Japan. Outside of the 25-mile limit of the treaty ports, foreigners were forbidden to form partnerships with Japanese nationals, buy property in Japan, own stock in a Japanese concern, or rent property for business purposes.

Side by side with these political-economic reforms, Meiji officials made their imprint on the cultural sphere.

Cultural Reforms

Prior to the Meiji Restoration in 1868, there were three cultural currents in Japan: (a) The *kokugaku* (National Learning) school, which was equated with the neo-Shinto movement of exalting the emperor as the legitimate heir to imperial charisma; (b) the *yogaku* (Western Learning) school, which encouraged seeking knowledge from all over the world for the purpose of maintaining national prosperity and defense; and (c) the *jugaku* (Confucian Learning) school, whose ethics remained as the only meaningful norm for family and other social relations (Kitagawa, 1966).

In early Meiji, the call for cultural borrowing from the West and the fast pace of industrialization led to a modernist movement and a new generation of Westernized intelligentsia in urban areas. This new generation demanded liberty, equality, and human dignity; some even proposed declaring Japan a Christian country so that it could further enjoy the boons of modernization. Furthermore, the Westernized intelligentsia criticized Shintoism as an ideology justifying the political monopoly by a few men surrounding the throne; it condemned Confucianism as unprogressive in the sense that it looked for a model of the new society in the past (Jansen, 1970).

The attacks from the Westernized intelligentsia, naturally, aroused fear and resentment among conservative elements in the government. However, many Meiji officials realized that Shinto, important though it was as the foundation of the new Japan, lacked the intellectual and moral content that was necessary for strengthening the nation. On the other hand, the moral codes of Confucianism, despite their effectiveness in social control, were of Chinese rather than Japanese origins and thus were inappropriate for promoting Japanese nationalism and moral order. The strategy for the Meiji officials, then, was to seek alliance with the Confucian scholars, redefine the national origins of Confucianism, and absorb Confucian moral values into Shinto ideology.

With the consent of leading Japanese Confucian scholars, Confucianism was quickly transmuted from a semireligious, ethical system based on the teachings of Chinese sages into an indigenous Japanese ethic fused with Shintoism. This blending of Confucianism and Shintoism was further institutionalized through the promulgation of the constitution and the Imperial Rescript on Education in 1890, which enforced a new morality based upon both the Shinto sense of respect for the emperor and the Confucian concept of filial piety. Thereafter, Shinto was elevated to the position of state religion above all other religions, and Christianity became a popular target for discrimination (Jansen, 1970; Kitagawa, 1966).

By the 1890s these far-ranging cultural, economic, and political Meiji policies had transformed Japan from a state in the external arena to a semiperipheral state in the capitalist world economy.

FROM EXTERNAL ARENA
TO SEMIPERIPHERAL ZONE

Core Domination

During the late 19th century, Japan was still under political-economic domination by Western core states.

Politically, Japan was forced to sign unequal treaties which granted foreigners the following privileges: Treaty ports of Yokohama, Kobe, Hakodate, Niigata, and Nagasaki were opened for foreign trade and residence. Extraterritoriality was established and the government lost the right of jurisdiction over foreigners in Japan. Western states were granted most-favored-nation status, whereby any subsequent privileges granted to one nation would automatically accrue to others. Japan's tariff autonomy was abolished and tariffs were fixed at 5% (Moulder, 1977).

Also, the Japanese economy was adversely affected when it was first incorporated into the world economy. Due to the lack of tariff control, there was a massive importation of foreign goods. By the first decade of the Meiji period, Western dress, food, and even architecture had become common in Tokyo. This led to the outflow of specie overseas, the draining of the government's specie reserves, and currency depreciation. Since the land tax was a money payment that remained constant from year to year, any depreciation in the value of money meant a corresponding loss of revenues for the government. The samurai also were impoverished because their income consisted of the fixed interest on government bonds. In addition, the influx of foreign products led to the ruin of the Japanese handicraft industry. For example, foreign machine-made cotton yarn was not only stronger but also much cheaper than native

Japanese yarn. The income of the peasantry declined as it was hit hard by the falling off of handicraft employment (Smith, 1955).

However, despite these political and economic problems, Japan had not fallen to the status of a periphery in the world economy.

Semiperiphery, Not Periphery

Politically, Japan was a semiperiphery because it still possessed a strong state capable of building a wealthy nation. The Meiji state had the capacity to abolish feudal domains, centralize the administration, dissolve feudal classes, institute educational reforms and universal conscription, create a constitution, set up a new land tax system, promote strategic industries, subsidize pilot projects, protect its domestic market, blend Confucianism with Shintoism, and elevate Shintoism to state religion.

In addition, the Meiji state had the capacity to suppress domestic rebellions. The peasants—hit hard by bad harvests, low market prices, the destruction of handicraft industries, high and rigidly fixed money land taxes, and growing debts—rose up against the state in 190 revolts in the first decade of the Meiji period (Norman, 1975). But the Meiji state easily suppressed these revolts because of their scattered nature and the increasing effectiveness of the conscript army. The samurai, too, rose up in protest as the majority found that they had no military role to play in the new society, as they lost their social privileges, and as they became more and more impoverished. The samurai-led revolts in the mid-1870s also were easily suppressed because the Meiji armies had superior weaponry and controlled communications and the seas (Kublin, 1949).

Furthermore, the Meiji state had the capacity to engage in territorial expansion. Between 1871 and 1876, the Meiji state undertook a series of bold and well-coordinated diplomatic and military ventures in East Asia. It forced the Ryukyu Islands to terminate its tributary missions to China, sent an expedition to Taiwan, and imposed a treaty upon Korea virtually at gunpoint, thereby squarely challenging China's hitherto undisputed supremacy in East Asia (Kim, 1980). The Korean military expedition was especially interesting because it shows how foreign and domestic issues became entwined in Japan. Those who endorsed the Korean expedition argued that it would pacify the samurai, channel their energy toward national defense, and serve as a springboard toward a national samurai army. Those who opposed the Korean expedition argued that it would lead Japan into poverty and give Britain a pretext to invade Japan (Crowley, 1966).

Finally, the Meiji state should be viewed as a semiperiphery because it had begun to achieve diplomatic parity with Western core powers. The predatory expansion toward weak East Asian neighbors and the implementation of a modern constitution made it possible for Japan to renegotiate the unequal treaties began in 1892. Japan successfully pushed the Western nations to end extraterritoriality in 1899, and although full tariff autonomy would not come until 1911, Japan had already become a full member of the world economy's interstate system by the 1890s (Jansen, 1970).

Economically, Japan can be described as a semiperiphery because it was able to protect its domestic market from foreign domination. Western investments in Japan turned out to be few and far between; Western loans to Japan were minimal; there was no drain of resources through indemnity payments, as there had been in China. Moreover, the sudden increase in demand for such export commodities as tea and silk boosted their prices and led to an economic boom. In the late 19th century, when industrialization was gaining momentum, Japan was exporting raw materials and manufactured goods in more or less equal amounts (Moulder, 1977).

Culturally, too, Japan should be classified a semiperiphery. There was no treaty obligation to tolerate Christianity, and Western missionaries were still not permitted to freely travel or to purchase property in the interior of Japan. Instead of abandoning native Japanese culture, the Meiji officials revigorated Shinto through fusion with Confucian moral values.

What, then, explains this great escape of Japan from peripheralization—a fate that has haunted most Third World countries? Why was Japan able to transform so quickly into a modern, capitalist state while China failed to do so?

CONCLUSION: JAPAN'S GREAT ESCAPE

To a certain extent, Japan's path of development was similar to that of China. Both countries were at the external arena of the world economy in the early 19th century; both were forced to be incorporated into the world economy under "unequal treaties"; both states still possessed a fairly high degree of capacity to initiate domestic reforms in response to the challenges from the world economy by the late 19th century.

But Japan and China were also quite different, especially in the areas of preincorporated legacy, agents of incorporation, initial responses to incorporation, and resultant state capacity. First, with regard to the countries' preincorporated legacies, China was a world empire at the external arena in East Asia, but Japan was not. As a Middle Kingdom, China established a Sinocentric world order and extended its Confucian civilization to its tributary states. It was only natural that China's bureaucrats and landed upper class were reluctant to borrow techniques and values from the "barbarians." By contrast, Japan had often been at the receiving end of cultural borrowing. Beginning with the Taika Reforms in the 7th century, Japan had a historical legacy of easing the pain of importing new institutions from other countries.

Moreover, the structure of the governing elite in the two countries was also different prior to their incorporation. In Qing China, the central state and the landed upper class had developed a close alliance, and it was this state-upper class alliance that upheld the Chinese empire from completely falling apart in the midst of foreign aggression and domestic antisystemic movements. In Tokugawa Japan, however, there was the deep cleavage between the Tokugawa government and the outer feudal domains. It was this elite cleavage that energized the samurai in the outer feudal domains to promote reforms during the Meiji revolution.

Second, with regard to agents of incorporation, China was attacked by Britain, and Japan negotiated with the United States. Britain was a hegemonic superpower in the world economy; it was attracted to the rich resources and huge market in China. Thus, Britain was determined to use force to open China. On the other hand, Japan was challenged by a Western power that had yet to exercise its military domination in faraway East Asia—the United States. Moreover, as the Western powers were preoccupied with China, they did not find Japan attractive in terms of either its resources or its markets. The result was that Japan experienced relatively less foreign domination and draining of resources than China had in the latter half of the 19th century.

Third, with regard to incorporation responses, the Chinese were confronted with the Taiping Rebellion, but the Japanese achieved the

Meiji Restoration. In China, the end of the dynastic cycle and the regional shift of foreign trade from Canton to Shanghai resulted in large-scale peasant uprisings. Whereas in Japan, the young samurai, after they saw what the foreigners had done to China, quickly evoked national sentiments to promote the Meiji Restoration.

Finally, with regard to resultant state capacity, the Chinese state had a relatively weaker capacity to promote semiperipheral ascent than the Japanese state. Because the Chinese state was weakened by both foreign domination and peasant rebellions, it could at best put forward a mediocre Self-Strengthening Movement. By contrast, the Japanese state, avoiding both strong foreign domination and large-scale peasant rebellions, and spurred by a feeling of the imminent threat of colonialism and the urgency of national survival, was able to carry out the far-ranging Meiji reforms within a short period. Here the historical irony is that in China, the "weak" Qing state was strong enough to suppress the challenges from the peasant rebellion, thus precluding a fundamental restructuring of state organization and power. Whereas in Japan, the weak Tokugawa government quickly crumbled in the face of a nationalistic movement from the outer feudal domains, allowing a strong Meiji state to emerge and institute a variety of reforms. Had the Tokugawa government been able to hold onto power and defeated the insurgency, the course of Meiji history might have been quite different.

It must be noted that our explanation of Japanese and Chinese development differs from the literature's. On one hand, there is the traditional societies theory (Azumi, 1974; Fairbank et al., 1978; Levy, 1955), which argues that since external impacts on Japan and China were similar, the fact that Japan developed while China did not must be attributed to such traditional institutions as feudalism. On the other, dependency theory (Moulder, 1977) has taken the opposite argument, saying that because the overall economies of Japan and China were quite similar before the mid-19th century, their divergent developmental outcomes must be due to their varying degrees of external domination. In contrast to such emphasis on either external or internal factors, this chapter argues that the divergent paths of Japanese and Chinese development must be explained by the complex interrelations among factors such as preincorporated legacy, agents of incorporation, initial responses to incorporation, and resultant state capacity after these two countries had been incorporated into the capitalist world economy.

Obviously, this different mode of incorporation had great impact on the subsequent development of both Japan and China, as will be explained in the next section.

PART III

Regionalization

Whereas the Qing empire put up only a modest state-sponsored industrialization in the second half of the 19th century, Japan was on its road toward a robust industrialization and ascendance to semi-peripheral status in the world economy.

In world-systems analysis, semiperipheral states have two distinctive features. First, semiperipheral states have a fairly even mix of core-like (high-wage and highly profitable) and peripheral-like (low-wage and not very profitable) products. Thus, they stand between the core states and the peripheral states in terms of kinds of products they export and the wage levels and profit margins they have. Furthermore, they trade or seek to trade in both directions, behaving like cores when trading with peripheral states and like peripheral states when trading with cores. Second, semiperipheral states actively intervene in the economy in order to protect and improve the relative position of the enterprises (and populations) located within their territories. Thus, semiperipheral states have formulated such strategies as import-substitution, invitation, and self-reliance to promote development.

In this respect, the Meiji state was instrumental in propelling Japan to semiperipheral status in the mid-19th century. However, by the 1890s, this nascent semiperipheral state in Japan was beginning to feel the constraints of limited territory, a small internal market, and poor resources. What new policy, then, should the Japanese state adopt in order to sustain its industrialization toward the 20th century?

Again, this timing is crucial because it helps to explain how world-system dynamics had influenced Japan's developmental strategy during this period. By the late 19th century, the world economy reached a downward phase, marked by stagnation and contraction of the global market. In addition, Great Britain was no longer a hegemon, as its industrial and military supremacy were increasingly challenged by rival core powers. In order to overcome stagnation, core states competed with one another for new colonies and investment rights in the periphery. Therefore, rather than continuing the mode of market incorporation in the mid-19th century, Western core states practiced territorial annexation and colonialism by the end of the 19th century. Furthermore, instead of advocating the doctrine of free trade, Western core states preached the ideologies of nationalism and racism, as they sought their "place in the sun," fulfilled a "manifest destiny," assumed a "civilizing mission," or acted as a "chosen people" (Bergesen, 1982; Borthwick, 1992).

Observing this global trend toward colonialism, the Japanese state developed a regionalization strategy of empire-building in East Asia. In world-systems analysis, a region of the world economy refers to a zone of multiple states, which, although fully integrated into the world economy, also manifests a high degree of integration of production processes within its bounds, and thus approaches the situation of being a single, fairly large state. For Wallerstein (1991a, p. 6), regionality is a means through which a semiperipheral state establishes a niche for itself in the world economy.

China, in this respect, again became a necessary component of Japanese regionalization strategy because of its cheap labor, abundant resources, and huge market potential. However, as a nascent semiperipheral state and a "late imperialist," Japanese continental expansion was naturally challenged by Western core powers, leading to a new wave of territorial annexation in East Asia at the end of the 19th century.

The next two chapters will discuss the origins, the nature, and the impact of Japan's regionalization strategy on East Asia. Chapter 4 will show that this regionalization strategy affected not only Japan proper but also its colonies in Korea and Taiwan as well; Chapter 5 will argue that this regionalization strategy sped up the Communist revolution in China.

4. Japan and Its Colonial Empire

With the achievements of the Meiji Restoration, Japan aspired to be the equal of Western powers in the world system. In due course, Japan developed a regionalization strategy to attain upward mobility through the domination of East Asia. This strategy of ascent inevitably pushed Japan into imperialism, and clashes with Western powers, and eventually dragged Japan into the disastrous Pacific war that almost destroyed all its achievements in previous decades. Meanwhile, the people of the Japanese colonies and even in Japan suffered a great deal in sustaining Japanese imperialism in the world system. Although Japan became increasingly an industrial power with heavy industrial production, the cycles and crises in the world economy, as well as the power struggles in the interstate system, impinged more deeply on Japan than before. Financial crises, industrial riots, political assassinations, and military coups were commonplace events during this period. It was no accident that the most severe depression in the 20th century finally brought Japan into the war. In this chapter, we shall review Japan's rise and fall in the world system from 1895 to 1945, beginning with the impact of Japanese colonialism on Korea and Taiwan.

THE FORMATION OF THE JAPANESE EMPIRE

Precolonial Taiwan and Korea

During the Qing dynasty, Taiwan mainly exported rice to mainland China in exchange for basic consumption commodities. But there was no real boost in the Taiwanese economy until the Treaty of Tientsin in 1858, which opened up Taiwan to Western commerce and diplomacy (Dai, 1985). Then tea suddenly became the leading export item for Taiwan in the 1870s, and "indeed for much of the last half of nineteenth century the level of activity in the tea industry determined the general economic prosperity of the island" (Ho, 1978, p. 20). The export of sugar, especially directed to Japan, also became increasingly important in the second half of the 19th century. The growth of Taiwan's export economy during this period was phenomenal, and the value of its exports amounted to 15.6% of Japan's by 1893.

After Taiwan had been incorporated into the capitalist world economy through export agriculture by the late 19th century, it had attained a relatively high level of development in production and commodity exchange. Taiwanese big landlords engaged in plantation business, and merchants collected crops from the countryside and processed them into exportable commodities (Dai, 1985). Sugar refining, for example, moved away from household production to workshop manufacturing, and specialization in different stages of the sugar production process also developed.

In contrast, economic development in Korea by the late 19th century lagged behind that of Taiwan. Despite the gradual loosening of central control by its government, Korea experienced little structural change prior to opening to foreign trade in 1876 (Zo, 1978). Before that period, Korea was still predominantly a subsistence agrarian economy, where private ownership of land and free peasantry had appeared as late as the 18th century. Korea's level of commercialization and urbanization was certainly behind that of Taiwan in this period. Korea's traditional handicraft industry made little progress after an initial spurt in the 18th century, and foreign trade was insignificant and officially prohibited until 1876. Because business activity was largely represented by peddlers, there was the lack of a strong merchant class as well as the absence of a geographical urban center of merchant activities comparable to Canton or Osaka (Eckert, 1991; Henderson, 1968). As Mason et al. (1980, p. 70) aptly put it: "Korea at the time of the arrival of the West appears to have been something of a commercial backwater in comparison to its East Asian neighbors."

Nevertheless, by the late 19th century, Korea had become the focal point upon which the two East Asian states—China and Japan—collided.

The Sino-Japanese War in 1894

Because Korea was China's vassal state, the Qing government was determined to protect it from being taken over by other foreigners. Japan, on the other hand, wanted to "open" Korea because of its strategic location at the tip of the Sea of Japan. In 1876 Japan forced Korea to sign the Treaty of Kanghwa, which opened two Korean ports to Japanese trade. After then, Japan's shipping companies began to dominate the foreign trade for Koreans; Japanese large-scale fishing enterprises overwhelmed the Korean small fishermen; and the growing export of Korean rice to Japan impoverished the Korean economy.

In 1894 Korea suffered the Tonghak Rebellion, which demanded an end to rice exports to Japan and a complete restructuring of power in Korea. Unable to suppress the Tonghaks, the Korean King Kojong turned to China for help. However, when China was about to send troops and a fleet to Korea, Japan reacted immediately by landing its own invasion force at Inchon. Without a declaration of war, Japanese warships intercepted and destroyed the Chinese fleet in the Yellow Sea. After a series of swift victories, the Japanese not only drove the Chinese forces northward out of Korea, but also captured the Chinese naval base of Port Arthur on the Liaodong Peninsula, as well as Taiwan (Borthwick, 1992, p. 149). At this point, China desperately sought terms of terms to end the Sino-Japanese War.

The Treaty of Shimonoseki in 1895 required China to pay Japan a crushing indemnity of 230 million taels (360 million yen). In addition, China had to recognize Korea's "independence," as well as cede Liaodong Peninsula, the Pescadores Islands, and the island of Taiwan to Japan. Furthermore, the cities of Suzhou, Hangzhou, Chongqing, and Shanxi were now opened to Japanese trade and manufacture. By virtue of the most-favored-nation clause, the other 13 Western powers also gained the same right (Thomas, 1984).

As Duus (1988, p. 5) remarks, the victory over China in 1894 was a shock to the Japanese that had a decisive impact on the subsequent historical development of Japan up to World War II. In regard to the economy, the sudden inflow of Chinese indemnity money not only paid for the cost of the war, but also helped finance Japan's development of heavy industry, especially iron and steel. In addition, the indemnities enabled Japan to shift to the gold standard; the opening of China's market provided an additional stimulus for Japan's textile industry; and the Japanese government began to more actively promote the export of manufactured goods. By 1895 there was no question that Japan's industrial revolution was well under way; Japan was becoming a semiperiphery. In politics, too, the year 1895 marks the beginning of a shift away from rule by the Meiji oligarchies to a new generation of political leaders drawn from the military, the civil bureaucracy, and the political parties.

In foreign policy, Japan emerged from the war as an empire, possessing Taiwan and becoming involved in intrigues in Korea. As Iriye (1970, p. 138) points out:

> Securing firm control over Korea became the cardinal goal of Japan's foreign policy. The army and navy had to be expanded to defend the new empire and prepare for contingencies in the Korean question. . . . Above all, the Japanese viewed their country as an imperialist . . . as a respectable participant in the game of imperialist politics.

Japan's victory and the acquisition of Taiwan had triggered a new wave of scrambling for concessions by the Western states. For example, France extended its control from northern Indochina to South China, including the lease of Guangzhou Wan. Germany established itself in the Shandong Peninsula and obtained the lease of Kiachow Bay. Russia acquired the Liaodong Peninsula. Britain obtained the lease for the New Territories north of Hong Kong as well as the lease for Weihaiwei. Facing this new wave of imperialist expansion in China, what was Japan's strategy for imperialist expansion?

The Regionalization Strategy

Its new semiperipheral position in the capitalist world economy at the turn of the 20th century greatly influenced Japan to adopt a regionalization strategy of imperialist expansion. First, Japan could only afford to invade its weaker neighbors. Unlike the core imperialist powers who commanded colonies around the globe, Japan as a semiperiphery had yet to develop a strong military to exert its influence beyond East Asia. As a result, Japan's strategy was to turn its East Asian neighbors into colonies and therefore markets for its nascent manufacturing industries; Japan also could extract foodstuff and raw materials from its new colonies.

Second, in terms of timing, Japan was a "late imperialist." After Japan became a semiperiphery and strong enough to develop imperialist ambitions, it found itself already surrounded by Western imperialist powers and their Asian possessions—Russia in Manchuria, Germany in northern China, Britain in central China, and France in southern China. As a result, Japan's imperialist expansion in East Asia would inevitably bring Japan into open conflict with the Western core states.

Third, in terms of power, Japan as a semiperiphery was still not strong enough to impose its wishes over the Western core powers. Although the main thrust of Japan's expansion had been directed at Korea, the Liaodong Peninsula, and Beijing [Peking], this military strategy had risked dangerous international repercussions. As a result, although the Liaodong Peninsula was awarded to Japan in the Treaty of Shimonoseki in 1985, within 3 months the "Triple Intervention" by Russia, Germany, and France forced Japan to retrocede Liaodong to China, which, in turn, was soon forced to lease the peninsula to Russia, to the suppressed fury of Japan. Immediate strategic and diplomatic circumstances, therefore, determined that Taiwan—whose occupation was least likely to provoke core resentment—would become the first outright possession of the Japanese colonial empire.

Fourth, in terms of security, Japan as a semiperiphery still worried about core domination. In this respect, Korea was of critical strategic importance to Japan. Korea was long perceived by Japan as "a dagger to the heart of Japan." If controlled by a hostile power, it would be a potent threat. If, on the other hand, Japan controlled Korea, the latter could be used as a springboard to further expansions in mainland China. In order to compete effectively in interstate rivalry, the logical move for Japan was to turn Korea into its colony. Thus 10 years after the "Triple Intervention," Korea was finally declared a Japanese protectorate after Japan defeated Russia in 1905. Korea was formally annexed and became a

Japanese colony in 1910. Both Taiwan and Korea remained Japanese colonies until the Allied forces defeated Japan in the Pacific war in 1945.

Finally, in terms of imperialist ideology, Japan's semiperipheral status in East Asia amidst Western imperialist powers led Japan's leaders to adopt what Duus (1988, p. 7) calls, "a curious form of anti-imperialist imperialism. They could run with the hare or hunt with the hounds, as external circumstances and internal interests dictated." On one hand, as the first Asian nation to modernize and successfully resist Western political and economic encroachments, Japan served as a model and aspiration to anticolonial movements throughout Asia. For example, Chinese nationalists like Sun Yat-sen sought refuge or support in Tokyo. As a result, the Pan-Asian idea that Japan, as the first successful non-European modernizer, was obligated to assist its less fortunate Asian neighbors, enjoyed wide currency from the beginning of the 20th century onward. On the other, as Japan further acquired its own colonial territories in Korea and southern Manchuria in the early 20th century, Japanese leaders came to share the same ambitions as those of Western imperialist states. In this respect, Japan's foreign policy was characterized by both anti-imperialist, Pan-Asian rhetoric and the imperialist rhetoric of continental expansion.

THE COLONIZATION OF TAIWAN AND KOREA

Political Domination

The first task of the Japanese colonizers was to construct a new administrative machinery that would allow them to exercise effective control over the Taiwanese and Korean polity. Following the annexation, the entire administrative and political setup of Chosen (the Japanese name for Korea) and Taiwan were duly overhauled in the following three ways.

First, there was an important component of repressive apparatus within the two colonies. The Japanese imperatives of exerting colonial control and suppressing local rebellions caused a steady increase in the power and number of the police forces. For example, the police force in Korea rose from 1,717 men in 1906 to 6,222 in 1911, and further to 14,000 by 1919 (Henderson, 1968, p. 79). Throughout the colonial period, these police forces assumed an ubiquitous presence at the local level and performed many public functions on behalf of the colonial state.

Second, there was the supreme power and autonomy of the colonies' governor-general (Beasley, 1987). In place of the king, the governor-general became the vortex of the colony of Chosen. Internally, the governor-general exercised almost absolute control of his bureaucracy. He appointed all officials and had extensive power over both civilian (including police and judiciary) and military affairs. Always a career military person, the governor-general was responsible directly to the Japanese emperor and was not even subject to the control of his home government. The autonomy of the Korean colonial administration was further augmented by the appointment of prominent individuals (such as Japanese ex-prime ministers) to the post of governor-general (Hong, 1980).

Third, there was the closure of the colonial states from indigenous populations. In Korea, the process of political exclusion started by eliminating the *yangban* governing class, initially by pensioning off officials of the Yi bureaucracy. During the colonial period, about half of the bureaucrats were Koreans; but, with very few exceptions, they held only minor posts. Even Koreans with higher positions were carefully kept from posts of substantive power (Kim, 1973).

In sum, an overdeveloped colonial state apparatus had emerged in Taiwan and Korea. Both the Taiwanese and the Korean people were excluded from the apparatuses' top echelons, and these people were largely deprived of opportunities to learn the "secrets" of modern administration. As a result, Japanese colonialism left behind an awesome institutional state structure that was highly autonomous from the local society.

Economic Exploitation

As Ho (1978, p. 32) observes, the Japanese colonial governments in Taiwan and Korea had two principal economic objectives: (a) to promote domestic sugar and rice production and export them to Japan; and (b) to keep local economic power in Japanese hands.

First of all, a system of "colonial exchanges" was instituted between the colonies and Japan proper. Before the colonization, Taiwan's external trade was mainly directed toward China, but that declined dramatically after Japanese annexation. The influence of Japanese banks, trading companies, and direct investment certainly contributed to the dominance of Japan in the colonies' external trade, but perhaps the most important mechanism was the building of a Japanese colonial trading bloc by means of tariffs. On one hand, high import tariffs were imposed on non-Japanese foreign imports into Taiwan, and exports from Taiwan to these foreign countries were taxed heavily. On the other, "transfers" (i.e., exports) from Taiwan to Japan were partially exempted from export duties. As a result of this trading bloc, Taiwan's transfers to Japan in 1928 were almost three times greater than Taiwan's trade with other countries (Yanaihara, 1956, p. 59). In Korea, Japan did not impose protective tariff barriers until 1920 in order not to offend the foreign core powers who had kept a watchful eye on Japanese rule in Korea. Nevertheless, even without official Japanese intervention, trade with Japan still accounted for the bulk of Korea's total foreign trade (Myers & Peattie, 1984).

Examining the structure of such colonial trade further testifies to the mechanisms of colonial exploitation. Exports from Taiwan and Korea to Japan were predominantly foodstuffs (rice and sugar), but imports from Japan were mostly manufactured products. Thus Ho (1984, p. 348) remarks that for much of the colonial period before the Pacific war, Korea's and Taiwan's economic positions in this empire were mainly as agricultural appendages of Japan. Through supplying inexpensive rice, sugar, and other foodstuffs to Japan, Taiwan and Korea helped support Japan's growing industrial population and prevented Japanese domestic industrial wages from rising rapidly. In turn, the colonies also served as captive markets for Japanese manufacturing industries.

The second economic objective of having the colonial states of Taiwan and Korea was to concentrate economic power in Japanese hands. Therefore, the formation of an indigenous entrepreneurial class in the colonies' modern sectors was never encouraged. For instance, the formation of purely Korean- or Taiwanese-owned corporations was subjected to official approvals, which were rarely granted. Even after this regulation was eventually repealed in the 1920s, the official policy was to encourage small-scale handicraft industries, such as mats and alcoholic beverages, that would not enter into competition with Japanese companies (Zo, 1978).

Class Collaboration

Another distinctive feature of the colonies under Japanese rule was class collaboration in the countryside. The first measure undertaken by the colonial state was the implementation of the land survey in the colonies. The land survey helped to remove the top layer of absentee landlords from the land-ownership system as well as to confer the right of land ownership to the cultivating landowners, so the colonial state could extract taxes directly from them. By guaranteeing property rights to these new landlords, the colonial state thus developed a class collaboration with the latter. As Cumings (1984, p. 491) points out, "the Japanese wanted to keep the landlords in the countryside to control their communities and to market their agricultural products." Through the landlords, cash crops were thus extracted from the peasants and turned into exports to Japan.

Nevertheless, the specific role of landlords in the process of colonial exploitation differed in the two colonies. In Korea's Yi dynasty, private property rights (including landholding rights) were ill defined and all land was officially owned by the king. As a result, large plots of Korean land without clear land ownership were expropriated during the land survey by the colonial government and allocated to Japanese companies. Most Korean peasants who had only cultivating rights were also deprived of any claims to the land (Y-S. Chang, 1971). On the other hand, because private land ownership was so well developed in Taiwan, there was no massive appropriation of land by the colonial state, unlike in Korea (Dai, 1985).

Furthermore, the Japanese colonial state also employed different strategies toward the Taiwanese landlords and the Korean *yangban* elite. In the case of Korean, *yangbans* were encouraged to stay inland and given little incentive to diversify their economic activities. However, because Taiwanese landlords had ample experience in export agriculture and were eager to cooperate with Japanese companies, the colonial state sought to harness the capital of big Taiwanese landlords and channel it to such domestic processing industries as the sugar-refining industry. This small group of Taiwanese "collaborator-entrepreneurs" later diversified their investments into other industries and financing, and they rose into prominence in the colonial business world (Gold, 1988, p. 109).

Indigenous Antisystemic Movement

Despite efforts to secure the support of the landlord class, Japanese colonialism had aroused indigenous resistance in both Taiwan and Korea because the colonial state was harshly authoritarian and exploitative.

In Taiwan, in response to the news of colonization, some members of the local gentry and administration proclaimed the independence of Taiwan and the establishment of the Taiwan Republic. Local militia fought long and cruel guerrilla warfare against the Japanese contingent in Taiwan. Even after the collapse of the republic 6 months after its establishment, the guerrilla activities and local uprisings, especially by aborigine tribes, continued for at least 6 more years. Nevertheless, by the late 1910s, the Taiwanese majority began to tolerate the Japanese presence and passively succumbed to the idea of colonial rule (Peattie, 1988).

In the case of Korea, however, Peattie (1988, p. 266) points out that, "the Japanese were faced with a virtual war of popular resistance in the years between the establishment of the protectorate and the annexation of the peninsula into the empire." Between 1907 and 1911, participants in the armed resistance movement increased to 143,690 persons, and there were almost 3,000 clashes between the Japanese army and Korean insurgents. Then the fires of Korean national hatred against Japanese colonialism continued to smolder until they burst out anew in 1919. Crying "Long Live Korean Independence," the March First Movement in 1919 was a protest of national proportions. Only the most drastic Japanese measures, the massive presence of the Japanese army, and the imprisonment of the leadership of the resistance finally brought the Korean people to sullen obedience. By their own account, the Japanese killed more than 7,500 Koreans and wounded another 16,000 during the suppression of the March First Movement, but the numbers were probably far greater than the Japanese official estimate (Borthwick, 1992, p. 194). A segment of the Korean armed insurgents, however, retreated to the border between Korea and Manchuria, where it continued to wage armed struggles against the Japanese (Mu & Sun, 1992).

What explains the bitterly anti-Japanese sentiments of the Korean people in contrast with the passive acceptance of Japanese colonialism in Taiwan? According to Peattie (1988), "there was, first, the historic animosity between the Korean and Japanese people dating back to Hideyoshi Toyotomi's invasion of the peninsula in the sixteenth century which had left a legacy of destruction and a tradition of Korean hatred. . . . " Second, there was the factor of Korean cultural autonomy. Whereas Taiwan had never existed as more than a political subdivision and cultural appendage of China, Korea had been a country with its own culturally rich tradition. Moreover, Korea had been a unified country, and its modern national consciousness had been beginning to develop. As Lee (1973, p. 275) notes, "Japan, through her conquest and rule of Korea, awakened and sustained Korean nationalism. Japan provided the negative and yet the most powerful symbol of Korean nationalism, a national enemy." Third, in Korea, there was an economic foundation for anti-Japanese sentiment. Compared with the Taiwanese under Japanese rule, the Korean people (the *yangban* landlord class, the small businessmen, and the peasants) fared worse in nearly every economic category. For example, because all rice surpluses produced in Korea were shipped directly to Japan, the consumption of rice by Koreans actually dropped during the colonial period (Peattie, 1988, p. 257).

In short, during the first phase of colonial rule in Taiwan and Korea, the Japanese had imposed a repressive government, relied upon the landlord class to extract food and raw materials for exports, and faced strong resistance movements from indigenous peoples. The intensity of Korean resistance movements, as well as the powerful currents of political change in the Japanese homeland and the capitalist world economy, began to halt the regionalization project of the Japanese state by the late 1910s.

REGIONALIZATION HALTED

Toward Global Cooperation

On balance, World War I was highly profitable for Japan. Borthwick (1992) notes that while Europe remained mired in the exhausting and destructive struggle, Japan continued to build its economy rapidly. Its entrepreneurs had benefited from the boom in global economic demand. In addition, the withdrawal of Western powers from East Asia prompted the Japanese state to expand its control from Taiwan and Korea to mainland China. After joining the Allies and declaring war against Germany, Japan immediately seized the German concessions on China's

Shandong Peninsula. Duus (1988) further points out that the absence of countervailing Western power had emboldened Japan's new attempts to secure a hegemonic position in China, first through the Twenty-One Demands and then through the Nishihara loans. In the aftermath of World War I, Japan therefore had become a strong regional power in East Asia.

In response to this increasing Japanese dominance, there emerged a new mode of agreement by Western core powers toward Japan's position in the world economy. This is because a new world order was emerging. The war signaled the end of British hegemony and the rise of the United States as the leading core power in the interstate system. Under American leadership, especially under Woodrow Wilson, ideals of liberal internationalism and the right to national self-determination resurfaced, symbolized by the formation of the League of Nations in 1920.

During the Washington conference of 1921-1922, the major Western powers further managed to establish the basis for military equilibrium in East Asia to avoid the excessive build-up of the Japanese navy and to halt Japan's regionalization project. First, the conferees decided to create a new multilateral arrangement involving France, Great Britain, Japan, and the United States. This new arrangement was a means to dissolve the British-Japanese alliance that had prevailed for the previous 2 decades. Second, after losing this premier ally, Japan was forced to accept a war fleet size that was inferior to that of the British and the Americans (a ratio of 5-5-3). This decision was aimed at diluting Japan's capacity to influence the events in East Asia, and especially at trying to restrict the special interests that Japan wrested from China. Third, after achieving a balance of power in East Asia,

> the emphasis from now on was on obtaining, preserving, and extending economic rights and interests. The diplomacy and economic expansion were to be conducted within the framework of international cooperation, in particular cooperation with the United States, the country viewed as the initiator of the new order. (Iriye, 1974, p. 243)

Under such a liberal world-economic order, Japanese peaceful economic competition among nations, through international cooperation and multilateralism, was seen as highly beneficial. Thus instead of competing with Western core states for colonial conquests in East Asia, Japan wanted to prosper by increasing its global exports, especially to the

United States, the richest economy in the world at the time. In exchange for refraining from military aggression toward China, Japan expected an increase in trade to follow from more friendly relations. Thus, Japan was committed to economism and internationalism throughout the 1920s (Iriye, 1974).

Economic Transformation

A significant transformation of the Japanese economy had occurred during this period of liberal world-economic order. First, the share of the primary sector in the economy began to fall behind the secondary sector's share. Second, the emergence of electrification made its impact on the economy, leading to not just the growth of electrochemical industries but also the mechanization of smaller-scale industries. Third, stimulated by the world wars, the share of Japan's heavy chemical industries in its domestic economy doubled from 15.9% of total manufacturing output in 1900 to 31.2% in 1938 (Minami, 1986, pp. 127, 133). The expansion of Japan's steel industry, in particular, was able to not only meet increasing domestic demand, but also increase its export volume in the world market.

All in all, Japan in this period exhibited the following characteristics of a semiperipheral economy: First, Japanese exports to core countries were very different in composition from its exports to peripheral countries. For the core countries as a whole, Japanese exports were predominantly light manufactured products (such as raw silk and silk products), accounting for some 73% of total Japanese exports. Japan also had a high degree of dependence on the American market even among core countries. Exports to the United States made up 24.3% of all of Japan's exports, and 67.5% of exports to all core countries. The pattern of exports to the peripheral countries, in contrast, was diametrically different. For its colonies and China (Japan's informal empire), more than one third of all Japanese exports were heavy industrial products (machinery in particular). Thus, although Japan's pattern of exports to core countries exhibited traces of peripheral status, Japan appeared as a core in its pattern of exports to the peripheral countries.

Second, Japanese imports also reflected a similarly triangular relationship. Imports from Europe were largely machinery and chemical products; imports from the United States were split between industrial products and raw materials (raw cotton, wheat). From the developing countries, Japan imports were almost exclusively foodstuffs and raw materials (Senkyu Hyakku Niju Nendaishi Kenkyukai, 1983, pp. 36-38).

Third, Japan's pattern of borrowing served as more evidence of its semiperipheral status. During the early 20th century, when Japan began to expand abroad, its imperialist ventures had to be financed by borrowing from Western core states. For example, the money Japan lent to the Chinese warlord governments was actually European money borrowed by Japanese government banks. As soon as the Russian-Japanese War had begun, the Japanese government had to raise loans in the money markets of New York and London. Many expenses of the Russian-Japanese War had to be paid out of foreign loans. Even in the 1920s, a large share of foreign loans raised was used to finance imperialist activities, such as the establishment of the Manchuria Railway Company and the Oriental Development Corporation (Duus, 1984, p. 161).

Fourth, the emergence of a dualistic industrial structure (small family firms versus giant corporations called *zaibatsu*) in Japan's economy in this period is another indication of its semiperipheral development. The economic power of the *zaibatsu* was largely exercised through *zaibatsu*-controlled banks. During the Meiji era, the largest *zaibatsu* had acquired control of the largest banks. During the Taisho period, the *zaibatsu* banks had a surplus of capital, which allowed them to lend to or invest in non-*zaibatsu* firms, and periodic financial crises in interwar Japan helped to weed out smaller and poorly managed banks. By exerting a larger degree of control over their financial capital, the *zaibatsu* could extend their influence to other firms and other sectors. In particular, during and after the First World War, the *zaibatsu* made forays into heavy industries, which required large doses of capital investments. The result was an upsurge in concentration of capital in the Japanese economy. Between 1920 and 1935, the share of the largest 1% of firms in the total capital of all Japanese corporations rose from 44.9% to 65.6% (Sato, 1981, p. 19). Oligopoly developed in many industries, such as heavy chemicals, machinery, shipping and shipbuilding, and the modern food-processing industry.

The disproportionate growth of the large enterprises, however, did not preclude the persistence of the small-scale sector. In the interwar period, distress in the countryside and the resultant rural-urban migration led to the further growth of small-scale traditional industries. The new urban migrants looking for jobs in the city were too numerous to be absorbed into the modern industries. Thus, the surplus labor force had no choice but to enter such traditional low-status service-sector jobs as itinerant peddling, street vending, and barbershops (Minami, 1986). Furthermore, Duus (1976, p. 178) points out that small enterprises survived because they served as suppliers or subcontractors for large companies, performing certain production operations less expensively in their small workshops than larger firms could in their factories. In some areas, the flexibility and specialization of small manufacturers even offered them a competitive advantage over larger ones. It is estimated that between 1916 and 1935, the share of the "modern" sector in employment barely increased from 10.6% to 12.1%, but the small-scale "traditional" sector grew from 36.1% to 41.5%, thereby absorbing much of the decline in the primary sector (Nakamura, 1983, p. 29). Even in manufacturing alone, 58.3% of the labor force in the private manufacturing industry in 1930 was employed in the small-scale sector, with fewer than five operatives (Lockwood, 1954, pp. 202-203).

The dualistic industrial structure was also reproduced in the labor market, due to the scarcity of skilled labor and the oversupply of unskilled workers in the early 20th century. In order to dampen high labor mobility and maintain skilled workers, a more paternalistic employment system took shape in the interwar period: lifetime employment, higher wages, a seniority-based wage system, and more fringe benefits. Among the larger firms in the industrial sector such practices were increasingly being applied to white-collar employees; in the large manufacturing firms, especially in the capital-intensive heavy industries, skilled workers received these benefits as well. Subsequently, wage differentials emerged among workers in different industries as well as in firms of different sizes (Taira, 1970).

Finally, the contradictions of Japanese semiperipheral development are also revealed by the acute agrarian problems during the interwar years. The First World War bought prosperity to the Japanese countryside as it did to the rest of the economy. The fortunes of the agrarian sector were reversed, however, by the onset of the postwar depression and the slump in agrarian prices. In order to sustain capital accumulation, to prevent urban wages from rising further, and to help maintain political stability, the Japanese state solved the food problem by further integrating Japan proper with its colonies. A crash program was adopted to increase agricultural production in the colonies, as well as food im-

HELEN-JEAN MOORE LIBRARY
POINT PARK COLLEGE

ports from the colonies to Japan. The program succeeded quite well, and the Japanese empire attained a higher degree of self-sufficiency in food production. Nevertheless, cheap food imports from the colonies left the Japanese peasants facing continual stress due to depressed agrarian prices (Patrick, 1971, p. 218). The only source of alleviation for the countryside was the growth in silk exports. Sericulture, however, made peasant households more vulnerable to fluctuations in the world economy than before.

By the 1920s the Japanese began to feel the political effects of these economic transformations.

Taisho Democracy

In the first 2 decades of the 20th century, an expanding urban middle class was formed, consisting of professionals, journalists, and civil servants. Having more education and improved living standards, this class wanted the government to serve its interests better and be more responsive. In addition, the growth of industry and commerce fostered a class consisting of big business and numerous small entrepreneurs, which also began to try to increase its influence over the government. Most members of this class were anxious to keep their tax burden from rising, and they did not want to divert expenditures from civilian and economic construction to military purposes. They wanted assistance from the government but not high-handed interference. To the emergent middle class and the bourgeoisie, a party government was a means to ensure that their interests were heard inside the state. As an indication of their influence, the composition of the Seiyukai, one of the two major political parties, began to change in favor of those with bureaucratic and business backgrounds (Duus, 1968, p. 14).

Between 1913 and 1918, Seiyukai party leaders were also given minor positions in the cabinet as a token of their support. Finally, the appointment of the Seiyukai president as premier in 1918, and the formation of a cabinet with a majority of Seiyukai members, were generally hailed as the beginning of parliamentary democracy in Japan; hence the label "Taisho democracy." The resemblance to parliamentary democracy was reinforced by the emergence of two-party competition between the Seiyukai and the Kenseito. From 1924 to 1932, the two parties alternated to organize the cabinet, and leaders from the two parties took turns as premier. In 1925 universal manhood suffrage was established, further increasing the democratic elements of party governments.

The democratization of the Taisho era coincided with changes in the state's economic policy. After initial ventures by the Meiji state, the scale and scope of public ownership of business enterprises declined in the early 20th century. In Lockwood's (1954, p. 508) words, the public sector "never bulked large in the prewar Japanese economy in quantitative terms, whatever their importance in other respects. They went little beyond what was then regarded as the conventional sphere of public responsibility in most industrial countries." Changes in the economy also enabled the state to "retreat" selectively from the economy. The boom during the First World War solved many of the problems in the economy. Japan's exports surged, reversing the previous deficits of international balance of payments. Despite the frequent financial crises in the 1920s, the Japanese economy still grew at a rate faster than most European economies. The growth of the *zaibatsu* and other large-scale enterprises, on the other hand, limited the state's ability to intervene in the economy. For example, the failure of the government to deflate the economy after rampant inflation during the First World War was largely the result of its inability to control the privately owned banking industry. The Japanese central bank was unable to put a grip on the rash credit policies of large *zaibatsu*-owned banks (Allen, 1962, p. 101).

In addition, Taisho democracy was accompanied by the rise of social unrest and socialism. The expansion and concentration of a urban proletariat during the First World War boom laid the foundation for a labor movement. The number of factory workers increased by 60% between 1914 and 1919 (Duus, 1968, p. 122). The growing affluence and stability of the skilled working class in large enterprises, as a result of the emergence of a dualistic labor market, created a nucleus for labor protests. Rampant inflation during the war excited the working class into action. The postwar recession further intensified labor militancy by forcing the workers to protest against layoffs, retrenchments, and rationalization measures. As a result, toward the end of the war, there was a major increase in the number of strikes, from only 50 strikes involving 7,900 workers in 1914 to 497 strikes involving 63,100 workers in 1919 (Yamamura, 1974, p. 308). Strikes temporarily subsided afterwards, falling below 300 cases a year, but again surged in the late 1920s. Labor organizations mushroomed in the late 1910s under the leadership of left-wing intellectuals. By 1926 about 488 labor organizations had been formed, claiming 284,739 members. In the heavy industries, union participation was especially common. A number of national federations were also formed (Duus, 1968, p. 124). The countryside was similarly affected by growing social unrest. Tenant farmers quickly organized themselves to seek redress for their economic deprivation. The number of tenant unions increased from 50 in 1908 to 1,530 in 1923. By 1927 a total of 365,332 (or 9.6% of all) tenant farmers belonged to unions. Tenancy disputes also shot up from 408 in 1920 to 2,751 in 1926 (Kobayashi, 1983, p. 283; Waswo, 1982, p. 367).

Political tolerance in Japan proper during the Taisho era, as well as the March 1919 crisis in Korea and the death of the incumbent military general in Taiwan, provided opportunities for the democrats in the Japanese government to push toward a more liberal administration of the colonies in the 1920s.

Liberalization and Resistance in the Colonies

As Peattie (1988, p. 234) points out, the first step was to abolish or limit military administration in those colonies where it still existed, because it had proven both oppressive and unresponsive to civilian populations. In Taiwan, Prime Minister Hara was successful in attaining this objective, and there was a decade and a half of civilian administration for the colony. In Korea, during the decade of "cultural rule" (*bunka seiji*), Korea was granted a number of modest reforms designed to permit greater self-expression for Koreans, abolish abuses in the judicial system, eliminate discrimination in the treatment of Koreans in public service, equalize educational and economic opportunities, promote agriculture and industry, and generally give Koreans a greater voice in the management of their own affairs (Brudnoy, 1970).

In response to these modest liberal reforms, a second wave of nationalist movements emerged in the Japanese colonies in the 1920s. In Korea, there were culturally oriented consciousness-raising activities in the form of a "New Life" movement and a "buy Korean" movement in the 1920s. Under Russian influence, Korea also developed a socialist movement. A provisional Korean government in exile was established in China in 1919, whereby Syngnam Rhee was elected president (Nahm, 1988, pp. 317-319). In Taiwan, there was a reformist movement which demanded the establishment of a legislative assembly. Japan-educated professionals, landlords and merchants formed the backbone of the movement, petitioning the Japanese government 15 times between 1921 and 1934. Toward the mid-1920s, as it became apparent that the petition movement was not bearing fruit, more radical movements appeared. The emergence of socialist movements in China and Japan also contributed to the radicalization of Taiwanese nationalism (Weng, 1992, pp. 32-35).

This period of so-called Taisho democracy and liberalization, as Gordon (1991) explains, is best characterized as a system of "imperial democracy." It is imperial in the sense that the system had its roots in the oligarchic consolidation of imperial sovereignty, the rise of capitalism, and the beginnings of imperialism in the late 19th century. The changes in this period are also democratic because of the genuine movement toward more popular participation in Japan proper and the colonies. As such, the system is contradictory because it was committed to both national glory and widened participation. By the early 1930s, however, the "liberal" interlude in the Japanese empire had come to a close. The combined weight of world depression, economic dislocation within Japan proper, and the assassination of Prime Minister Hara had led to the winding-up of civilian rule in the colonies, and to a call for ultranationalism, militarism, and continental expansion at home. This renewed pursuit of regionalization appeared in the building of an East Asian Co-Prosperity Sphere.

BUILDING AN EAST ASIAN
CO-PROSPERITY SPHERE

World Depression and Ultranationalism

As Nakamura (1988) remarks, while the impact of American's Wall Street panic of October 1929 was still reverberating throughout the world, Japan was plunged into a severe depression. As the Western core states began dumping their exports abroad and Japan's domestic demand declined, Japanese heavy industries were force to reduce their workforces in order to rationalize production. Numerous small enterprises went bankrupt. Workers were forced to take sharp cuts in wages. Hardest hit, however, were the farm villages, by the sudden drop in the prices of key commodities such as rice and silk cocoons. The distress of farm households was matched by growing unemployment in metropolitan areas.

During the 1930 depression, right-wing ultranationalism became increasingly popular. Beasley (1963, p. 237) argues that "the resulting movement embraced conservatives, professional patriots, agrarian idealists, advocates of state ownership and social revolutionaries, all contributing in some measure to the aggressive 'ultranationalism' of the nineteen-thirties." For these ultranationalists, the economic and political problems of Japan were the results of following the path of Westernization. Thus, the growth of labor unrest was attributed to the spread of Western capitalism, which led to concentration of wealth in the hands of *zaibatsu* and profiteers; the agrarian depression and the emergence of tenancy disputes were said to threaten the very foundation of the Japanese society; and parliamentary democracy was chastised for the corruption of party politicians.

Militant nationalism crystallized around such ultranationalist thinkers as Kita Ikki (Wilson, 1969). For Kita, the Meiji constitution had to be suspended because it was modeled upon the Western model. The monarchy had to be reconstituted as the symbol of national unity. The economy had to undergo socialist reform. Industrial capital had to be nationalized and put under state control; social reform had to be implemented by establishing workers' ownership of enterprises. As Najita and Harootunian (1988, p. 721) point out, Kita's thinking was decidedly anti-Western because the "ultimate aim of socialism in Japan was to force the retreat of the West and to create a new civilization based on the revival of all of Asia."

In the early 1930s, ultranationalists seized upon rising social tensions during the depression to attack party politicians. Inspired by a romantic view of selfless devotion to the state and the emperor, they resorted to terrorist tactics to overthrow the parliamentary government. They favored direct action; a series of terrorist assaults on key political leaders was waged by right-wing military officers. For example, after he retired from office, Prime Minister Hamaguchi Osachi was shot dead by a right-wing youth. With the support of such ultranationalists, the military's influence within the government was greatly enhanced, and there was a renewed push toward Japanese expansion into continental Asia.

Manchukuo and Continental Expansion

Japan's continental expansion started with an initiative by the Guandong army, which originally was merely a garrison in the Guandong Leased Territory on the strategic Liaodong Peninsula. This Guandong army often acted independently of the Tokyo government to extend Japan's influence in Manchuria. In the so-called Manchurian Incident in 1931, Lieutenant Kawamoto Suemori of the Guandong army set off an explosive to blow up Japan's own railroad tracks near Mukden, an incident for which the Japanese Guandong army then blamed the Chinese. This permitted the Guandong army to claim self-defense and advance beyond its zone. By 1932 all Manchuria lay under Japanese military control. In defiance of League of Nations condemnations, the Japanese installed China's last emperor Puyi as head of the new puppet state "Manchukuo" and issued the Japanese yen as its currency (Borthwick, 1992, p. 203). A "Japan-Manchukuo Economic Bloc" came into being in the 1930s, following the worldwide trend of creating a "sterling bloc" centered on Great Britain and the Commonwealth, and a "dollar bloc" centered on the United States. Thus, the era of international cooperation in the 1920s was replaced by the era of closed economic blocs in the 1930s.

In 1934 the Guandong army marched further south and established a de facto sphere of influence in northern China. After broadening this into the "Japan-Manchukuo-North China Economic Bloc," the army developed plans for obtaining from northern China raw materials such as iron ore, coal, and salt, which were in short supply in Manchukuo. In 1937 the army drew up another plan to expand direct military preparations for the expected outbreak of war with Western core powers, expand the chemical and heavy industries, and establish a firm base for munitions production. Japan proper was to provide 6.1 billion yen of the needed capital for this army plan, and 2.4 billion yen was to come from Manchuria and northern China (Nakamura, 1988).

The establishment of Manchukuo and continental expansion played a role in Japan similar to that of the New Deal in the United States. The reflationary effects of increased military expenditures and increased war production revived the Japanese economy from stagnation. In addition, the war had led to increasing state intervention into Japan's economy (Hata, 1988).

Because Japan's full-scale war with China started in 1937, the Japanese economy was administrated with the sole objective of meeting its military demands. Japan continually strengthened its economic controls by giving priority to allocating limited materials and capital to meet military demands. As Nakamura (1988) reveals, the Diet in 1938 enacted the National General Mobilization Law, which gave the government sweeping powers:

> (1) The establishment of firms, capital increases, bond flotations, and long-term loans came under a licensing system; (2) the government was empowered to issue directives concerning the manufacture, distribution, transfer, use, and consumption of materials connected with imports and exports . . . and (3) the government was also empowered to issue directives on the conscription of labor power, the setting of working conditions, the disposition of firms' profits, the use of funds by financial institutions, the administration, use, and expropriation of factories and mines, and the formation of cartels. (p. 481)

In 1940, because of the increasing squeeze on consumer goods as well as poor rice harvests, Japan instituted a rationing system for rice, matches, and sugar, and also imposed fixed prices on key commodities.

Observing Nazi Germany's successful invasion of France and expecting the imminent defeat of Britain, Japan's military drew up plans to invade Singapore and the Dutch East Indies, to gain access to abundant supplies of raw materials such as oil, rubber, and tin. In 1940 Japan further advanced into northern French Indochina and signed a treaty of alliance with Germany and Italy. In response, the United States tightened its export restrictions against Japan, froze Japanese assets in America, and imposed a total embargo on petroleum exports to Japan (Nakamura, 1988). Unable to persuade the Americans to accept Japan's dominating role in China and Southeast Asia, Japan launched a surprise attack of Pearl Harbor on December 7, 1941.

After Japan superseded the European powers as the most dangerous imperialist state in Asia, the Pan-Asian ideas that had enjoyed currency at the turn of the 20th century acquired new vigor in the notion of the Greater East Asia Co-Prosperity Sphere (Crowley, 1970):

> We must show the races of East Asia that the order, tranquility, peace, happiness, and contentment of East Asia can be gained only by eradicating the evil precedent of the encroachment and extortion of the Anglo-Saxons in East Asia, by effecting the real aim of the co-prosperity of East Asia, and by making Nippon the leader of East Asia. (p. 238)

The Transformation in Korea and Taiwan

As Japan plunged into the Pacific war, its central concerns were economic consolidation of the empire and the integration of its colonial economies to meet the wartime requirements of Japan proper. Accordingly, the colonial governments of Korea and Taiwan drew up plans for major industrialization programs and downgraded agricultural production as an economic priority (Peattie, 1988). In both Taiwan and Korea, therefore, industrial facilities were created to produce the raw materials— petrochemicals, ores, and metals—needed by Japanese heavy industry.

These industrial efforts were pushed further ahead in Korea than in Taiwan, owing to superior natural resources in the Korean peninsula. Peattie (1988, p. 258) points out that with the Sino-Japanese War in full swing in the late 1930s, Korea increasingly became a logistical base for Japanese military operations on the continent, and Korea's industrial plants turned to the task of keeping Japan's armies in China supplied.

In addition, with the outbreak of the Pacific war in 1941, Japan's manpower needs increased dramatically. To fill the demand for workers in factories in Manchuria and Japan, millions of Koreans and Taiwanese were seized from their families and sent off to work far away. Borthwick (1992, p. 200) reports that in 1944, at the war's peak, fully 16% of the Korean population—4 million people—had been deported from Korea to Japanese labor camps.

How then should we assess Japan's impact on Taiwanese and Korean development? On one hand, the Japanese contribution seems to be quite positive. The economies in colonial Taiwan and Korea ended up having respectable growth rates; both countries emerged from Japanese rule with efficient and productive agricultural systems, modern banking and

monetary systems, educational and administrative facilities, and factories. On the other, on top of the enormous human costs of Japanese
colonial repression, Peattie (1988) argues that Japanese policy, by keeping power out of the hands of the Taiwanese and Koreans, constrained
the development of a modern entrepreneurial class in both Taiwan and
Korea. In addition, because industrial and administrative positions were
so often filled by Japanese during the colonial period, few indigenous
technicians or managers were available to either country, which resulted
in massive dislocations in the economies of Taiwan and Korea when the
Japanese withdrew.

CONCLUSION

From a broader perspective, the Pacific war was a result of Japan's
strategy of semiperipheral ascent in the interwar period. Japan had
chosen to pursue an expansionist strategy of development by the 1890s.
In order to overcome the dual constraints to development—the scarcity
of national resources and the small size of the domestic market—Japan
took on a regionalization strategy. It sought to build up an Asian regional
empire in order to make available the supply of major staple imports, as
well as markets for its nascent manufacturing industries, especially textiles. Taiwan and Korea mainly served the former purposes; continental
expansion catered more to the latter.

As we have seen, such a strategy of regional dominance halted during
the 1920s. The Western core powers at the Washington conference
induced Japan to accept an inferior war fleet and to engage in international cooperation rather than regional rivalry. Echoing President Wilson's call for democracy and domestic pressures from the emergent
Japanese middle class, there was a brief era of Taisho democracy in Japan
proper, providing political tolerance for the many social movements to
emerge. The liberals in Japan then pushed for civilian rule in Taiwan and
Korea.

However, the world depression in the 1930s and its dislocations in the
Japanese economy led to the emergence of ultranationalism, militarism,
and the end of modest liberal reforms in the colonies. The depression
testified to the vulnerability of Japan in the world economy and accentuated Japan's desire for regional integration. Japan stepped up conti-

nental expansion to China and initiated expansion to Southeast Asia. The idea of a Great East Asian Co-Prosperity Circle was also raised to rationalize Japan's empire-building efforts. When the United States cut off the supply of military-related exports to Japan, most notably oil, the latter could see no alternative but to fight for a high level of integration with the resources-rich Southeast Asia by eliminating the American presence in the region.

By the time of its defeat by the United States in 1945, Japan had lost 3 million lives, and its economy was in ruin. Nevertheless, Nakamura (1988, p. 492) suggests that "the conditions for sustaining postwar economic growth were already sprouting among those ruins." For instance, the wartime munitions industry provided the prototype for the chemical and heavy industrial sector. Links between big factories and small business that developed in the munitions industry also became the basis for the postwar subcontracting system. Administrative guidance by government ministries—a fundamental characteristic of the postwar developmental state—was also a legacy of the wartime controls.

Obviously, Japan's regionalization project had a significant influence on China's development. This will be the focus of the next chapter.

5. The Sino-Japanese Wars and the Chinese Communist Revolution

The regionalization strategy of Japan had greatly shaped China's path of development in the following three ways: (a) While Japan emerged after the first Sino-Japanese War in 1894 as a full-fledged imperialist state building up a colonial empire in East Asia, China experienced rapid foreign political, economic, and cultural encroachments after losing the war. (b) Nevertheless, as a result of Japanese rivalry with other core powers in East Asia, Chinese nationalist movements, and cyclical opportunities in the world economy, these factors had contributed to the consolidation of state power under the Nanjing [Nanking] regime of the Guomindang [Kuomintang or KMT; hereinafter GMD], and to the achievement of substantial economic growth during China's Republican period. (c) Despite the above progress toward state building and economic growth, the global depression in the early 1930s, the continental expansion of Japan to Manchuria, as well as the second Sino-Japanese War from 1937 to 1945 had led to the degeneration of the GMD regime, the slowing down of industrialization, the increase of rural pauperization and the worsening of agrarian class relations. This created a space for the Chinese Communist Party (the CCP) to mobilize the peasantry through nationalism and ultimately seize state power in 1949. In this chapter, we are going to account for China's turbulent development trajectory from 1894 to the first half of the 20th century.

THE DOWNFALL OF THE CHINESE EMPIRE

Political Encroachment

After being defeated by Japan, China was required by the Treaty of Shimonoseki, in 1895, to pay Japan a crushing indemnity of 230 million taels (360 million yen). In addition, China had to recognize Korea's "independence," as well as cede Liaodong Peninsula, the Pescadores Islands, and the island of Taiwan to Japan.

The aftermath of the first Sino-Japanese War, therefore, witnessed the political dismemberment of the Chinese empire. In order not to lose grounds to the Japanese, each Western power immediately sought to define a sphere of influence in China within which it would have the exclusive right to build railways and engage in exploration and mining. For example, France extended its control from northern Indochina to South China, including the lease of Guangzhou Wan. Germany established itself in the Shandong Peninsula and obtained the lease of Kiaochow Bay. Russia acquired the Liaodong Peninsula. Britain obtained the lease of the New Territories north of Hong Kong as well as the lease of Weihaiwei.

In addition, exclusive arrangements on Chinese territories were often guaranteed by means of bilateral agreements among the Western powers, with or without China's knowledge. For instance, Iriye (1970, p. 140) notes that "a French-British agreement recognized their respective spheres of influence in China, and a German-British agreement assigned Shandong as Germany's sphere of interests and the Changjiang [Yangtze] as British's, while a Russian-British pact defined the mutual limits of railway concessions in North China."

Due to this scramble for concessions by the foreigners, China was close to political colonization by 1899. Then came the 1900 Boxer Uprising, through which a secret society of traditional martial arts experts led an antiforeign rebellion. After the Boxers were defeated by an alliance of Western forces, the Chinese government was forced to pay a huge indemnity of 450 million taels (Moulder, 1977, p. 117). The indemnity payments served to drain China's economic resources and slowly suffocated its political system.

Economic Encroachment

Up until 1894 the Chinese government had generally been very reluctant to borrow money from abroad because of fear of foreign control. However, between 1894 and 1911, China borrowed seven times more than it had borrowed in the entire previous century of contact with the West. Beginning in 1897 these loans required annual repayments. According to Thomas' (1984) calculation,

> loans to pay the 1895 indemnity cost about 17 million taels per year by 1898, while the Boxer indemnity added another 18 to 23 million taels per year . . . and by 1902, indemnity payments required over 40 percent of China's central government revenue. . . . From 1897 on, and particularly after 1902, China's government was in a continuous state of bankruptcy. (p. 113)

In exchange for the loans, the Chinese government was forced to grant railway and mining concessions to foreigners. By 1911, 41% of the railway mileage in China was owned by foreigners, and the reminder had largely been built by the Chinese government with foreign loans. Foreign loans had strings attached, such as giving foreign agents a monopoly over construction and control over the administration and part of the profits until the loans were paid off. In order to ensure that China would pay back the loans, the foreign customs revenues, the salt revenues, and even internal customs taxes were taken as security for loans. In this respect, Young (1970, p. 154) remarks that Chinese sovereignty was diminished in the handling of maritime customs funds, in the ownership of railways and mines in the country, and in the control of salt revenues during the early 20th century. Foreign power seemed to be present everywhere and to fill all the vacuums left by such internal disruptions as the Boxer Uprising.

Desperately striving for more revenues, the Chinese government had tried five times since 1896 to gain the necessary unanimous consent of the foreign powers to raise tariffs. But British merchant pressures blocked approval of four of these Chinese requests for a tariff increase. No increase was permitted until the 1902 Mackay Treaty, which allowed an increase in tariffs from 3% to 4% in exchange for Chinese reductions in provincial and local trade taxes. In this respect, the result was little net increase for the Chinese domestic economy, but simply a shifting of revenue from the provinces to the central government (Thomas, 1984, p. 114).

Unable to raise tariffs, the Chinese government was then forced to raise internal taxes to meet the loan and indemnity payments. This had an adverse effect on the domestic Chinese economy, as silver payments to foreigners reduced the amount of silver in China, fueled inflation, and contributed to the failure of many traditional banking institutions. The financial distress of the Chinese government also prevented it from providing the necessary economic resources and political support for the self-strengthening enterprises. The indemnities and foreign loans deprived China of capital that could have been used to develop Chinese-owned enterprises. Numerous Chinese businesses were in danger of failure due to lack of capital after 1897. Moreover, imposing new taxes on these enterprises caused a loss of confidence among the Chinese merchants, making them hesitant to invest in new or even existing state-connected industries. Furthermore, after the 1895 Shimonoseki Treaty allowed the foreigners to set up manufacturing facilities in China, China became effectively deprived of control over its own domestic markets. By 1897 cotton goods imports had surpassed opium as the largest Chinese import, and foreigners took control of much of China's cotton goods import-substitution market (Thomas, 1984, pp. 115-123).

Cultural Encroachment

After 1900 Western culture had become dominant among the urban intelligentsia as indigenous Confucianism retreated. One channel for expanded Western cultural influence was the rapid expansion of missionaries in the early 20th century. In 1889 there were only 1,296 foreign missionaries, 37,287 claimed communicants, and 16,836 students enrolled in missionary schools. By 1919 there were already 6,636 foreign missionaries, 345,853 claimed communicants, and 212,819 enrolled in missionary schools. In addition, increasing numbers of Protestant missionaries moved beyond the evangelical limits of the 19th-century mission compound to participate actively in community educational, medical, and philanthropic work (Feuerwerker, 1976, pp. 42, 49).

The retreat of Confucianism can also be seen through the educational reforms of the Qing government in the first decade of the 20th century. Before 1900 Confucianism was still highly respected and used as a bulwark to resist Western ideas and values. Even while schools for teaching foreign languages and Western learning were being established, recruitment into the civil service continued to be dominated by the old examination system. Beginning in 1901, however, the examination system was dismantled in a series of rapid moves. It was ruled that the selection of the official elite was to be accomplished through a comprehensive system of new schools and through study abroad. As a result, there was a great spurt in the creation of modern schools, and thousands went abroad for study, especially to Japan.

As Young (1970, p. 158) points out, "the real revolution accompanying the abolition of the examination system was in the realm of political attitudes and values. It was an abandonment of the centuries-old belief that only years spent with the Confucian classics truly qualified one for political leadership." The culturally refined literati from the landed upper class who had dominated for a millennium were suddenly seen as anachronistic. Instead of relying upon Confucianism and the literati, the Qing government was now looking for specialists trained in Western knowledge, because it believed that only people endowed with such talents could handle the imperialist threat. The bonds between the landed upper class and the Chinese state via Confucianism were therefore completely torn apart through the abolition of the old examination system.

After downgrading Confucianism, the Qing government tried to invoke patriotic sentiments in an effort to rally the Chinese population to meet the foreign threat. Now children had to learn mathematics, geography, science, and above all, nationalism. Young (1970) reveals that

> the textbooks published between 1903 and 1906 for the new school system stressed China's territorial losses in the nineteenth century, the unequal treaties, the free wanderings of missionaries in the interior, the humiliation of the Boxer affair, the importance of racial conflict and competition, and the virtue of military valor. (p. 158)

However, the reforms of the Qing government were too little and too late.

The Collapse of the Imperial Bureaucracy

The social support of the Qing government was rapidly eroded by the accelerated pace of foreign domination by the turn of the 20th century. First, China's humiliating defeat in the Sino-Japanese War and the scramble for concessions afterwards destroyed much of the political legitimacy of the Qing government. Second, huge indemnity and loan payments forced the Qing government to cut expenses, fire officials, and decrease salaries. These financial pressures greatly exacerbated existing patterns of customary corruption as officials accepted bribes, sold official positions, and traded long-term concessions in exchange for short-term income. These actions made the Qing government even less popular than before. Third, under the growing financial burden, friction between the central and provincial governments increased. For instance, this occurred when three fourths of the financial responsibility for the Boxer indemnity was passed on to the provinces, upsetting the local governments' balance of revenues and expenses; and when the terms of the 1902 Mackay Treaty dictated that the central government could receive an increase in tariff rates only in exchange for decreased provincial taxation of trade (Thomas, 1984, pp. 117-118). Fourth, increasing taxes on the self-strengthening enterprises and abolishing the old examination system broke the old stable alliance between the Qing government on one hand, and the merchants, the industrialists, and the landed upper class on the other.

Still, it was the Qing government's own reforms that triggered its final collapse. In addition to the new schools that specialized in Western education, the Qing government set up a "New Army" to train modern officer corps. Then the Qing government undertook the creation of representative assemblies, through which it hoped to mobilize the landed upper class in an advisory role to support the imperial government. In this "constitutional reform," elections for provincial assemblies were scheduled for 1909, and a national assembly was to be elected in 1910, to plan for a parliament to be established in 1917. As Young (1970, p. 165) remarks, the Qing government "dug its own grave with the reform movement." In the Qing government's new schools, Western-educated students developed nationalist views that were hostile to the alien Manchu dynasty. In the Qing New Army, officers were absorbed into the framework of the regionally based armies remaining from the

Taiping Rebellion. And Qing-initiated constitutionalism not only politicized the landed upper class, but also provided it with a class organization to safeguard its provincial and local class interests at the expense of the central government (Skocpol, 1979, p. 78).

As a result, when the Wuchang uprising occurred on October 10, 1911, no economic class or social group came to the Qing government's rescue. Within the next few weeks, the military governors who commanded the New Army forces and the landed upper class-merchant leaders in the provincial assemblies quickly declared their independence from the central government, leading to the Revolution of 1911. After the central imperial bureaucracy was dismantled, power came to rest primarily in the regionally based New Army factions; and warlord rivalries intensified as the armies and their commanders competed for territories and resources (Skocpol, 1979, pp. 79-80).

In sum, China could no longer remain a unified empire in East Asia. In the midst of the scramble for concessions, China had no central state to defend its own interest; its economy was under foreign domination; and its Confucian culture was in retreat. Did it mean that China had fallen to the status of a periphery?

INCOMPLETE PERIPHERALIZATION

In the literature that is sympathetic to dependency theory, the prevailing view is that China increasingly resembled a colony or a periphery by the early 20th century. The famous quotation is Sun Yat-sen's remark that "China was not the slaves of one country, but of all and therefore was worse off than a colony because there was no one paternalistic power to whom she could turn for mercy" (Thomas, 1984, p. 112). In the old historiography of the Chinese Communist Party, China was characterized as "semi-colonial and semi-feudal," and its economy was on the verge of bankruptcy (Wright, 1992, p. 13).

However, in a world-systems analysis that highlights imperialist rivalry, antisystemic movements, and cyclical rhythms, China's peripheralization was incomplete. Despite strong foreign domination in China's political, economic, and cultural spheres, there was still room for China to strive for upward mobility in the capitalist world economy in the early 20th century.

Imperialist Rivalry

First of all, the very multiplicity of China's imperialist dominators and their interests in East Asia limited the extent of their power. An imperialist state could not extend its power too far without infringing upon the prerogatives of another. For instance, although the Sino-Japanese War involved only the two combatants, its aftermath concerned other imperialist powers. As Iriye (1970) observes:

> Russia, France, and Germany directly influenced the shape of the peace when they objected to Japan's acquisition of the Liaodong Peninsula and forced it to renounce that territory in return for an increase in China's reparations payments. This tripartite intervention revealed the interrelatedness of European and Asian politics. Russia feared that Japan's foothold on the continent would menace its own designs in the Maritime Province, Korea, and Manchuria. Germany was interested in promoting Russian intervention in East Asia so as to divert the latter's attention from Europe. France acted with Russia to show solidarity with its ally. Britain did not act, as it was immobilized by pressures from the three powers to join them and from Japan to repudiate them. (p. 138)

Later, during the scramble for concessions in the late 1890s, Great Britain decided to support China's independence. Britain opposed China's total disintegration because colonization would harm British commercial and strategic interests. Britain wanted to avoid the protectionist tariffs that had been established in French and German colonies in Africa—tariffs that had prevented the expansion of British trade (Thomas, 1984, p. 111).

Finally, China's independence was guaranteed by the U.S.-promoted Open Door policy of 1899, which the British had inspired. Under this policy, the imperialist powers agreed to share equally the benefits of occupying China, rather than to divide China into separate colonies or fight to make China an exclusive colony of one country. Instead of carving China up into spheres of influence, the American policy therefore stressed the equality of commercial opportunity and, eventually, China's "territorial and administrative entity" (Iriye, 1970, p. 140).

In 1917, U.S. President Wilson further called for a doctrine of national self-determination. To the Japanese, "Wilsonianism become little more than a clever ideological ruse designed to check the growth of imperial Japan, to protect the semicolonial rights of the Western powers in China, and to promote Sino-Japanese hostilities" (Crowley, 1970, p. 239). Nevertheless, during the Washington conference of 1921-1922, Japan was forced to pledge its respect for Chinese sovereignty and the Open Door policy in exchange for naval security with respect to the Anglo-American powers.

Due to these intense imperialist rivalries, the political peripheralization of China was incomplete. As Feuerwerker (1976) remarks:

> Perhaps it was too big for any one [state] to swallow, and—misleadingly— too dazzling a prize for satisfactory division of shares to be worked out, given the rivalries and constraints of the pre-World War I international system. China's sovereignty might be derogated, but it never came near to being extinguished. In whatever manifestation he presented himself, the foreigner in China had always to acknowledge that there was a Chinese authority, central or local, with which he had to contend. (p. 1)

If political peripheralization was incomplete, so was economic peripheralization. This was because imperialist rivalries also provided the cyclical opportunity for industrialization and the growth of the Chinese capitalist class.

Cyclical Opportunity

In the early 20th century, the Chinese capitalist class began to emerge amid foreign economic domination. Its golden opportunity was World War I, as the Western powers, focusing their energies on imperialist rivalries in Europe, significantly reduced their economic involvements in China. As Borthwick (1992) points out:

> Chinese entrepreneurs soon replaced the European imports and services for which there continued to be a growing demand in China. Chinese banks sprang up: savings banks, postal banks, and credit cooperatives all serving an expanding economy. By 1920 a National Banker's Association formed to enforce standards and help maintain currency stability. Chinese exporters and processors of raw materials prospered from the global increase in prices created by the Great War. Even Chinese currency appreciated due to the rise of silver prices on the world market. (p. 189)

Borthwick (1992) notes the overseas origins of the Chinese capitalist class. For example, many successful business families in Shanghai got their start outside of China in overseas Chinese communities:

> The Jian family began a shipping empire out of Guangzhou in the nineteenth century, moved into massive cigarette exports to Southeast Asia of the Nanyang Brothers Tobacco Company which grew to challenge the might British American Tobacco Corporation. Similarly, the prosperous Kwok family started its entrepreneurial life in Sydney, Australia and maintained close ties to the branches of the family as far away as the Philippines and Fiji. (pp. 189-190)

The growth of the Chinese industrial economy was further assisted by robust antisystemic movements within China during the early 20th century.

Nationalist Movements

First of all, after 1905, China experienced a new spurt of nationalist movements stimulated by the Japanese defeat of Russia. Japan's victory laid to rest the fiction that the white race was superior to Asians, and it showed that an Asian state could defeat a European state. This event greatly boosted the confidence of the Chinese: They were convinced that they could also develop into a strong state, as Japan had done. Soon afterwards, a Right Recovery movement began: a Chinese nationwide effort to resist the development of foreign concessions, to purchase back concessions or rights lost to foreigners, and to promote Chinese-owned industrial enterprises. The movement produced impressive results. An estimated 549 private and officially sponsored manufacturing and mining enterprises, with a total estimated capitalization of 80 million taels, were initiated between 1895 and 1913 (Thomas, 1984, p. 153).

Second, there were numerous boycotts against foreign goods. It started with the 1905 boycott of American goods in a protest against increasingly blatant, racially biased U.S. immigration rules. It was followed by a boycott against Japanese goods in the Tatsu Maru incident in 1908, and another boycott against Japanese goods in the "Twenty-One Demands" incident in 1915. Then there were at least five boycotts directed against Japan, one of them also against Britain, in the 1920s. The

Chinese capitalist class was, of course, very active in promoting these boycotts to enhance its interests; but these boycotts did have widespread support from other classes (students, intellectuals, and workers) and generally spread quickly to major Chinese cities. As a result, the boycotts were quite effective in reducing foreign control over Chinese industries. For example, whenever there was a boycott against Japan, Japanese exports and imports into China plummeted (Liao, 1990, pp. 62-83).

Third, there was the May Fourth Movement in 1919. Several thousand students from Peking [Beijing] universities gathered in a massive demonstration on May 4, 1919. The students protested the Versailles Peace Conference for confirming Japan's claim to the German-held territory on China's Shandong Peninsula. The students were shocked to find out that Japan had signed a secret covenant with Britain, France, and Italy as early as 1917, to guarantee its claims over Shandong after the war was over. Thus, the slogans of the students read: "The loss of Shandong means the destruction to the integrity of China's territory," "Don't forget our national humiliation," "Struggle for sovereignty—throw out the warlord traitors," "Boycott foreign goods" (Schell & Esherick, 1972, pp. 61-62).

The historical significance of the May Fourth Movement is that a new generation of students and intellectuals had been galvanized to the calling of nationalism to save China (Zarrow, 1994). Before 1919 this new generation was attracted to the universalism of the West. It proposed total Westernization and the brutal, wholesale repudiation of Confucianism. It idolized the "Mr. Democracy" and "Mr. Science" of the West, and it condemned such Chinese traditions as arranged marriages. However, after the massive demonstrations in 1919, there was a rapid radicalization of nationalist leaders. Disappointed by the decision at the Versailles Conference, many radical students and intellectuals began to perceive the West as agents of imperialism, rather than as representatives of science and democracy. Inspired by the Bolshevik Revolution in Russia, and grateful for Lenin's offer to give up nearly all the old claims of the czar's sphere of influence in China, many Chinese students and intellectuals were drawn to Marxism and Lenin's theory of imperialism. Since 1919, Marxism had come to dominate every sector of intellectual life. The Chinese Communist Party (the CCP) was founded in 1921 (Bianco, 1971, pp. 27-52).

Finally, the Nationalist Party (Guomindang—the GMD) had also turned to the new Russian Communist regime for help. Sun Yat-sen, the founder of the GMD, had been organizing uprisings to overthrow the Qing dynasty since the 1890s. Although Sun was finally successful in getting rid of the imperial bureaucracy and was made the first president of the new government in 1911, warlord opposition immediately forced him to step down, and he fled to Japan. The failure of the Western powers to aid Sun and the GMD during the warlord era left him bitterly discouraged with parliamentary solutions to China's problems. As Sun wrote: "We have lost hope of help from America, England, France or any other of the great powers. The only country that shows any signs of helping us in the south is the Soviet Government of Russia" (quoted in Schell & Esherick, 1972, p. 69). In 1923 Sun signed an agreement with the Russians, promising them to allow members of the CCP to join the GMD in exchange for funding, arms, and advisers. In 1924 Sun adopted the "Three New Policies of the GMD": alliance with the Soviet Union, support for workers' and peasants' movements, and collaboration with the CCP. In the same year, a military academy at Huangpu, near Canton, was established to train cadres for the revolutionary army; this academy was under the leadership of a young specialist trained in Tokyo and Moscow named Chiang Kai-shek [Jiang Jieshi]. After Sun's death in 1925, the leadership of the GMD passed to Chiang.

In 1926 a unified GMD and CCP army launched a "Northern Expedition" against the warlords. Assisted by general strikes of workers, and in the face of a tremendous show of popular enthusiasm for the nationalist cause, many warlords gave up without a fight. The cyclical opportunity in the world economy, by contributing to the growth of an indigenous capitalist class, also strengthened the GMD's cause, because it was able to garner resources from the nascent bourgeoisie. After capturing Nanjing and Shanghai, however, Chiang suddenly moved against the CCP in 1927. Without warning, Chiang launched an armed attack against labor groups and the CCP in Shanghai, slaughtering several thousand people. The brutal suppression in Shanghai was soon followed by the elimination of labor leaders and Communists throughout the country. When Chiang was in complete control of the GMD, he set up a new government in Nanjing (Borthwick, 1992, pp. 183-184).

The Nanjing Government

In the late 1920s, as a result of imperialist rivalries, cyclical opportunity, and nationalist movements, the GMD was able to bring nominal political unity to China after decades of warlord politics. After driving out the Communists and banning labor strikes, the GMD established political order in the major urban centers.

Appealing to President Wilson's doctrine of national self-determination, and taking advantage of the new Japanese global cooperation policy in the 1920s, the GMD began to regain control over tariff protection from the foreigners. By the early 1930s, the GMD was able to gain real, though limited, autonomy to set levels of tariffs that might protect industry or maximize revenues, to benefit from the customs revenues (which became the mainstay of the GMD finances), and to control the actual customs operations by placing Chinese staff in senior positions (Wright, 1992, p. 22).

In addition, the GMD formulated economic policies that were in accord with capitalist interests. The suppression of the working class eliminated strikes and industrial disturbances. A National Economic Council was established in 1931, to direct the economic reconstruction of the country. The currency system was unified, with the virtual elimination of the tael in 1933 and the adoption in 1935 of a modern paper money system. Tariff autonomy was achieved and indirect taxation increasingly rationalized and centralized. And the government experimented hopefully with an annual budget (Feuerwerker, 1968b, p. 51).

Nurtured by the above policies, the Chinese industrial economy continued to grow. The impressive annual growth rate of 13.4% during and after World War I (1912-1920) was followed by an average annual growth rate of 8.7% from 1923 to 1936. In 1933 a survey recorded 2,435 Chinese-owned factories capitalized at Ch$ 406 million, with a gross output valued at Ch$ 1,114 million, and employment of 493,257 workers. These factories were concentrated in the coastal provinces, and especially in Shanghai, which accounted for 1,186 of the plants surveyed. For China proper alone, 78% of the output of the factory industry was accounted for by Chinese-owned firms. Certain industries, such as the cotton textile industry, grew rapidly and steadily and were not monopolized by foreign-owned firms. Even in the 1930s, China's cotton textile output was one of the largest in the world. Therefore, although China's

modern industrial sector in the 1930s was small in relation to the economies of the core states, it was neither inconsiderable nor without potential for further development as compared, for instance, with Japan in
1895 (Feuerwerker, 1977, pp. 17-39). Rawski (1989, pp. 344-345) further
argues that during the 2 decades up to 1937, the Chinese economy grew
on a substantial basis, with its GDP rising some 20% to 25% in inflation-
adjusted output per capita.

In short, a unified state, the recovery of tariff autonomy, developmental policies, and a rapid rate of industrial expansion are indicators of
incomplete peripheralization in China. If the Wilsonian global cooperation environment in the 1920s had persisted, China might have been on
its way to emerging as a powerful, industrial state, and East Asian history
since the mid-20th century would have to be entirely rewritten. However, the world economic crisis and the renewal of Japanese imperialism
in the 1930s had started a new phase of development in East Asia. Instead
of sustaining its trend toward state-building and capitalist industrialization, China suddenly moved toward communism in 1949. What then
explains this abrupt shift in path toward communism in the mid-20th
century?

ORIGINS OF THE COMMUNIST REVOLUTION

The Communist Revolution is such a complex event that it has to be
explained by a combination of the following factors: (a) The degeneration of the GMD's Nanjing government laid the foundation for the
Communist movement; (b) peasant pauperization and changing agrarian class relations in the 1930s provided the social supports for this
movement; (c) Maoism, the Red Army, and peasant mobilization provided the revolutionary ideology, organization, and strategy; and (d) the
second Sino-Japanese War provided the timing and the powerful catalyst
for revolution.

The Degeneration of the Nanjing Regime

There were two historical events that triggered the degeneration of
the Nanjing Regime. First, there was renewed Japanese imperialism.
Although thwarted by the Washington conference of 1921-1922, Japa-

nese continental expansion pressed with renewed vigor in the 1930s. In 1931 the Mukden Incident touched off the invasion of Manchuria, which in early 1932 became the Japanese puppet state of Man Zhou Guo [Manchukuo]. Then Japan tried to establish a second puppet state made up of the five provinces of North China. In response, nationalist sentiment and boycotts against Japanese goods swept through China. But Chiang Kai-shek ignored this surging nationalism in the early 1930s. Instead, his strategy was "Unification and then resistance" (Bianco, 1971, p. 144). Chiang wrote:

> You think that it is important that I have kept the Japanese from expanding during these years. I tell you that it is more important that I have kept the Communists from spreading. The Japanese are a disease of the skin; the Communists are a disease of the heart. They all say that they want to support me, but secretly they want to overthrow me. (Quoted in Schell & Esherick, 1972, pp. 91-92)

Not willing or able to stop the Japanese invasion, Chiang thus lost the support of the nationalist students, intellectuals, and workers. Many of them turned to the CCP for nationalist resistance, because it had officially declared war on Japan in 1932.

Second, there was the 1929 world economic crisis. Due to the reduction in demand in the capitalist world economy, there was a sharp drop in exports for certain Chinese industries. The Chinese silk industry, for instance, reduced its exports from 136,000 piculs in 1931 to 54,000 piculs in 1934, resulting in the closing of 160 out of 180 silk factories in central China (So, 1981, p. 47). In addition, starting in 1931, the capitalist countries successively abandoned the gold standard, thus causing the price of silver to rise again and commodity prices in China to fall, leading to an unprecedented serious economic crisis. The Japanese occupation of the vast markets and natural resources of northeast China, the dumping of foreign goods at cheap prices, and the import of smuggled Japanese goods further aggravated the economic crisis in China, resulting in more stagnating sales, factory shutdowns, and falling production (Wu, 1992, pp. 37-38). Due to the economic crises in the 1930s, the Nanjing government was under considerable financial stress. It began to increase excise taxes on consumer necessities and to borrow through high-interest bonds issued by government-controlled banks. These fiscal measures, as

Skocpol (1979, p. 250) remarks, restricted consumer purchasing capacity, destroyed incentives for saving and long-term productive investments, and alienated the capitalist class from the GMD. Needless to say, the GMD had no resources to deal with the enormous peasant problem in the countryside. The percentage of the national budget allocated to rural reconstruction was a meager 0.2% in 1931-1932, 0.5% in 1933-1934, 3.9% in 1934-1935, and 3.7% in 1935-1936 (Bianco, 1971, p. 110).

Failing to present itself as a nationalistic party to resist Japanese invasion, and lacking the resources to buffer the impact of the world economic crisis, the Nanjing government by the 1930s had to rely increasingly upon bureaucratic, moral, and repressive means to maintain political control.

Bureaucratically, the Nanjing government revived the traditional *Bao Jia* [pao-chia] system by extending the state from the county level to the village level. Through this "state involutionary process" (Duara, 1988), the Nanjing government hoped to get the peasant masses under more effective control and make the suppression of Communists much easier. However, this *Bao Jia* system failed to work. The local official positions were usurped by "local bullies." In the name of the GMD, the local bullies used their authority to tax the peasants illegally and to set up gambling, opium dens, and prostitution, so as to drain monies into their own hands.

Morally, the Nanjing government promoted the New Life Movement as an antidote to communism. The propaganda pamphlet, titled *On the New Life*, called for the following moral conduct: "Be clean. Do not spit in the streets. Button your suit properly. Stand up straight. Do not eat noisily. Do not drink, dance, or gamble. Shun high living and dissipation" (Bianco, 1971, p. 127). Confucian ethics of filial piety were also brought back in, as Chiang asserted: "To fulfill the principle of complete loyalty to the state and of filial piety toward the nation; to be altruistic and not seek personal advantage; to place the interests of the state above those of family; such is the highest standard of loyalty and filial loyalty" (quoted in Schell & Esherick, 1972, pp. 76-77). It is doubtful whether the old morality of Confucianism was able to provide adequate legitimacy in lieu of nationalism and effective political-economic programs.

Politically, as the Nanjing government lost dynamism, it became drained of all political vitality and degenerated into a series of cliques, focused through ties of personal loyalty on Chiang Kai-shek. As Skocpol (1979) remarks,

The "Generalissimo," directing the strategic Military Council, devoted most of his attention and skill to military campaigns against remaining warlords and the Communist "bandits." . . . Mass organizations were either allowed to atrophy or else were used purely for purposes of enforcing the depoliticization of workers, peasants, and students. (p. 250)

When students and intellectuals demanded national resistance, when critics pointed out the widespread corruption among government officials, and when peasants cried for relief from the oppressive taxes of government, Chiang's responses became increasingly authoritarian—censorship, prosecution, political prisoners, assassinations, and so on.

As a result of the degeneration of the Nanjing government, the peasant problem grew worse in the 1930s.

Pauperization and Changing Agrarian Class Relations

In the literature, there is a debate on whether peasant conditions were deteriorating before 1949. On one hand, Tawney (1932) and Chen (1936) emphasize rural poverty, landlord exploitation, and the backwardness of the rural economy during this period. On the other, Myers (1991) and Rawski (1989) provide the most bullish estimates on the success of the rural sector for this period in not only maintaining but actually raising per capita consumption.

Although the debate remains inconclusive due to the lack of solid empirical data (R. B. Wong, 1992), there is no doubt that the Chinese peasants experienced a sharp fall in income as a result of the contraction of export markets during the 1930s world depression. As Feuerwerker (1977) explains,

in this period of steeply falling prices, the farmer's fixed costs and the prices of manufactured goods tended to be more "sticky" than prices received for agricultural commodities which fell first and more rapidly. There was a clear tendency for farmers to cut back on cash crop production and return to the cultivation of traditional grain crops in response to the depression. Opportunities for off-farm employment, which had been essential to the family incomes of small farmers in particular, also may have declined temporarily after 1931 with a resulting flow of labor back to rural areas from the cities. . . . The outflow of silver from rural areas to Shanghai and other cities made it more burdensome for farmers to obtain loans. In sum, significant parts of the gains that had accrued to the agricultural sector during the previous long inflationary phase were lost in 1931-1935. (p. 48)

The world depression, falling prices, bankruptcy of cash crop exports, and reduction of off-farm employment had accelerated social stratification in the countryside. As Huang's (1990) "involutionary commercialization" thesis illuminates, the Chinese peasants turned to commercialized crop production for survival more than for capitalist profit. Without reserves and operating close to the margin of subsistence, the peasants often had to sell immediately after the harvest, when prices were falling. During the 1930s depression, therefore, many peasants fell into debt; they had to borrow, often at very high interest rates, to make ends meet. When they could not repay these loans, they had to transfer the titles to their land to landlords. The result was a growing unequal distribution of land ownership and the expansion of an impoverished, marginal peasant class at the bottom of the social hierarchy in the village.

Although this phenomenon had happened numerous times before, the collapse of the imperial bureaucracy and the involvement in the world economy brought several new features to the changing Chinese agrarian class relations in the 1930s. To start with, there was a delegitimation of the landlord class. In Imperial China, the landed upper class were esteemed scholar-gentry who were knowledgeable in Confucian classics, passed the examinations, and were recruited into the imperial bureaucracy. Although they extracted land rent from the peasants, the landed upper class protected the local community from the state's arbitrary taxation and also provided such vital services as welfare to the widowed, charity to flood victims, and sponsorship of the Chinese New Year festival. Nevertheless, by the 1930s, this esteemed landed upper class had left the local community, because its members were both attracted to the higher living standard in the treaty ports and frightened by the growing rural unrest in the countryside. These absentee landlords then relied upon their agents to collect land taxes for them.

By the 1930s the leadership of the local community was passed to a new group called "corrupt gentry and local bullies" (Zarrow, 1991). These new local leaders knew no Confucianism and performed no community services; they would not concede rent reduction nor extend loan payment deadlines in the case of bad harvests. Instead, they relied upon purely coercive means, such as *gong fu* [kung-fu] fighters and weapons to collect land rent, to engage in usury, to set up opium and gambling dens, and to impose arbitrary taxation. As Moore (1966, p. 220) laments, a sense of "felt injustice" must have been built into the Chinese rural social structure on the top of massive poverty and landlord exploitation.

In Imperial China, the above peasant grievances would fuel only minor revolts, because the peasants lacked ideology, organization, and local community-based autonomy to render their resistance revolutionary. In the 1930s, however, the emergence of Maoism, the Red Army, and the strategy of peasant mobilization had intensified the revolutionary potential in the Chinese countryside.

Maoism and Peasant Mobilization

After the 1919 May Fourth Movement, the Chinese students and intellectuals forsook Western science and democracy and adopted the science of revolution of Marx and Lenin. Leninism had a special appeal to the Chinese students and intellectuals because, as Borthwick (1992, p. 179) points out, it "provided a *doctrine* of imperialism which explained the basis of Western colonial behavior in economic terms, a firm *prediction* that such behavior was ultimately doomed, and a *methodology* for fighting back by means of a specialized, disciplined organization" (italics original). Following the doctrine of Leninism and Russian advisers, the radical Chinese students and intellectuals formed the Chinese Communist Party (CCP), organized workers in the cities, and worked with the GMD in the North Expedition to get rid of the warlords. However, in 1927, Chiang executed thousands of Communists and drove the Communist movement out of the cities. For years after 1927, recurrent attempts were made by the CCP to retake the cities, but all such attempts proved abortive and costly in human lives.

The late 1920s and the early 1930s were the period of wandering in the wilderness for the CCP. Here was a Communist party cut off from the cities and the working class, crouching in the shelter of a remote and hilly countryside, and working mostly with the poor peasants. It was under such aloofness from the capitalist world economy that Mao Zedong [Mao Tse-tung] formulated the original concept of the Red Army, the strategy of peasant mobilization, and a set of new values called *Maoism.*

First, Mao realized that it was of utmost importance for the Communists to develop a Red Army. As Selden (1966, p. 68) remarks, "without military forces of their own, wooing of the elite, creation of a party organization and leadership in the peasant and labor movement came to naught in the swiftly changing currents of warlord-Guomindang China." Different from the conventional army, which focused on technical training, the Red Army placed more emphasis upon ideological training. The aim of the Red Army was to educate all members of the military to cooperate for the achievement of party-defined purposes. In addition, the Red Army was trained to unite with the civilian peasantry. Basically, this meant treating peasant lives, property, and customs with scrupulous respect; the Army also engaged in production activities so as to supply themselves without burdening or violating the peasantry (Skocpol, 1979, p. 253).

Second, Mao realized the importance of peasant mobilization. In order to gain the active support of the peasantry, Red Army units promoted political education, party activities, and militia organization in the villages with which they had substantial contact (Blecher, 1986). For Mao understood that peasants could not just be forcibly drafted into professionally led standing armies; instead, they had to be persuaded to volunteer manpower and supplies to the Red Army. Peasants would not willingly and reliably provide such support unless the Communists fought in their interests, in a style that conformed to their local orientations. Thus Mao called upon the party cadres and the armies to carry out the "mass line." Mao wrote:

> This means take the ideas of the masses and concentrate them . . . then go to the masses and propagate and explain these ideas until the masses embrace them as their own, hold fast to them and translate them into action, and test the correctness of these ideas in such action. Then once again concentrate ideas from the masses and once again take them to the masses. . . . And so on, over and over again in an endless spiral, with the ideas becoming more correct, more vital and richer each time. (Quoted in Schram, 1969, p. 316)

Only when the peasants were satisfied with the CCP's grassroots participation did that later become "a fish swimming in the sea of the people."

Third, Mao formulated a set of new values to legitimize CCP activities. Usually called Maoism (Selden, 1979, pp. 12-20), these new values consisted of equality, mass participation, and self-reliance. With regard to equality, the rigid hierarchical class structure of traditional China embodied in the dominance of landlords over tenants, rich over poor, officials over the common people, the old over the young, and men over women gave way—often strikingly so—to more egalitarian practices in political, economic, and social life. For example, differences in rank and reward between officers and men in the Red Army were downplayed. With regard to mass participation, the mass line technique required that "leaders must be pupils as well as teachers of the masses." Party cadres and officers in the Red Army were sent to work in the fields in order to learn from the peasantry. On the other hand, the masses were organized into peasant organizations, militia units, and, in the case of activists, party members. With regard to self-reliance, Mao believed that each local community could develop on its own without outside help. What was needed was to mobilize local resources, develop grassroots leadership, and invoke the spirit of collectivity.

With the Red Army, the strategy of peasant mobilization, and the new values of legitimacy, the CCP was able to utilize peasant grievances in the countryside and wage a civil war with the GMD. Nevertheless, up until the early 1930s, the forces of the CCP were still too weak to provide a serious challenge to the GMD. Facing the GMD's 75 divisions of German-trained and -equipped troops in 1933, the CCP at best narrowly escaped annihilation, by relocating its base from Jiangsi to Yenan through the famous Long March. In this respect, although the CCP had found the right peasant formula, it still had to wait for a historical opportunity in order to fully develop this revolutionary potential in the countryside. Fortunately for the CCP, the second Sino-Japanese War provided such a golden opportunity.

The Second Sino-Japanese War (1937-1945)

In the Xian [Sian] Incident of 1936, Chiang Kai-shek was kidnapped by one of his warlord allies while on a visit to Xian, and was released only when Chiang publicly agreed to establish an anti-Japanese United Front with the Communists. No sooner had the Nationalists and the Communists formed their second alliance then Japan unleashed a full-scale invasion of China in 1937. In 2 years, Japan ended up occupying the treaty ports, the industrial centers, the capital, and the richest and most populous parts of China. Then Japan went on to establish colonial regimes in the Dutch East Indies, Malaysia, Singapore, the Philippines, and French Indochina in the early 1940s.

The second Sino-Japanese War, from 1937-1945, empowered the Communists in the following ways. First, it considerably enlarged the space through which the CCP could expand its political and military activities. The Japanese forces were swallowed up in the vastness of China, and they did not have the manpower to effectively control the countryside, where Communist guerilla bases multiplied rapidly during the war years. Moreover, as Meisner (1970) points out,

> the retreat of kuomintang [GMD] military forces to the west in the face of invading Japanese armies, and the concurrent collapse of Nationalist governmental authority in much of China, allowed the Communists to break out of their remote sanctuary in Shensi and expand their military and political influence through vast areas of the countryside in northern and central China. . . . The gradual growth of peasant-supported Communist political and military nuclei in many parts of China during the war years was to prove decisive when the revolutionary struggle with the Guomindang was resumed with full fury in 1946 in a massive civil war. (pp. 278-279)

Second, the war enabled the Communists to present themselves to the Chinese populace as nationalists (Johnson, 1962). Although it was nationalism that drove many students and intellectuals to Russian communism during the 1919 May Fourth Movement, during the second Sino-Japanese War, when communism was blended with nationalism, it was able to extend its appeal to the Chinese population. Posted as the leaders of patriotic resistance against the Japanese, the Communists became saviors of the Chinese in the areas liberated from Japan. Thousands of students went to Yenan to work with the Communists for patriotic resistance; patriotic propaganda, with its reduction of land rent program, was much more successful in winning over the peasants than the agrarian revolution had been several years before.

Finally, the second Sino-Japanese War had greatly weakened the GMD. Bianco (1971, p. 159) asserts that it was during this external war that the Guomindang lost the Chinese civil war. The second Sino-Japanese War exposed the weakness of the GMD's military forces, particularly its faction-ridden and incompetent command structure. In addition, this war touched off China's greatest inflationary rates of all time. The loss of major sources of revenues (customs duties were now collected by the Japanese), and the need to finance increased wartime expenditures with the resources of a few poor provinces in the interior, laid the roots of this inflation. This inflation not only produced the usual consequences of widespread financial speculation and corruption, but also affected intellectuals and government workers badly, because they depended on a fixed salary. When the resultant protests arose at the end of the war, the GMD resorted again to authoritarian means of suppression, further alienating itself from the middle classes.

In sum, the second Sino-Japanese War weakened the GMD regime and sped up the triumph of the Communists by providing new political space for the expansion of the Communists and enabling them to present themselves as patriotic resistance leaders.

CONCLUSION

Due to geopolitical dynamics in the East Asia region, the historical development of China was closely intertwined with that of Japan, from the turn of the 20th century through the end of the Pacific war.

In the first Sino-Japanese War, in 1894, Japan won. Japan's economy got a boost from the huge indemnities received from China; Japan recovered tariff autonomy and began to stand on equal footing with the Western powers; and Japan started to engage in the regional domination of East Asia. On the other hand, China lost the war in 1894. This led to a scramble for concessions, the weakening of the Chinese economy, the retreat of Confucianism, and finally the collapse of the Qing dynasty. Nevertheless, this peripheralization of China was incomplete. Due to imperialist rivalries, nationalist movements, and cyclical opportunities, the Nanjing government was able to put forward another mediocre attempt to unify the Chinese state and to regain tariff autonomy.

However, the second Sino-Japanese War, from 1937 to 1945, altered the paths of development of Japan and China. During the 1930s depression, Japan was prompted by ultranationalism and militarism to invade Manchuria and mainland China in order to build a Greater East Asia Co-Prosperity Sphere. This time, however, Japan lost the war, resulting in the American Occupation and Japan's forsaking militarism. On the other hand, the second Sino-Japanese War stripped bare the contradictions of the GMD regime, aggravated the peasant problem in the Chinese countryside, provided more political space for the CCP to operate, and enhanced the "nationalist" call of the Communists. Without the Sino-Japanese War, the Communist Revolution still might have happened because of the deep-rooted peasant problem and the active intervention of the Communists. But the revolution would certainly not have happened so quickly in 1949, and it probably would not have been so radical. In this respect, the second Sino-Japanese War set the timing for and acted as a powerful catalyst in speeding up the revolutionary process.

After the second Sino-Japanese War, the development of China and Japan went in separate ways. In the 1950s the nascent Chinese Communist regime was forced to withdraw from the capitalist world economy, and the defeated Japanese government was designated as the junior partner of the American hegemony. Needless to say, these new paths of Chinese and Japanese development have profoundly transformed the geopolitics of the East Asian region. The next three chapters will examine the three different strategies of ascent by East Asian states in the postwar era.

PART IV

Ascent

The landscape of East Asia in the 1970s contrasted dramatically with that in the early 20th century. Before World War II, mainland China was on the brink of becoming a periphery; Korea, Taiwan, and Hong Kong were colonies; and Japan was merely a semiperiphery. A few decades later, however, Japan quickly emerged as a core state; mainland China and North Korea became socialist semiperipheries; and Hong Kong, South Korea, and Taiwan had moved up to capitalist semiperipheries.

The above path of East Asian development then illustrates an important point in world-systems analysis: Although the world economy has a constant trimodal structure of core, semiperiphery, and periphery, the distribution of nation-states in the trimodal structure is not static. Mobility in the world economy is indeed possible, both in the upward direction (a periphery moving to semiperipheral status or a semiperipheral moving to core status) and in the downward direction (a core moving to semiperipheral status or a semiperipheral moving to peripheral status).

In this respect, the crucial research questions to be addressed are: What explains the general pattern of ascent in East Asia from 1945 to the mid-1970s? Why did the East Asia states exhibit not one, but three different paths (capitalist core, socialist semiperiphery, and capitalist semiperiphery) of ascent?

It is necessary to bring in the changing world-system dynamics in the mid-20th century so as to understand the pattern of ascent in East Asia. After World War II, the United States emerged as the new hegemonic power in the capitalist world economy. This postwar American hegemony, however, was different from the previous empire-building projects, because it did not rest upon territorial exclusivity like the old European colonial system had. As Cumings (1993, p. 31) points out, this American hegemony can be called an "open-door empire." On one hand, it was like an empire "policed by a far-flung naval and military basing system and by penetration of allied defense organizations. On the other, the American hegemon advocated "free investment" for transnational corporations (Arrighi, 1994a). In addition, the United States promoted such new ideologies as democracy and modernization in order to decolonize the Third World nations from the European core states. Under American leadership, the postwar world economy thus became much more liberal, multilateral, and interdependent. This new world order under U.S. hegemony led to an unprecedented expansion of the capitalist world economy. From 1950 to the mid-1980s, world merchandise exports increased about nine times in volume (Grimwade, 1989, pp. 51-53).

The main concern of the United States toward East Asia in the late 1940s was how to prevent the further spread of communism from mainland China to other parts of the region. Therefore, in contrast to the previous Japanese strategy of regionalization, the American strategy of containment called for a polarized East Asian region, divided between the socialist camp of mainland China and North Korea on one hand and the capitalist camp of Japan, Taiwan, South Korea, and Hong Kong on the other.

The next three chapters will explain how the global dynamics and geopolitics in East Asia since the late 1940s profoundly shaped the paths of development of mainland China, North Korea, Japan, and the newly industrializing economies of Taiwan, South Korea, and Hong Kong.

6. The Socialist Trajectory of China and North Korea

THE SOCIALIST STATE IN WORLD-SYSTEMS PERSPECTIVE

Most researchers—Marxists and conservatives alike—tend to treat socialist states as highly autonomous entities with ample freedom to formulate revolutionary developmental strategies. However, from a world-systems perspective (Arrighi, 1991; Chase-Dunn, 1982, 1990; Wallerstein, 1982b), socialist states are still situated within the capitalist world economy, and their activities are very much constrained by the interstate system of the capitalist world economy.

In fact, as early as 1974, Wallerstein (1979, p. 90) already proposed a provocative thesis that "establishing a system of state ownership within a capitalist world economy does not mean establishing a socialist economy." Because the capitalist system is composed of owners who sell for profit, the fact that an owner is a group of individuals (such as a joint-stock company) or a sovereign state (such as a so-called socialist state), rather than a single person, makes no essential difference. A state that collectively owns all of the means of production is merely a collective capitalist firm as long as it remains a participant in the market of the capitalist world economy.

This basic premise of the world-systems perspective opens up many new research agendas on socialist states. First, it helps to look into the global and regional dynamics that are shaping the trajectories of socialist states, including the cyclical pattern of the capitalist world economy, the reaction of core states to socialist revolutions, and the impact of regional blocs on socialist state development.

Second, after identifying the above dynamics, the world-systems perspective directs researchers to examine the interactions between global and regional forces on the changing path of national development. Although global dynamics provide the general structural context for development, it is still national actors who select their own strategies, make their own choices, and pick their own paths of development. As such, it is important to look into how national actors, such as classes, status groups, states, and parties, have responded to world-system dynamics in explaining the particular trajectory of a socialist state.

Third, the world-systems perspective identifies two phases of a socialist state's trajectory, *withdrawal* and *reintegration*: (a) Immediately after the socialist revolution, there are usually intensive hostilities from the advanced capitalist states (the cores), forcing the nascent socialist state to withdraw partially from the world economy. Constantly harassed by core states and facing imminent invasion, the nascent socialist state is pressured to build up its military sector, mobilize the grassroots population for defense, and turn to other socialist states for protection (Kraus, 1979). (b) It is only after core hostilities subside and the socialist state consolidates its rule that the latter is allowed by the core states to be fully reintegrated into the world economy. The socialist state is then able to reestablish diplomatic ties with the core states, borrow money from the World Bank, and engage in exports and imports in the world economy. In this second phase, the socialist state faces fewer dangers of military invasion and more dangers of economic domination by the core states.

Finally, the world-systems perspective highlights the contradictory (revolutionary versus mercantilist) objectives of socialist states. Wallerstein (1990) points out that socialist revolutions first originate as antisystemic movements, which aim to capture the nation-state and use it as a means to transform the capitalist world economy. In this respect, socialist states initially fuse with revolutionary objectives, aiming to eliminate the exploitation, injustice, and domination in the world economy. Nevertheless, once socialist states are in power, one major objective becomes to stay in power, and this is dependent not merely on domestic political forces but also on outside political forces. In order to gain acceptance in the interstate system, therefore, most socialist states pull back from their revolutionary promises. No longer aiming to transform the world economy, socialist states merely hope to catch up with advanced capitalist nations and achieve upward mobility in the world economy—a developmental strategy that Wallerstein (1982b) labeled as *mercantilism*. Thus the slogan "socialism in one country" emerges in socialist states, and mercantilism becomes their paramount strategy of development. The historical dilemma for socialist states, then, is whether to choose revolutionary objectives or mercantilist strategies in pursuing development in the capitalist world economy.

In sum, in contrast to conventional researchers who treat socialist states as highly autonomous and independent, world-system researchers have contributed to developmental theories by emphasizing the structural constraints imposed by the capitalist world economy upon socialist states' development. The merit of the world-systems perspective, therefore, is to draw our research to such agendas as the global context of the capitalist world-system, the interaction between world-system dynamics and national forces, the two phases of socialist development, and the contradictory developmental objectives (revolution versus mercantilism) of socialist states.

This chapter will utilize the above insights developed by world-systems researchers to study the changing trajectory of socialist China from 1949 to the present. It will focus on how Chinese actors made strategic choices between mercantilist strategies and revolutionary objectives in responding to the various constraints imposed by the capitalist world economy in the past four decades. Finally, it will discuss to what extent the Chinese socialist path of development is similar to the North Korean socialist path.

MERCANTILISM: 1949–1955

The Regional Context

After World War II, the number one aim for the United States at that time was how to contain the spread of communism in the free world. Consequently, the United States responded to the Chinese Communist Revolution with intense hostility.

The United States sent warships to patrol the Taiwan Strait and supported the defeated Nationalist Party (GMD) in Taiwan, sent soldiers to fight against the Communists in Korea, supported counterrevolutionary activities in China, froze mainland Chinese assets in the United States, imposed an economic embargo on mainland Chinese products, prevented mainland China from gaining a seat in the United Nations, and waged ideological attacks on Chinese and Soviet "Communist totalitarianism" in the mass media. This period, of course, was remembered as the Cold War.

Intense hostility from the United States served to preclude certain developmental options for socialist China. Cut off from contacts with capitalist core states, the Chinese socialist state could not possibly pursue either export-oriented industrialization (due to the closure of Western markets) or import-substitution (due to the economic embargo). Thus, socialist China was forced to miss the golden opportunity of achieving ascent during this upward phase of the world economy.

Furthermore, this global context also induced socialist China to seek help from its socialist allies. Soviet political support was instrumental in fending off capitalist core hostilities; and Soviet economic aid, loans, and technology were badly needed to rebuild China's war-torn economy. Therefore, despite the differences between the Chinese Communist Party (the CCP) and the Soviet Communist Party on revolutionary strategy— the former favored guerrilla warfare, and the latter favored urban insurrection—the Chinese developed an alliance with Soviet Russia in the early 1950s and hailed the Russians as their "big brother."

In this period, the paramount objective for the CCP was to rebuild the war-torn economy. After engaging in World War II, the civil war, and the Korean War, the CCP naturally had to make economic reconstruction its top priority in order to pull China out of poverty and backwardness. But how could China carry out this mercantilist strategy without getting fully involved in the capitalist world economy?

State-Building

The mercantilist strategy's success lies in a strong state with full capacity to restructure the economy and society. Although the CCP was skillful in rural peasant mobilization, it had little experience in urban management. After the Communist Revolution in 1949, the CCP needed to develop an administrative system to handle the burgeoning responsibilities of coordination and economic management in the cities. In addition, the political order had to be strengthened to confront the "imperialist enemies" without (notably during the Korean War) and the "counterrevolutionaries" within (notably the remnants of GMD opposition).

To cope with an increasingly wide range of state functions, the CCP adopted the Leninist model for state building. As White (1983) points out, the Leninist model

> was elitist in conception (notably the notion of vanguard party) and authoritarian in operation, with very limited provisions for intraparty democracy. It advocated a tight concentration of decision-making power in the hands of a supreme leader and his cohorts and offered scant provision for effective mass participation in or control over the state machine. (p. 28)

Because of the fusion of functions and the overlapping of personnel among the CCP, the state bureaucracy, and the army, there was an excessive concentration of power in the vanguard Leninist party. Only political organizations (like peasants' associations, labor unions, and women's associations) formally sponsored by the CCP were allowed to operate; other organizations were either made ineffective (like the small democratic parties) or simply banned from operation (like the GMD).

Finally, this Leninist party-state was all powerful in the sense that it extended both vertically and horizontally to every sphere in Chinese society. Vertically, the Leninist party-state was the first Chinese government that was able to exert its political control all the way down to village, family, and individual levels. Horizontally, there was a great expansion of state functions. The Leninist state did not just collect tax and keep social order, it also oversaw such functions as education, health care, marriage, culture, economic policy, and so on.

Such a strong state allowed the nascent Communist regime to carry out the following mercantilist programs.

Developmental Objectives and Programs

First of all, the CCP nationalized foreign property and GMD property to eliminate the economic bases of imperialism and the GMD's bureaucratic capitalism. Then the CCP carried out land reform to redistribute land ownership from the hands of the "feudal" landlords to the peasants.

But, at the same time, the CCP also made it clear that the interests of the rich peasantry, small merchants, industrial capitalists, and the new middle class would be protected in order to promote economic growth (Selden, 1979).

In the early 1950s, after the conclusion of the land reform, the CCP set up its First Five-Year Plan, modeled after those of the Soviet Union. The CCP wanted to imitate the Soviet success in transforming a weak, poor periphery into a strong socialist state on equal footing with capitalist core states. Hence, the First Five-Year Plan focused on heavy industrialization rather than on light industry and agriculture, urban development rather than rural development, and coastal provinces rather than heartland provinces. The rationale was that heavy industrialization in coastal cities would be the quickest path to transforming China into a strong, wealthy nation-state in the world economy (Kaple, 1994).

Although there were radical proposals for rural collectivization and nationalization of urban industries, the CCP did not adopt these proposals in the early 1950s because it preferred gradual, voluntary advances. The CCP thought that it might require three more 5-year plans before industrialization and mechanization could provide the technical foundations for large-scale collective agriculture (Selden, 1983).

Ideology and Social Supporters

Because mercantilism was the goal of Chinese development in this period, revolutionary socialist objectives had to be delayed. The program that justified this mercantilist strategy was "New Democracy," which aimed to get rid of only imperialism, bureaucratic capitalism, and feudalism, but not minor commodity production and industrial capitalism.

In this mercantilist phase, therefore, the CCP developed a united front to promote industrialization. Although unskilled workers and poor peasants were mobilized as the chief supporters of the party, the CCP also called upon rich peasants, industrial capitalists, small merchants, the new middle class, and overseas Chinese to contribute to national development.

Dilemma

In the early 1950s, state-building and the mercantilist strategy worked well to enhance both political stability and economic growth. First, hostilities from core states and the prospect of external invasion helped stimulate Chinese nationalism, unifying different classes behind the CCP to build a strong, wealthy nation-state. Second, land reform redistributed resources to the peasantry and raised its standard of living. Finally, mercantilism resulted in the expansion of the minor production sector. With the endorsement of the CCP, rich peasants were motivated to expand agricultural production and engage in rural industry; small merchants were willing to work harder; and small capitalists were able to reap more profits than before, because of the absence of market competition from foreign and bureaucratic capitalists.

Nevertheless, the momentum of mercantilism seemed to threaten the revolutionary objectives of the CCP by the mid-1950s. Heavy industrialization failed to provide enough jobs for the growing urban population; the Soviet model was urban-focused and biased against the peasantry, the group from which the CCP obtained its political support; and land reform had led to growing class inequalities, with rich peasants beginning to take advantage of their poorer neighbors. If this mercantilist trend continued, it would lead China away from the revolutionary goals that the CCP had been striving for since the 1920s. As a result, Mao Zedong [Mao Tse-tung], the chairman of the CCP, decided in the mid-1950s to drop the Soviet model and promote a program that grew out of the CCP's revolutionary struggles in the countryside.

REVOLUTIONARY SOCIALISM: 1956–1977

The Regional Context

Many of the regional dynamics in the previous period were still active in this period. The United States was still highly hostile to China and later even intensified its military involvement in Vietnam and Southeast Asia; many capitalist states in East Asia began to industrialize as a result of American support.

However, this phase was distinguished by an intense rivalry between China and its socialist "big brother." In the late 1950s, China criticized the Soviet invasion of Hungary and Khrushchev's denunciation of Stalin, and the Soviet Union was annoyed by the CCP's new rejection of the Soviet development model. In the early 1960s, after the two socialist states openly condemned one another for betraying Marxism, the Soviet Union withdrew all its technical staff from China. Finally, in the late 1960s, the two socialist states almost went to war because of a series of border disputes.

No doubt impelled by what he termed Soviet "imperialism" and "revisionism," Mao wanted to speed up China's revolutionary process and promoted a Chinese style of socialism.

Developmental Objectives and Programs

As a result, there was a drastic shift in China's developmental objectives by the mid-1950s. The Soviet mercantilist model was discarded, as the CCP believed that revolutionary socialism had to be achieved before industrialization and mechanization.

First, during the "socialist high tide" in the mid-1950s, the CCP quickly instituted collectivization of agriculture in the countryside and nationalization of industry in the cities. With the expansion of the rural collective sector and the urban state sector, most Chinese resources were allocated through a unified state plan. Subsequently, markets and the private sector played reduced roles in the Chinese economy.

Second, during the Great Leap Forward in the late 1950s, the CCP attempted to combine rural collectives into communes, thus containing both agricultural and industrial activities, relying upon local resources and grassroots mobilization, and retaining a high degree of autonomy from the central government (Selden, 1979).

Finally, during the Cultural Revolution between 1966 and 1976, there were attempts to establish a truly egalitarian society (Pye, 1991). It was not just the new middle class and the industrial capitalists who were attacked, but also the party officials "who were carrying the capitalist road." Through the new institution of the May 7 Cadre School, even the veteran party leaders and state officials were sent to the countryside to do "labor" so as to be educated by poor peasants (Blecher, 1986).

In addition, the Chinese state changed its developmental strategy. Instead of relying on external support (such as Soviet aid, technology, and expertise), the CCP focused on domestic resources. The CCP put forward a "self-reliance" model of development, stressing national autonomy, pride in being a poor country, mass mobilization, and labor-intensive industries.

Furthermore, the CCP also changed its priorities in regional development. During the Cultural Revolution, the new emphases were on developing rural areas rather than urban areas, and heartland provinces rather than coastal provinces. By establishing rural communes dispersed all over the heartland provinces, the CCP hoped that it could avoid economic ruin due to external invasions from either capitalist core states or rival socialist states (Naughton, 1991; Riskin, 1987).

Ideology and Social Supporters

During the Cultural Revolution, the ideology of Maoism was transformed into a state religion that affected the basic way of life in Chinese society. Mao was worshipped as a god; he became the "greatest leader," the "great helmsman," and the "greatest teacher who would live for a thousand years;" his "little red book" of *Quotations from Chairman Mao Zedong* became a bible read by his loyal Red Guard followers. Everyone claimed to be a Maoist, was faithful to the values of Maoism (including egalitarianism, selflessness, collectivity, and serving the people), and practiced "struggle, criticism, and transformation" in mass meetings. Furthermore, every institution in Chinese society was revamped according to the ideals of Maoism. For example, Pfeffer (1972, p. 638) points out that the new educational goals during the Cultural Revolution included: (a) greatly increasing the enrollment in schools of children of poor peasants and workers; (b) making education serve the concrete needs of the masses of people; (c) reducing the technocratic elite's status and hierarchical control of education; and (d) putting politics in command of education, which meant inculcating in those connected with the educational system Maoist revolutionary values, methods, and goals as the salient standard for judging all other theories and practices.

These revolutionary socialist programs and ideology thus called for a different group of class supporters for the CCP. Although mercantilism depended on the support of rich peasants, skilled workers, small merchants, the new middle class, and industrial capitalists—who were overall relatively more productive—revolutionary socialism tended to rely upon poor peasants and unskilled workers—who were the disadvantaged masses in the class hierarchy. During this phase of revolutionary socialism, therefore, entitlement programs for job security, housing, child care, and pensions were granted to the urban working class; social programs in education, health care, and welfare became increasingly available to the peasantry.

Attacking the State

This revolutionary socialist ideology inevitably came into conflict with the authoritarian, elitist state that was instituted during the previous mercantilist phase. The Maoists perceived the Cultural Revolution as embodying a new form of revolutionary mass movement, involving extensive democracy and the "four big freedoms" (big contending, big blooming, big debate, and big-character posters). The Cultural Revolution was radical in two senses: It encouraged the formation of partially autonomous mass organizations, and it was directed at "enemies" inside the CCP and the state machinery.

Between late 1966 and early 1967, mass organizations increased their power and the CCP lost control over the Cultural Revolution. As White (1983, p. 48) recalls, this radical phase culminated in the January Revolution in Shanghai in 1967, when the established party-state apparatus was replaced, through violent power seizures, by a coalition of mass organizations welded together in a Paris-style Shanghai People's Commune. However, Mao rejected the Commune model because it was "too weak when it comes to suppressing counterrevolution." Subsequently, Mao formulated a new state using "three-in-one" combinations in revolutionary committees, which brought the young Cultural Revolution Red Guards into an uneasy juxtaposition with the army and the veteran cadres.

Dilemma

Politically, Mao hoped that the Cultural Revolution would create some form of partially autonomous mass power that could act as a check on the state bureaucracy, authoritarianism, and elites, as well as forming an important part of the grassroots political base. However, inspired by Mao's call for revolution, many radical Red Guards wanted more than the sharing of power with the army and the veteran cadres in revolutionary committees. Instead, they wanted to smash the old state machinery and replace it with their own organs of mass power. However, fragmentation prevented the radical Red Guards from forming a unified political force. The Red Guards were torn by factional struggles, small-group mentality, idealism, and violence-prone struggles. Furthermore, after long periods of struggling among themselves, many Red Guards became disillusioned with Maoist ideals. And long periods of Red Guard factional struggles alienated the general population, making them highly cynical about the slogans of class struggle and absolute egalitarianism. It seems ironic that in just a few years, the charismatic calling of Mao and the intense ideological struggles of the late 1960s were quickly replaced by the widespread political alienation and disillusionment of the mid-1970s.

Economically, compared to the peripheral states in Africa and Asia and the debt-ridden states in Eastern Europe, the Chinese program of revolutionary socialism must be considered a success. Two decades of institutional transformation, mass mobilization, and infrastructure investment produced a significant growth rate (an average of 4% to 5% gained in GDP per year). Socially, as Selden (1993) points out, China achieved basic food self-sufficiency for nearly 1 billion people in a society with a class structure that yielded relatively egalitarian distribution of income and services, particularly in the cities. Moreover, by the early 1980s, with life expectancy at 68 years, an average daily diet of 2,600 calories, and high levels of literacy and health care, in important respects China's social profile bore a resemblance to those of countries with far higher income levels. In addition, Arrighi (1991) points out that China did much better than the populous India in terms of a relatively egalitarian wealth distribution. Therefore, through its revolutionary program, China emerged from a century of foreign domination and a succession of costly wars as a socialist semiperiphery in East Asia.

However, the economic program of revolutionary socialism had its limitations. Despite its economy's impressive growth rate, China's per capita annual income was still less than $350, due to the extraordinary growth of its population, from around 500 million in 1953 to 1 billion in 1980 (Selden, 1993). Thus, China still ranked among the poorest nations in the world, and the standard of living of its people remained very low. It seemed that the strategy of mass mobilization, which enabled China to solve the problem of starvation and inequality, was unable to propel China to catch up with the capitalist core states, or even to catch up with the newly industrializing semiperipheral states, in terms of per capita income.

Consequently, the tasks of promoting economic growth, providing more consumer goods, raising the standard of living, and the like became increasingly pressing for the CCP after the first wave of revolutionary fervor died down in the 1970s. But the centrally planned economy was unable to tackle these mercantilist problems. For example, state enterprises were highly inefficient and paid little heed to productivity, because they had been operating under a "soft budgetary constraint" and could always rely on the state for more credits if they ran into losses. State enterprises also tended to stockpile more resources and manpower than necessary, leading to waste, misuse of resources, and acute shortages of raw materials. In addition, workers had little incentive to work harder, because revolutionary socialism guaranteed job security and fringe benefits regardless of job performance, and because there were few consumer goods that they could spend their salaries on. Furthermore, without the support of a new middle class of technologists (such as engineers, computer programmers, and nuclear scientists), and without technology imported from abroad, Chinese technology was falling further behind that of the capitalist core states.

In short, by the 1970s Chinese revolutionary socialism had already outlived its historical mission of building a strong state to provide the basic living requirements of the world's largest population. Using such programs as the Great Leap Forward and the Cultural Revolution, the CCP tried to stave off various attempts to bring mercantilism back to China in the late 1950s and the early 1960s. However, with the passing away of the old revolutionary generation, and with the changing situation in the world economy, the CCP was no longer able to withstand another assault from mercantilism in the late 1970s.

THE RETURN TO MERCANTILISM: 1978–1986

The Regional Context

The late 1970s was a period of declining American hegemony. Economically, the United States faced the problems of inflation, low productivity, and recession. Its products could not compete with Japanese and German manufactures in the world market. Politically, the United States was still plagued by its defeat in Vietnam and its failed attempt to fend off global Soviet expansionism. At this historical juncture, the United States welcomed China back to the world economy. China could be a new regional power to balance Soviet military expansion and Japanese economic expansion in East Asia. Moreover, the vast Chinese market, cheap Chinese labor, and abundant Chinese raw materials and minerals could considerably increase the competitive power of American industry in the world market.

For its part, the CCP was attracted to the economic success of its East Asian neighbors. With U.S. support in the 1950s and the 1960s, Japan, South Korea, Taiwan, Hong Kong, and Singapore had become highly industrialized, and their people enjoyed a much higher living standard than those in China. Thus, the CCP saw an opportunity to follow the path of its successful neighbors to engage in export-oriented industrialization.

While being drawn to the United States and its East Asian neighbors, the CCP was also becoming highly dissatisfied with its former socialist allies. By the end of the 1970s, the economies of the socialist states in Eastern Europe were in disarray, haunted by foreign debts, low growth rates, and declining living standards. This failure further convinced the CCP that it was necessary to bring mercantilism back in order to rejuvenate the stagnant Chinese economy.

Developmental Objectives and Programs

During this period, China's top priority was to develop productive forces as rapidly as possible. The slogan was "Four Modernization"—to modernize agriculture, industry, science and technology, and the military to catch up with the capitalist core states. In order to carry out this developmental objective, the CCP promoted an open-door trade policy and brought market forces back in (Chossudovsky, 1986).

First, China decided to open up the economy for foreign trade and investment. As a result, its foreign trade volume grew by leaps and bounds, rising from slightly more than US$20 billion in 1978 to more than US$111 billion in 1989 (Yang, 1991, p. 42). After it became a certified player in the world economy, China began to gain access to supplier credits subsidized by foreign governments. Total lending to China by the World Bank in the 1979-1982 period was US$2.7 billion per year; by 1987 and 1988, this figure had risen to US$5.8 and US$6.5

billion, respectively (Perkins, 1991, p. 272). China also opened four Special Economic Zones and 14 coastal cities to attract direct foreign investment. In particular, at the beginning China also encouraged joint ventures with foreign firms. By 1990 China had attracted about US$16 billion of foreign investment (Battat, 1991, p. 1; Lall, 1991, p. 3). Full reintegration into the world economy, therefore, had opened up many new channels for China to obtain foreign currency, foreign loans, foreign advanced technology, and foreign management know-how.

Then the CCP tried to bring market forces back in. In the countryside, communes were dismantled. Peasant families were given plots of land to cultivate, and they were responsible for their own gains and losses. They were also encouraged to sell their products to rural markets, engage in rural industries, and seek work in nearby township enterprises. In the cities, urban youths were encouraged to engage in small-scale trading activities or to set up their own small shops (like barbershops and restaurants), especially when they could not find employment in the state sector. State and collective enterprises were asked to contract out their unprofitable operations to small enterprises or temporary workers. The state hoped that, as the reforms progressed, a private sector that absorbed surplus labor and paid attention to market forces would gradually emerge alongside the state and the collective sectors.

Rebuilding the State

In order to carry out the above mercantilist programs, the CCP had to rebuild the state out of the chaos and mass organizations of the Cultural Revolution. No sooner had Mao passed away, in 1976, then the radical leftists of the Cultural Revolution (the so-called "Gang of Four") were arrested and their Red Guard followers purged from the CCP. In late 1978, Deng Xiaoping [Deng Hsiao-ping] quickly emerged as the new strongman in the CCP and instituted four political reforms to strengthen the CCP and to reshape state-society relationships.

First, the new CCP emphasized collective leadership. In order to avoid the concentration of power in the hands of a single supreme leader like Mao, the CCP now stressed the collective decision-making processes of the Politburo. Also, no central party leader was allowed to wear multiple hats, such as holding the post of the chairman of the party, the premier of the state, and the commander of the army at the same time. Second, to avoid the turmoil and violence of the Cultural Revolution, and triggered by the need to set up joint-venture laws with foreign corporations, the CCP instituted a number of legal system reforms, including a call to abide by "the rule of law," the creation of an independent judiciary, the expansion of the legal profession, and the emergence of a whole body of commercial law. Third, the CCP made a modest attempt to move toward a Western electoral model. Competitive elections at the county level first took place in 1980. There was also an attempt to strengthen the National People's Congress, so it would not be merely a rubber stamp for the CCP. Finally, members of the new middle class were recruited into the party on a massive scale, resulting in the professionalization of the Chinese Communist Party (Nathan, 1990).

Because of these political reforms in the party-state, state-society relationships transformed correspondingly. Wormack (1984) suggests that "a zone of indifference" has been created in Chinese society to distinguish the public from the private sphere. Subsequently, there has been more personal freedom in the private sphere, where there has been a visible relaxation in behavior so that nonconformity is even tolerated. For example, now evening newspapers provide more entertaining and thought-provoking fare, reporters make investigative forays, and journals feature open debates among experts.

Ideology and Social Supporters

The return of mercantilism necessarily called for a revision in CCP ideology. First, Mao and Maoism were attacked. Chairman Mao was criticized for behaving like a feudal emperor who imposed his wishes on the population without regard to their general welfare. The Cultural Revolution was seen as 10 years of disaster for which Mao was fully responsible. The values of egalitarianism, collectivism, and mass participation were seen as excessive and unrealistic. Second, as a result of this "de-Maoism," there was a promotion of materialistic ideology that emphasized productivity, incentives, expertise, technology, modernization, and catching up with the West. Third, there was a promotion of consumerism and of aiming for a higher standard of living. Thus, soap operas, sitcoms, quiz programs, dancing girls, and fashion shows came to dominate Chinese prime-time television along with, of course, a goodly dose of competitive sports. Rock-and-roll, disco dancing, and karaoke singalong now dominate musical films, and boy-meets-girl romances among upwardly mobile entrepreneurial types account for a good share of new films (Hinton, 1993, p. 99).

Consequently, there was a shifting of class supporters toward mercantilist forces. In order to promote the Four Modernization, the CCP turned to foreign capitalists, overseas Chinese, rich peasants, small merchants, industrial capitalists, and members of the new middle class for help. Underscoring this urge toward modernization was the CCP's motif that "it is not shameful to get rich, so long as you earn your profit through hard work."

Dilemma

Nevertheless, politically the modest reforms toward Western electoral democracy were only halfhearted, because they were only instituted at the county level, because there were no real elections at the provincial level and above, and because the CCP still fully monopolized political power at the top level of the state bureaucracy. In addition, although there were more freedom and relaxation in the political sphere, there were still no constitutional guarantees protecting individual rights and the civil society; the CCP still upheld the ideology of Marxism-Leninism-Maoism and the so-called dictatorship of the proletariat.

Nevertheless, due to post-Mao factors such as the rapid expansion of higher education, the exposure of college students to Western democratic values, and the infiltration of the new middle class into the CCP, there emerged in the past 2 decades a democratic movement challenging CCP rule. Initiated by the Democracy Wall Movement in 1978, another democratic movement sprang up between late 1986 and early 1987. Although both movements were suppressed easily because of their small size, lack of organization, inappropriate protest strategies, and lack of supporters in Chinese cities, these movements laid the foundation for later large-scale protests, as seen in the 1989 Tiananmen Incident.

Economically, the renewed promotion of mercantilism was also halfhearted because it rested upon the foundation of state capitalism. Although a significant private sector had emerged, the Chinese economy was still dominated by state enterprises. Although markets flourished and some prices moved up and down according to supply and demand, most prices and the circulation of key commodities were still regulated by the state. What the CCP tried to accomplish in this phase was to open some space for mercantilist forces to operate, hoping that this limited dose of mercantilism would be sufficient to stimulate efficiency, productivity, and profitability in the state sector.

In the short run, this mercantilist program worked remarkably well. The Special Economic Zones grew from market towns to modern cities in a few years (So, 1988). China also experienced rapid growth in manufactured exports; between 1978 and 1988, total Chinese exports rose from US$9.75 billion to US$47.5 billion, increasing at an annual average rate of 17%. Of this total increase of US$37.8 billion, US$28.6 billion was accounted for by a rise in the export of manufactures. This performance was not far below those of South Korea and Taiwan during the same period. In addition, China saw a dramatic increase in agricultural production. Between 1978 and 1984, grain output averaged an annual rate of increase of 5%, and rural net per capita income tripled from 134 to 398 yuan (Perkins, 1991, p. 270, 274; Selden, 1988, p. 551). More consumer goods were available in the private sector, and the Chinese population enjoyed a higher standard of living than before.

In the long run, however, this mercantilist program ran into structural problems. Because the enthusiasm of the peasantry could not continue forever, agricultural output reached its limit by the mid-1980s. Unless the peasantry decided to promote mechanization and rationalization of production, agricultural output would not increase further. But the dismantling of communes and the division of collective farms into small family plots had already precluded this mechanization and rationalization option (Putterman, 1993).

Then American and Japanese capitalists started to complain about the Chinese bureaucracy, which set up numerous regulations on labor mobility, profit remittance, tariffs and quotas on foreign imports, and so on. Core capitalists, of course, wanted China to play the role of periphery and accept foreign domination without resistance. But the CCP preferred to play the role of a semiperipheral actor so as to retain a higher degree of autonomy. As a result, American and Japanese investment slowed down considerably by the mid-1980s, occupying only 11.4% and 9.5%, respectively, of total direct investment in China (Perkins, 1991, p. 273).

Finally, the coexistence of the state sector and the private sector created new problems for the Chinese economy. The expansion of the private sector aggravated the shortage of resources and drove up prices in the market. This resulted in a highly unbalanced dual-pricing system, with the prices set by the state through administrative means being much lower than the prices set by the market through supply and demand. Because CCP officials possessed the necessary political connections to obtain scarce resources at state-set prices (Bian, 1994), they could easily make a big profit by selling the resources at market prices. In this way, enterprise profits were earned as much by getting political connections, access to scarce resources, and subsidized credits as they were by improving technology, cutting production costs, and increasing sales. Without reforming the dual-pricing system, and without severing the ties between the enterprises and the state, Chinese enterprises could not possibly become a truly capitalist economic entity disciplined by market profitability.

CHINESE SOCIALIST TRAJECTORY:
ITS RELEVANCE FOR NORTH KOREA

This chapter applies the world-systems perspective to study the Chinese socialist trajectory. The merit of this perspective is that it opens up new research agendas on how world-system dynamics (such as cyclical trends in the world economy, links between capitalist core states and socialist states, and regional blocs) might affect developmental objectives (mercantilism versus revolution) as well as various phases of socialist development.

This chapter also shows that socialist China initially adopted a mercantilist strategy borrowed from the Soviet Union in the early 1950s in order to promote postwar economic recovery. But socialist China decided to drop mercantilism in the mid-1950s because it did not fit with the CCP's revolutionary heritage. The Soviet invasion of Hungary and Khrushchev's denunciation of Stalin further convinced the CCP to speed up revolutionary socialism through programs of self-reliance, collectivization, egalitarianism, and mass mobilization. Nevertheless, with the reduction of capitalist core hostilities, with the passing away of the revolutionary generation, and with the desire to catch up with the living standards of its successful East Asian neighbors, socialist China returned to mercantilism in the late 1970s, opening some space for small commodity production and using foreign trade and technology to stimulate its stagnant economy. Because the coexistence of state socialism and a burgeoning private sector could not solve the old problems of low productivity and declining worker motivation, the CCP was tempted in the late 1980s to use such radical measures as enterprise, price, and political reforms to dismantle the various institutions of state socialism. Such a showdown between wholesale mercantilism and state socialism, however, led to an economic crisis (runaway inflation) and ultimately a political crisis (the Tiananmen Incident). In the early 1990s, therefore, the CCP reevaluated the mercantilist strategy and finally decided to create a hybrid socialist-commodity economy, strengthening the state to promote export-led industrialization, and relying upon the proposed benefits of national integration with Taiwan and Hong Kong to boost its economy and political unity. This zigzag trajectory of the Chinese social- ist state, of course, would be incomprehensible unless researchers lo- cated it at the juncture of world-system dynamics and domestic forces (such as classes, the party, the state, etc.).

To what extent, then, is this Chinese socialist trajectory relevant to the experience of sister socialist state North Korea? Researchers can easily find similarities between the Chinese and the North Korean paths of socialist development. First, North Korea also started with a phase of mercantilism in the late 1940s. Land reform was carried out, creating an economy of private small farming; Soviet aid and technology were sought, and the Soviet model of heavy industrialization was adopted. Likewise, there was a strong move toward economic reconstruction, especially after the disasters inflicted by the Korea War. For instance, it is said that in Pyongyang only two buildings remained intact, and the Pyongyang population was reduced from 400,000 to 80,000 (Foster-Carter, 1978).

Then, like its Chinese counterpart, North Korea shifted to revolution- ary socialism in the late 1950s. Withdrawing from the capitalist world economy and taking advantage of the disputes between its two socialist neighbors (the Soviet Union and China), North Korea was able to for- mulate its own "Juche" brand of socialism. As Perry (1990, p. 182) points out, "Juche can be defined broadly as self-identity and autonomy . . . mastery of revolution and reconstruction in one's own country . . . holding fast to an independent position, rejecting dependence on oth- ers." With Juche ideology, Kim Il Sung and his party thus had a free hand in restructuring the North Korean economy and society. In 1961 a "Dae-an Work System" (DWS) of industrial management was set up to replace the Soviet one-man responsibility system. The DWS stressed collective management by the Factory Party Committee; used "speed battle" to mobilize the materials, funds, and labor; and looked upon workers as endowed with revolutionary passion for moral reasons (Kang, 1989). Again, as in China, the North Korean revolutionary socialist program performed well in the early phase and was sometimes even labeled "the Korean miracle" (Robinson, 1965). But it began to show problems of low productivity and slow growth rates in the early 1970s, giving rise to the view that the positive potential of mass mobilization had been exhausted (Kahng, 1991).

In order to stimulate lagging industrial growth, North Korea also adopted a halfhearted mercantilist program in the early 1970s. It first went on a buying spree for foreign machinery, exporting minerals and metals as payment. As Perry (1990, p. 179) explains, the "oil crisis, coupled with falling prices for what they had to sell, led to trade imbalances, foreign debt, and eventual default on that debt. Hard currency shortages have led to notorious difficulties for North Korean diplomats abroad . . . " Impressed by the initial economic success of Chinese mercantilism in the early 1980s, North Korea tried again to reestablish economic links with the world economy by enacting a new joint-venture law in 1984, with special emphasis on the inducement of Western technology and capital investment (Yu, 1987). In its Third Seven-Year Plan, proposed in 1987, North Korea further called for financial accountability and relative autonomy of state enterprises, material incentives of labor, reduced scope of central planning, and promotion of foreign direct investment (Kang & Lee, 1991). These mercantilist programs, however, could only be described as halfhearted, because they did not attract any significant foreign investment (except those from the Japanese ethnic Koreans), and because it was doubtful whether the call for enterprise reforms was ever carried through (Mazarr, 1991; Perry, 1990).

What distinguished the North Korean socialist trajectory from the Chinese one, therefore, is that the former was able to maintain revolutionary socialism much longer than the latter. To understand why this is so, it is helpful to point out that even today North Korea is still ruled by first-generation revolutionaries, who are incapable of repudiating past revolutionary programs because they are personally responsible for them. Members of the North Korean government have been in office for decades, so any mistakes that have occurred during this period through the revolutionary socialist program are directly attributable to them (Mazarr, 1991). In addition, there have been no large-scale opposition movements in North Korea, and there are no immediate prospects of any. As Mao's position had been while he was alive, Kim Il Sung's position in North Korea remained preeminent, and his strong state was able to suppress any organized dissent swiftly (Phipps, 1991). As such, there had not been any substantial policy change toward mercantilism within the lifetime of Kim Il Sung.

While North Korea remained a "hermit kingdom," the world around it was changing dramatically in the late 1980s. Beginning in 1988, North Korea received one diplomatic setback after another. It started when the socialist states in Eastern Europe established diplomatic relations with South Korea, surely a severe blow to Pyongyang. Then China and South Korea agreed to open trade offices in their respective capitals, followed by the Soviet Union's announcement of formalizing diplomatic relations with South Korea in September 1990 (Rhee, 1991). Meanwhile, North Korea's efforts to improve its relationships with the United States and Japan did not make much headway.

These diplomatic setbacks, together with its suffocating economy, are sure to put pressure on North Korea to lean further toward mercantilism. Learning from the Chinese trajectory, North Korea may push for a socialist-commodity economy, combining mercantilism and state socialism. Furthermore, North Korea may play the national unification card to promote both economic growth and political unity. Right now, North Korea nears a critical juncture where difficult choices must be made. Only time will tell what choices North Korea leaders will make.

In sum, the Chinese and North Korean experiences reveal the prospects as well as the limitations of the socialist state's path of development in the world economy. Although a strong state was built and revolutionary socialism was tried in both cases, China and North Korea were forced to adopt mercantilism and enter the capitalist world economy as a result of contradictions built into the strategy of socialist ascent. Meanwhile, alongside Chinese and North Korean struggles to maintain semiperipheral positions in the world economy was Japan's miraculous postwar ascent to the core. This will be our topic in the next chapter.

7. The Corization of Japan

The rise of Japan from the ruins of World War II is one of the spectacular comeback stories in modern East Asian history. This chapter argues that the rise of American hegemony and the changing geopolitics in East Asia were instrumental in forging Japan's domestic conditions for high-speed growth.

FROM RAGS TO RICHES:
THE SPECTACULAR JAPANESE COMEBACK

When the Japanese surrendered in 1945, they found their economy utterly stricken. Japan lost its colonial possessions of Taiwan, Korea, and Manchuria, which were lifelines for the Japanese economy. Allied carpet-bombing destroyed most of the nation's industrial facilities, and resource depletion from wartime production campaigns immobilized the rest. Industrial production had fallen to one third of the production level of the mid-1930s. Also looming was the specter of mass unemployment due to the sudden flooding of the job market created by the disbanding of the military forces and the return of about 1.5 million people from abroad.

Yet in a space of less than 3 decades, Japan not only recovered from its wartime destruction but became an economic powerhouse in the world economy. The following are some indicators of the upward mobility of Japan from a semiperiphery in the first half of the 20th century to a core in the second half of the 20th century.

First, there was the exceptional economic growth rate of 10% per annum from 1953 to 1973 (Boltho, 1975, p. 8). In fact, the economy expanded so rapidly that all Japanese government economic plans made in this period underestimated the country's growth rate. As a result of this exceptional growth rate, the real GNP of Japan surpassed West Germany's by 1968, making the Japanese economy the second-largest in the world.

Second, there was tremendous growth in Japanese exports. From the 1950s onward, Japan's exports grew twice as fast as world trade as a whole. In addition, the dominant trend in postwar Japan has been the replacement of low value-added, light-industrial exports with high value-added, heavy-industrial ones. Thus, machinery and transport equipments' share among Japanese exports surged from 12.3% in 1955 to 40.5% in 1970, whereas the share of other industrial products (such as textiles) fell precipitously from 70% to 46.8% in the same period (Nakamura, 1981, p. 60). Furthermore, there was a shift in relative importance of different export markets. Although Japan in its early postwar years could only export to Asian and other developing countries, the significance of these markets among total Japanese exports declined rapidly thereafter. By the 1970s the United States and Europe had become the largest customers for Japan's exports (Allen, 1981, p. 163).

Third, due to its strong exports, Japan began to run consistent trade surpluses in its international balance of payments. Very soon, Japan was transformed from a debtor nation in postwar years into a creditor nation in the late 1960s. With its balance of payment bottleneck overcome in the late 1960s, the amount of Japan's direct foreign investment exploded and reached US$26,809 million in 1978 (Allen, 1981, p. 173). The fastest area of growth in Japan's foreign investment was registered in Southeast Asia and East Asia, where Japan emerged either as the largest foreign investor or as the second-largest investor, behind the United States (Halliday & McCormack, 1973).

Finally, Japan was similarly transformed from an aid recipient in postwar years to an aid donor in the 1970s. In the form of development loans and export credits (rather than grants), Japanese foreign aid increased from US$360.7 million in 1964 to US$1,824 million in 1970 (Halliday & McCormack, 1973, pp. 25-26). By 1970 Japan had overtaken West Germany and Britain as aid donors to become the second-largest aid donor (after the United States) in the capitalist world economy.

How could the Japanese economy grow so rapidly after World War II? What explains this quick transition to core status in 3 decades? This chapter will chart the rise of Japan from the ruins of the war in the 1950s to one of the major economic powerhouses in the world economy in the 1970s. In the following sections, we will discuss four factors that explain this quick core transition; namely, the American hegemony; the Japanese developmental state; the Japanese industrial relations and subcontracting system; and the Japanese ideology of consensus, paternalism, and sexism.

AMERICAN HEGEMONY
AND THE JAPANESE ASCENT

Between August 1945 and September 1951, Japan was under the control of the United States, largely through the Supreme Commander for Allied Powers (SCAP) under General Douglas MacArthur. The primary aim of SCAP was to overhaul Japan's political and economic institutions so that it would not become a threat to world peace and American hegemony again.

Political Reforms

To SCAP, this aim would be politically achieved through liberalization, demilitarization, and democratization (Halliday, 1975; Stockwin, 1975).

First, as a result of the liberalization programs, all political prisoners were freed in 1945. Political rights—such as freedom of assembly and association as well as speech, press, and all other forms of expression—were granted to all Japanese citizens. The once-banned Japan Communist Party and other leftist organizations were now fully legal and free to espouse whatever political views they preferred, including Marxist class theory; labor unions could now bargain collectively with management (Fukui, 1992, p. 208).

Second, SCAP staged a purge of militarists from influential positions in the Japanese state and society: army and navy officers, bureaucrats, politicians, businessmen, journalists, and right-wing intellectuals believed to form the core of Japan's imperialism.

Third, a new constitution was prepared by SCAP in 1946 and enacted in 1947. The new Japanese constitution was basically modeled upon the American constitution, including its provisions for individual freedom and civil rights. The sovereign power of the Japanese state now resided in the will of the people instead of the emperor, who was now regarded merely as a symbol of the state. Naturally, the emperor cult was condemned, as were all other forms of ultranationalist ideology, including Shinto and Confucian dogmas (Fukui, 1992, p. 207). In addition, Article 9 of the new constitution stated that "the Japanese people forever renounce war as a sovereign right of the nation."

In 1947 the first postwar general election was held. Both the dominant prewar parties, the Liberal Party (Jiyuto) and the Democratic Party (Minshuto, previously known as Shimpoto or the Progressive Party) had been seriously weakened by the militarist purge, and their roles in the prewar government diminished their popularity among the electorate. As a result, the Japan Socialist Party (JSP) in 1947 was able to form a coalition government and elected a socialist prime minister for the first time in Japanese history. For a time, at least, it seemed that the political reforms initiated by SCAP really opened up the Japanese political system for popular participation.

Economic Reforms

In order to stem the rebirth of Japanese imperialism, SCAP had called for reforms in the economy as well as in the polity. Japan was asked to pay for the wartime damages it had inflicted upon other countries. To do so, industrial equipment in Japan was to be removed and shipped to other countries as war reparations. Such a policy, it was believed, would keep Japan economically weak and hence unable to carry out other imperialist ventures.

Between 1945 and 1947, SCAP further implemented three major reforms to "democratize" the Japanese economy (Nakamura, 1981, pp. 23-30). First, there was the antitrust program. Because the *zaibatsu* controlled the lion's share of the economy when the war ended and were regarded as the principal agents of Japanese imperialism, SCAP set out to dissolve the *zaibatsu*. SCAP ordered the holding companies controlling the *zaibatsu* to auction off their shares, thereby dissolving the *zaibatsu*. As part of the program, *zaibatsu* leaders were purged and barred from holding positions in the economy. To prevent the future reappearance of *zaibatsu*, the Elimination of Excessive Concentration of Economic Power Law was enacted in 1947 in order to break up monopolistic companies. The Anti-Monopoly Law was also passed to help maintain competitiveness in the economy.

Second, SCAP instituted land reforms in the countryside. Because the plight of tenant farmers and the agrarian crises were regarded as major sources of militarism in prewar Japan, SCAP issued a directive to carry out a thorough land reform in 1946. All land owned by absentee landlords was confiscated without compensation and resold to tenant farmers at a low price. Land holdings above one *cho* (1 *cho* = 2.45 acres) were bought up by the government to be resold to the former tenants. Thus, between 1946 and 1950, the percentage of farmland being cultivated by tenant farmers dropped from 46% to 10% (Nakamura, 1981, p. 27).

Third, SCAP reformed industrial relations. With the passage of the Labor Union Law in 1946, workers gained the rights to associate and to engage in collective bargaining. SCAP encouraged the formation of unions and required employers to cooperate with this law. The percentage of unionized workers increased from zero in 1945 to almost 60% in 1949; the number of unions increased from none to 34,688 in the same period (Halliday, 1975, p. 207; Ito, 1992, p. 55). SCAP also attempted to improve the previous harsh working environment, through the Labor Relations Adjustment Act of 1946 and the Labor Standards Law of 1947. In this new, more relaxed labor atmosphere, industrial disputes and strikes were frequent amidst runaway inflation and food shortages.

The Reverse Course of Occupation

Had the United States insisted on implementing its economic and political reforms in Japan, as originally planned, during the early postwar years, Japan might not be able to transform into a core so rapidly. But there was a curious twist in East Asian history in 1947, as the United States suddenly reversed itself and dropped most of its Japanese economic and political reforms.

By late 1947, the Americans' reformist zeal began to ebb as the Cold War began heating up. In that year, Mao's Liberation Army was gaining ground in China. In 1948, in response to the Soviet blockade of West Berlin, the United States carried out a massive airlift. Correspondingly, the overriding objectives of the American Occupation of Japan shifted from reform and punishment to restoration and rehabilitation.

Hence, many earlier reforms were rolled back. In early 1947 SCAP, weary of the surge in labor militancy under the leadership of leftist political organizations, banned a planned general strike on February 1, 1947. In August 1948, the rights of public employees to strike and bargain collectively were revoked. The antitrust reforms were also halted. Originally 325 firms were targeted for antimonopoly actions; by 1948, only 18 companies were actually split up into smaller units. More important, SCAP terminated the reparation and removal program in 1947, because by then the important goal was to rebuild Japan's economic power in order to support U.S. domination in Asia.

The Strategy of Containment in Asia

One of the most influential figures in U.S. postwar diplomacy, George Kennan is widely credited as a key architect of America's policy of containment in Asia during the 1950s (Borthwick, 1992, p. 391). In Kennan's original formulation, this policy called for the coordinated use of political, economic, and military influence to prevent the expansion of Communist control in vital regions (mostly Japan and the Philippines) in Asia.

However, from the 1950s onward, there was an increasing emphasis on military containment rather than political and economic containment; and the "vital regions" had extended beyond Japan and Philippines to include the entire perimeter in Asia-Pacific. As Borthwick (1992, p. 392) explains, this shift of emphasis reflected the burgeoning Soviet military growth and the rapid spread of communism in China, Japan, Korea, and Vietnam. In addition, the United States could expect little military or political support from its World War II allies who had become exhausted and dispirited. The British, French, and Dutch began to lose hold over their Asian colonies as they struggled to rebuild their nearly bankrupt, war-torn economies.

Under this containment strategy, the goal of the United States was to build Japan up as a bulwark against the spread of communism in Asia, and as a critical element in a U.S.-led world economy. George Kennan, who played the key role in pushing through this reverse course in Japan, explained this goal succinctly: "The changes in occupation policy that were now required were ones relating to an objective—namely, the economic rehabilitation of Japan and the restoration of her ability to contribute constructively to the stability and prosperity of the Far Eastern region" (quoted in Halliday, 1975, pp. 187-188).

Nevertheless, due to the loss of the Japanese empire after the war and the coming to power of socialist regimes in China and North Korea, the United States had to come up with a new way to incorporate Japan into the world economy. Eventually, the United States decided to cut off Japan from socialist Asia and incorporate it into the American-led capitalist regional economy in East Asia and Southeast Asia. The resultant arrangement was to develop a triangular relationship among the United States (the core), Japan (the semiperiphery), and Southeast Asia (the periphery) (Cumings, 1987). Although Southeast Asia had been controlled by other colonial powers (France, the Netherlands, and Britain) before the war, now the United States, as the new hegemonist, built up a new "dollar bloc" in the area. Under the new triangular structure, Japan would export industrial products to Southeast Asia and earn dollars in order to pay for imports from the United States. The United States, in turn, would import raw materials from Southeast Asia, as well as provide international aid to facilitate the triangular transactions (Shiraishi, 1989). As we will explain in the next chapter, the East Asian NIEs (South Korea, Taiwan, and Hong Kong) also were incorporated into this triangular commodity chain and turned into Japan's hinterland.

Had the United States nothing to fear from reviving Japan—its enemy during World War II? As Cumings (1987, p. 63) points out, although this postwar settlement aimed to revive the Japanese economy, it was also simultaneously designed to keep Japan under U.S. hegemonic control. Thus, Japan was to be ultradependent on the United States, or on American firms, for oil and security, and significantly dependent on the United States for food. Since 1945, Japan has had no military capability remotely commensurate with its economic power.

Meanwhile, although Japan's exports increased, which alleviated the nation's balance of payment bottleneck, rampant inflation was threatening the plans to revive the Japanese economy. To lay the foundation for future growth, SCAP executed the Dodge Plan in 1949. This plan, named after Joseph Dodge, an American banker serving as SCAP's adviser, was a full-scale deflationary scheme that sought to put Japan's economy back on a healthy course of recovery. The most important elements of the plan were to balance the government budget and cut spending drastically. State lending and subsidies to private firms also were curtailed. As a result, prices fell and a recession set in. When inflation finally came under control, a unified exchange rate was set at a low $1 = 360 yen in order to stimulate exports. Furthermore, under the pretext of rationalization and retrenchment, mass dismissals were carried out in both the public and private sectors. Left-wing and labor activists were purged, and pro-employer enterprise unions were established. Thus, it was only when the United States had reversed its reform policies that the rebuilding of Japanese capitalism began and democratization came to a full stop.

The American Origins of the Japanese Ascent

The United States exerted the following impacts on the Japanese economy: breaking up of some *zaibatsu*, granting special favors to Japanese corporations, an infusion of U.S. aid, relieving Japan of the burden of military defense, and creating a free trade global climate.

First, there were the effects of American tutelage in Japan after World War II. The *zaibatsu* were less destroyed than reformed, prospering again by the mid-1950s in a less concentrated form. The breaking up of some *zaibatsu*, nevertheless, had a significant impact on the structure of the postwar Japanese economy. It radically reduced the level of concentration as well as the dominance of the *zaibatsu* groups in the economy. This increased the number of companies operating in particular industries and encouraged new, smaller enterprises to grow—for example, the development of Honda in the auto industry. Although Japanese industries were by and large still oligopolistic in market structure, the level of competition increased greatly compared to the prewar period. Furthermore, fierce competition among the oligopolies induced them to embark on an aggressive drive to expand production capacities, exploit the latest technology, and emphasize high-rate capital formation, which, in turn, increased productivity by leaps and bounds. The purge of *zaibatsu* leaders also enabled a new generation of younger managers to rise to influential positions. "These men lacked the dignity and authority of their conservative predecessors, but they aggressively took up the challenge of meeting these new goals, and in many cases they succeeded" (Nakamura, 1981, p. 64). This perhaps explains the aggressive expansion and investment activities of Japanese enterprises in the postwar era.

Second, due to the significant geopolitical value of Japan in Asia, the United States was even willing to open its domestic markets to Japanese exports while tolerating the trade barriers of Japan for a long time. Cumings (1987) remarks that

> it was the great victor of the Occupation. Autonomy enabled Japan to pursue neo-mercantile policies of restricting entry to Japanese markets, resisting the intrusion of foreign capital, and providing various incentives and subsidies to restructure the industrial base in the 1950s, and conquer foreign markets in the 1960s and 1970s. (p. 64)

As a result, total foreign assets in Japan, even in the mid-1970s, were only about 2% to 3% of total assets. Few non-Japanese transnationals operated in Japan, and the major markets for foreign imports remained food and oil (Halliday, 1975, p. 283).

Third, the early infusion of American aid helped alleviate the worst postwar shortages. As part of its effort to rebuild the Japanese economy, the American government encouraged American companies to enter into alliances with Japanese corporations, to help them catch up with post-1930s technological developments. Though many American technologies imported into Japan were not the most up-to-date, they still enabled Japanese corporations to improve their productivity and competitiveness more quickly than expected. Furthermore, when Japan was suffering from the worst recession since the end of the war, induced by the Dodge Plan, the arrival of American industrial orders needed for the Korean War, through the so-called special procurement lifted the Japanese economy out of recession and put it on a course of rapid growth. Special procurement expenditures between 1951 and 1955 helped pay for about 30% of Japan's commodity imports. In 1952 and 1953, foreign exchange income from this source amounted to 60% to 70% of Japan's exports (Nakamura, 1981, p. 42). Several industries received great boosts from the Korean War boom. For example, the nascent automobile industry was greatly helped by American orders for military trucks used in the Korean War. Later, in the 1960s, the outbreak of the Vietnam War also benefited the Japanese economy, bringing as much as $1 billion a year to Japanese firms between 1966 and 1971 (Dower 1993, p. 13; Havens, 1987). Altogether, in the 20-year period from 1950 to 1970, U.S. aid to Japan averaged $500 million a year (Borden, 1984, p. 220).

Fourth, although the American imposition of demilitarization and the maintenance of U.S. military bases in Japan were regarded by some Japanese as an infringement of national sovereignty, relieving Japan's burden of military defense must be seen as beneficial to Japanese economic growth. "As a result, while other large countries were devoting between 4 and 7 percent of their GNP, and sometimes much more, to military expenditures, the Japanese were paying next to nothing" (Reischauer, 1988, pp. 316-317). Beneath America's military shelter, Japan was able to pursue an "economic growth first" strategy and devote almost all of its resources to economic reconstruction. In the postwar years, Japan spent less than 1% of its GNP annually on its small Self-Defense Force.

Finally, there was the relative liberalism in international commercial transactions under the U.S. hegemony. As a new hegemon, the United States made an effort to reduce barriers to trade all over the world, and backed this with U.S. political and military influence. As a result, world trade expanded tremendously. Japan's exports naturally benefited from this more open international commercial environment. On the import side, the liberal world economy also induced a continuous drop in raw material and oil prices in the 1950s and 1960s. Given Japan's virtually total dependence on imports of these commodities, and the importance of these commodities to Japan's industrial development, American hegemony had a very positive impact on the Japanese economy. With American hegemony enforcing the relatively "free" transactions in the world economy, Japan was able to obtain the requisite supply of critical inputs without having to resort to its prewar strategy of building an empire.

Among the benefits of American-led free trade was the fact that Japan had been able to return to the Southeast Asian and East Asian markets much earlier. Given the bitterness caused by Japanese imperialism, it is difficult to envisage these countries welcoming Japanese trade and investment in the early 1950s without the United States pulling the strings. For example, without American support, it would not have been possible for Japan to join the General Agreement on Tariffs and Trade (GATT) in 1955, which enabled Japan to enjoy the tariff concessions conferred by membership (Shiraishi, 1989).

The benefits of free trade would have been mitigated had there not been a major expansion in the demands for imports in Western core states. The wartime boom and the upsurge of workers' militancy had led to a new compromise between capital and labor. This led to the triumph of Fordism, with the twin pillars of mass production and high consumption as the engine of growth. The steadily improving real wages of U.S. workers, however, served to threaten the profit margins of firms producing consumer products at the lower end of the market. Competitive pressures then induced a major rise in consumer imports, capitalizing on the much lower wages elsewhere. Gradually, a new international division of labor emerged in the world economy, signified by a constant relocation of labor-intensive productions from the United States to Japan and then to other peripheral states (Frobel et al., 1980). The apparently insatiable American appetite for imports (from textiles to electronics to automobiles), under this new international division of labor, provided an excellent opportunity for the growth of manufacturing in Japan.

In sum, the reverse course of the U.S. Occupation and the special concessions that the United States granted to Japan during the early postwar years were instrumental in promoting the latter's rapid economic development from the 1950s to the 1970s. As Arrighi (1994b) points out, under U.S. hegemony, Japan thus got for "free" that economic hinterland it had fought so hard to obtain through territorial expansion in the first half of the 20th century, and eventually lost in the catastrophe of World War II. Nevertheless, in Kennan's original formulation, Japan was to play only a semiperipheral role in assisting the American hegemonic domination of East Asia. What, then, explains Japan's quick transition to core status and its eventual ability to challenge U.S. hegemony in the 1980s? To answer this question, researchers must examine some important Japanese institutions and ideologies.

THE DEVELOPMENTAL STATE

Johnson's Conception of the Developmental State

According to Chalmers Johnson (1982), the first feature of the developmental state (hereinafter DS), as its name implies, is its commitment to development. Johnson (1987, p. 140) points out that there is the "existence of a developmentally oriented political elite for whom economic growth is a fundamental goal." Sensing the constant cyclical contractions in the world economy, developmental elites within a state devise strategies to achieve economic growth and lift the national economy out of stagnation.

Second, the DS is committed to capitalist developmental strategies. As a capitalist state, the DS relies upon the market mechanism to achieve its developmental goals, motivate people to work, and foster efficiency. Therefore, the DS's actions tend to be market-conforming rather than market-displacing. The DS does not attempt to realize its objectives by command alone; instead, it seeks to manipulate the context through which the private sector makes its decisions in line with national goals.

Third, developmental elites in the DS possess the technical competence to formulate strategies for development because they were recruited "from among the technically most highly qualified people in the system" (Johnson, 1987, p. 152). Japan's MITI (Ministry of International Trade and Industry), for instance, was staffed by the best students from the best universities in Japan. Once they entered the bureaucracy, they normally stayed for most of their careers, thus developing expertise in their jobs and an esprit de corps with fellow bureaucrats.

Fourth, the DS is highly autonomous. In Japan, state policy was formulated and implemented by a highly autonomous corps of bureaucrats who had been shielded from the political pressures of various interest groups, due to the prolonged stability of the political system brought about by the dominance of the Liberal Democratic Party. As far as possible, the politicians "reigned but did not rule." Politicians let the bureaucrats alone to do the job of planning and steering economic growth.

Although it is not without its critics (because he might have overstated the autonomy and capacity of the Japanese state: see Friedman, 1988; Samuels, 1987), Johnson's developmental state thesis—that the state has played a crucial role in Japan's upward mobility to the core status— seems beyond dispute. Nevertheless, a development-oriented, market-conforming, competent, and autonomous state does not emerge out of nowhere and deliver economic growth when required. Crucial research questions that need to be addressed are: What are the historical origins of the Japanese DS? When did the DS emerge? And why was it so autonomous?

Wartime and U.S. Origins

World War II helped lay the foundation of the DS in Japan; during the war, there was a greater degree of state control over the economy. The Japanese state exercised direct control over many parts of the economy, through the wartime Commerce and Industry Ministry and Munitions Ministry. The experience of state intervention and close state-business cooperation during wartime mobilization shaped the effectiveness of the Ministry of International Trade and Industry's (MITI) policies in the postwar era. Furthermore, the Bank of Japan came to regulate closely the operations of the nation's private banks, and established the precedents for Japan's state-finance-industry relationship.

The reforms imposed by the United States during its occupation of Japan had further increased the power of the Japanese bureaucrats vis-à-vis the Japanese politicians and the bourgeoisie. Before World War II, the bureaucrats had to put up with rivalry among the political parties, the military, and the *zaibatsu* in their contest for power. The SCAP reforms and purges during the American Occupation, however, helped remove most influential politicians, smashed the military, weakened the *zaibatsu*, and dispossessed the landlords. In contrast, the bureaucracy, in particular MITI, was untouched by the Occupation reforms. Halliday (1975, p. 173) reveals that bureaucrats accounted for only 0.9% of the total number of people purged by SCAP. After eliminating the rivals of the bureaucracy, SCAP ruled Japan largely through the bureaucracy. SCAP's dictatorial style of rule, therefore, indirectly enhanced the authority of the Japanese bureaucracy. Finally, SCAP crushed the labor movement and rendered it unable to challenge the developmental policies of the bureaucracy.

Thus, the autonomy of the Japanese DS was considerably strengthened during the period of American tutelage. Subsequently, the DS was empowered to formulate many industrial and financial policies to promote Japanese development.

Industrial Policy and Product Cycle

Industrial policy

refers to a complex of those policies concerning protection of domestic industries, development of strategic industries, and adjustment of the economic structure in response to or in anticipation of internal and external changes which are formulated and pursued by MITI in the cause of the national interest. (Johnson, 1982, p. 26)

The basic assumption of Japan's industrial policy is a dynamic view of the world market, in which national competitive advantages of a particular industry come and go according to domestic changes and international technological and market situations.

Essentially, this entails a policy of "industrial targeting," or "picking the winners." After deliberations based on the possibilities and benefits of developing a particular new industry, MITI officials designate certain industries as strategic industries and draw up a plan for the nurturing of the industries. Johnson (1982) points out that

the tools in the hands of the economic bureaucrats included control over all foreign exchange and imports of technology, which gave them the power to choose industries for development; the ability to dispense preferential financing, tax breaks, and protection from foreign competition, which gave them the power to lower the costs of the chosen industries; and the authority to order the creation of cartels and bank-based industrial conglomerates . . . which gave them the power to supervise competition. (p. 199)

In the early postwar years, when light industries such as textiles, food, and beverages still accounted for the bulk of industrial output, the Japanese DS pushed ahead with heavy-chemical industrialization. World War II had greatly stimulated the development of heavy-chemical industry in Japan. Although most facilities were destroyed in the war, the knowledge and technology amassed in the engineers and workers in the heavy industries facilitated their rapid recovery. Five heavy-chemical industries were targeted in the 1950s for development: steel, shipbuilding, coal, power, and fertilizer (Rapp, 1975). Steel would prove critical to the recovery, due to the world steel shortage in the early postwar years; shipbuilding would help rebuild Japan's merchant fleet; coal and power would provide the energy for economic growth; fertilizer would be valuable for increasing agrarian output and cutting the need for agricultural labor.

By the 1960s, when the heavy-chemical industry became firmly established, the Japanese DS began to boost the development of new industries, such as synthetic textiles, plastics, petrochemicals, automobiles, and electronics. In effect, all the major industries developed in postwar Japan underwent a period of state nurturing and protection.

Furthermore, when an industry lost its competitiveness in the world market, the Japanese DS would also engineer an "orderly exit" of the industry from the economy, through such devices as recession cartels and rationalization programs. Cumings (1987, p. 65) explains that "moving out of declining into advanced sectors is much easier because powerful domestic business interests rarely clash, and a labor force lacking influence at the commanding heights can be eased out of old industries and retrained for new ones." Japan's flexible adjustment to product cycles, induced by changes in the world market situation and Japan's own competitive advantages, has enabled it to maintain its industrial power throughout the postwar decades.

Aside from successful industrial policy, the Japanese state also promotes a financial policy to facilitate a high rate of investment and capital formation.

Financial Policy and Capital Formation

For a high rate of capital formation to be possible, particular institutional mechanisms that transform household savings into investable capital are required. The Japanese DS promoted this financial policy through two channels.

The first was through the commercial banks. Commercial banks were more ready to transform savings into loans for their clients' long-term investment needs. Much of the explosive investment activity in this high-speed growth period were thus based on debt-financing. For the banks to be able to expand loans and advances to their clients, however, the Japanese state had to adopt the policy of "overloaning" to act as the final guarantor of the banking system. During the periods of capital shortage, the Japanese state increased "government loans to city banks (the twelve national banks to which the Bank of Japan extends loan privileges), who in turn distributed the funds to the industrialists who were clamoring for money to expand their facilities" (Johnson, 1982, p. 202). Due to the dependence of the banks on government loans, and the excess demand for loans by corporations, the banks followed government guidelines in rationing credits among different borrowers, thus enhancing the effectiveness of state industrial targeting.

A second channel of industrial financing was through the state's own financial institutions. After World War II, the Japanese state established an array of financial institutions with specific missions. Among these were the Industrial Bank of Japan and the Japan Development Bank, which provided long-term financing at low interest rates, and the Export-Import Bank of Japan, which financed export trade (Allen, 1981, pp. 56-57). A critical role was also played by the state's Postal Saving System, which amassed a large share of household deposit savings and put it into a Fiscal Investment and Loan Program (FLIP). The FLIP then was empowered to extend loans at low interest rates to public financial institutions, which in turn made loans to private corporations. Because of these institutions, the Japanese state was able to supply between 19% and 38% of industrial capital through its various special banks (Johnson, 1982, p. 210). The special banks' lending, as in the case of commercial banks, followed MITI's criteria; in the case of the Japan Development Bank, loan applications were actually reviewed by MITI for approval. As a result, strategic industries were favored and were able to finance their large-scale investment projects through low-cost government loans.

In sum, at the state level, Japanese developmental elites quickly seized the favorable postwar opportunity offered by the United States and instituted industrial and financial policies to strive for entry into the core. As the following section will reveal, there were similar efforts waged at the enterprise level.

INDUSTRIAL RELATIONS
AND SUBCONTRACTING SYSTEM

Dual Industrial Structure and Industrial Relations

In the chapter on Japan's regionalization effort, we noted the emergence of a dualistic industrial structure during the interwar period of the *zaibatsu*-related firms on one hand and the traditional small industries on the other. The duality became more pronounced after World War II. The development after the war of new large-scale *keiretsu* (enterprise groups), like Sony, Honda, and Toyota, along with the persistence of the old *zaibatsu* groups contributed to expansion of the large-scale sector. Nevertheless, this development of the large-scale sector did not lead to the demise of the small and medium-sized firms. The share of manufacturing firms with fewer than 99 employees dropped only slightly in the 1950s and 1960s, then rebounded in the 1970s. Consequently, small firms accounted for 60.9% of manufacturing employment in 1951, and they still hired 55.5% of all manufacturing workers in 1975 (Nakamura, 1981, p. 172).

In the large sector, industrial relations were characterized by enterprise unionism, lifetime employment, and seniority-based promotion and wage systems. In addition, there was a unique pattern of industrial subcontracting between enterprises in the large sector and those in the small sector.

In enterprise unionism, as Yoshinaga (1994, p. 10) points out, "unions became a part of the corporation, buying into the overall interests of management and the corporation, rather than serving as a non-corporate, cross-corporate voice of workers' interests." In the so-called Quality Control (QC) Circle, a small group of workers engaged on a daily basis in voluntary activities aimed at improving both the quality of their products and the management of their work through self-learning and mutual teaching. Through the QC circle, the corporation

> raises the standard of work performance by all employees, including the least able; under the group's collective pressure, all work overtime with nominal compensation, mavericks are brought into line, and recalcitrant dissidents—especially those who believe in class ideology—are forced either to change their ways or quit their job. (Fukui, 1992, p. 212)

In addition, although lifetime employment and the seniority-based wage system were introduced by management during World War II as means to recruit, train, and then keep scarce workers, they were again introduced by management in early postwar period as weapons to divide and rule labor. Fukui (1992, p. 213) laments that under such employment and seniority systems, job security, promotions, and wages now became subjects to be discussed and settled strictly by management and the employees of the given enterprise alone, and thus no business of outsiders. It has also been found that lifetime job security and age-based promotion and wage increases were granted only to the predominately male, "regular" employees in large enterprises, and a large number of temporary, part-time, female employees in these enterprises, as well as most of the workers in the medium and small enterprises and sub-

contractors, were excluded. It is estimated that the "Japanese employment system" covered less than one quarter of the labor force (Koike,
1988; Levine, 1989; Shimada, 1980). As such, these kinds of industrial
relations weakened working-class solidarity, cut down industrial disruption due to strikes, and promoted industrial productivity.

Subcontracting

Though the coexistence of large and small firms is hardly novel in
capitalist economies, Japan does stand out because of the presence of the
following pattern of subcontracting between large and small firms.

First, there was a dense network of subcontracting relations between
large and small firms. As Allen (1981) points out:

> For many years past it has been customary for the latter [large firms] to rely
> on subcontractors not only for parts and components but also as suppliers
> of services (for example, cleaning) within their factory. The result is that
> every large firm is the center of a constellation of small and medium firms
> which are, in greater or lesser degree, dependent on it for business. . . . Japa-
> nese small firms were very dependent on subcontracting, as about 70% of
> small manufacturing firms in the textile, electric machinery, machinery,
> clothing and steel industries produced via subcontracting relationships in
> 1966. (p. 122)

Second, the subcontracting relationship in Japan was also remarkable
in its continuity and stability. Often it was idealized "as a family relationship and is symbolized in terms such as parent company or child sub-
contractor" (Eccleston, 1989, p. 34). Subcontractors often produced
exclusively for one big company for a long period of time. For small
firms, such a relationship offered a steady stream of orders, and became
their only means of survival.

Third, subcontracting relations often went beyond merely buying and
selling. Parent companies could also assist their subcontractors financially or technically to help them to improve their methods of production. Thus, larger firms often kept a close watch on the internal
operations of their subcontractors. Parent companies would transfer
personnel, equipment, and ideas about organization to their own subcontractors, who in turn would do likewise, right down to the level of
the single-person firm.

This unique pattern of subcontracting has greatly strengthened the competitive power of the Japanese firms. It enabled large firms to expand production quickly at time of economic booms without directly bearing the responsibilities of the costs of expansion. When recessions came, parent companies could pass on the burden of adjustment to their subcontractors, hence buffering the vagaries of business fluctuations. Because parent companies often had numerous subcontractors at one time, they usually were in a more advantageous position and were able to extort concessions from their suppliers. This unequal exchange between the large and small firms can be regarded as a building block for the renowned flexibility of Japanese industries.

Another advantage of subcontracting, from the perspective of the large companies, was in labor costs. Large wage differentials between the large firms and the small firms were maintained in the postwar years. The average wage of firms with 30 to 99 employees was 67.3% of that of firms with 500 employees or more in 1950; it was 69.9% in 1970 (Nakamura, 1981, p. 164). The large wage differentials between large and small firms were a function of the rapid development of capital-intensive manufacturing in the postwar years, and the surplus supply of labor during the 1950s. In any case, the existence of such wage differentials enabled Japanese corporations to suppress the level of real wages in a period of high-speed economic growth.

However, as a result of intense interenterprise competition and rising wages, Japan's wages were no longer cheap by Third World standards. Furthermore, due to the oil shock and the sharp rise of the yen in the early 1970s, there was a rapid increase in the costs of production in Japan. Subsequently, the above economic pressures prompted Japanese corporations to engage in a transborder expansion into selected locations in East Asia.

Toward Transborder Expansion

Arrighi et al. (1993) point to the following characteristics of Japanese transborder expansion. First, Japanese enterprises had been far less insistent and reliant on majority ownership than U.S. and Western European companies. Thus, in 1971, minority ownerships and joint ventures accounted for about 80% of foreign manufacturing subsidiaries of Japanese firms, as opposed to 20% for similar firms of the United States and the United Kingdom.

Second, the great Japanese wave of transnational expansion in the early 1970s consisted primarily of transborder expansion of the subcontracting networks of trading companies and the activities of small and medium-sized subcontracting firms. As Woronoff (1984) observed, the small and medium-sized enterprises involved in transplanting would have been unable to move abroad on their own, had they not been assisted by the trading companies that were their suppliers or their customers, or both.

Third, most transplanting at the lower value-added end of the Japanese manufacturing apparatus occurred within Asia; Hong Kong, Taiwan, South Korea, and Singapore especially received a disproportionate share. What Japanese capital was seeking were locations close at hand with efficient, cheap, flexible labor supplies, and with a maximally privileged access to the United States and other core markets. From this viewpoint, Japan's former colonies of South Korea and Taiwan, which had as privileged an access to the U.S. domestic market as did Japan, and the city-states of Singapore and Hong Kong, were good locations.

As Arrighi et al. (1993) emphasize, this transborder expansion of the Japanese subcontracting system created conditions for the continuing vitality of the multilayered subcontracting system in Japan, speeding up Japan's economic ascent to the core. In addition to this subcontracting system, the ruling-class ideology of postwar Japan also helped promote the corization of Japan.

THE IDEOLOGY OF
CONSENSUS, PATERNALISM, AND SEXISM

The Ideology of Consensus

The core ideology of the prewar Japanese state was its commitment to building "a rich nation with a strong army." The basic ideological means to achieve this—the emperor cult, moral education, Shintoism, and Confucianism—were developed by the state and appropriated by the capitalists to train and tame the working class.

However, the postwar reforms put an end to the state's sponsorship of the exclusive nationalist ideology (ultranationalism) as well as militarism. The reforms also expanded the sphere of the civil society, free from state-imposed restrictions. As Fukui (1992) points out, thanks to these democratic reforms, there was

> a deeper penetration of society in general and the corporate world in particular by the anticlass ideology of consensus and cooperation. The promotion of the unionization of labor, land reform, emancipation of women, the democratization of the education system, and so forth, all contributed to the eclipse rather than the popularity of the ideology of class warfare, notably Marxism and its variants. (pp. 209-210)

Despite these reforms, however, the eventual triumph of the ideology of consensus can be seen in many important arenas, beginning with that of education. In 1954 Japan passed a pair of laws that made it illegal for school teachers either to make any political statement—such as criticizing a government, a political party, or a policy—in class or to engage in off-campus political activities. In 1957 the Japanese state established a uniform nationwide teacher evaluation system, directed at the left-wing Japan Teachers' Union. These reforms succeeded in sanitizing primary and secondary school curricula against class ideology. Another triumph of the ideology of consensus was the spread of paternalism in the corporate world.

Paternalism

Through the institution of enterprise unionism, corporate Japan cultivated the ideology of the company as a surrogate family to its employees. Abegglen (1973) remarks that the absence of status barriers in the company—marked by traditions such as an all-inclusive cafeteria, the presence of permanent employment, the seniority wage system, and the availability of other fringe benefits such as sports, hobby clubs, and company vacation resorts—are also conceived as traditional familism. Such benefits reinforce the loyalty of employees toward the enterprise and boost their willingness to sacrifice their own interests for the good of the enterprise.

Once the imagery of corporate paternalism was installed, employees were subjected to constant pressures to conform and obey company rules and orders. As Muto (1986) argues0:

> The "company world" is an institutional-cum-ideological device used to translate inter-enterprise competition (which was always sharp) into inter-worker competition. The big company is structured into a world within which the workers are coerced into sharing the fate of the company. Once workers are integrated into this "world," they are forced to compete with one another to achieve the goals set by the company. (p. 123)

This corporate paternalism has made interfirm mobility highly difficult. Once a worker joins a corporate family, the lifelong employment system and the seniority-based wage system make it hard for the person to quit and move to another company. Even when a worker is able to find a job in another company, it is very unlikely that the person could have the same level of pay and fringe benefits as before. Most important, other workers and managers, as well as personnel departments in the hiring firms, look on such a worker as "flaky," unreliable, and potentially troublemaking for not being able to stay at his or her former company.

The real "secret" of the Japanese corporate paternalism, then, must be found in the exceptionally effective system of social control over workers, forced to bond their own fates to that of their corporate families. As such, Muto (1986, p. 123) points to the positive impact of corporate paternalism on economic growth: "To the degree that management succeeded in preempting workers' resistance in the plants, it could feel free to implement technological innovations, expand the scale of production, and thus obtain special surplus value for reinvestment." The flexibility of the Japanese employment system was also enhanced by the traditional ideology of sexism.

Sexism

Women workers in Japan often engaged in low-skill and low-paying jobs in the labor market. Fukui (1992) laments that corporate Japan has deprived many working women of benefits given to their male counterparts. Women employees not only accounted for an overwhelming majority of those "regular" employees excluded from the systems of lifetime employment and seniority wages, but they also accounted for a large majority of "nonregular" employees hired on a part-time or temporary basis.

In addition, Arrighi et al. (1993) also note that corporate Japan practices discrimination against the employment of women in the top layers of the subcontracting system. Conversely, women always show up in the bottom layer of the subcontracting system—the female home pieceworkers. The hourly wages received by these pieceworkers are only about one fourth those of full-time male workers in the smallest enterprises, with 5 to 29 employees.

In this respect, Yoshinaga (1994) concludes that

> women employees, frequently saddled with the patronizing label of "office ladies" or OLs in white-collar Japan, suffer from lower pay than their male colleagues, fewer promotional opportunities within the management track, sexual harassment, pressures to quit and cast away their careers upon marriage and childbirth, sexism internalized and directed by other woman employees and managers as well as by males, and relatively low job security (since the majority of the dispensable "temporary employees" are women). (p. 16)

However, despite the ideology of consensus, paternalism, and sexism, and despite rapid economic growth in Japan, the Japanese people reacted vigorously to the contradictions brought about by the corization of Japan in the capitalist world economy. As a result, there has been a upsurge of antisystemic movements in Japan since World War II.

THE ANTISYSTEMIC MOVEMENTS

The Labor Movement

The first contradiction that Japanese society experienced was massive unemployment and rampant inflation right after the war. As soon as SCAP institutionalized its liberalization reforms, labor unions were formed, many strikes broke out, and the Japanese working class resorted to work-in or production control in the manufacturing sector. Japanese workers also demanded job security and a basic livelihood wage (Gordon, 1985, pp. 352-353).

In response, SCAP quickly rolled back some of the earlier liberal reforms in labor relations, and the Japanese capitalists immediately dismissed or purged militant workers in order to break the back of many radical unions that favored collective action. Moreover, the Japanese capitalists institutionalized the lifetime employment and enterprise unionism system, with the aim of containing collective bargaining at the enterprise level (Gordon, 1985; Moore, 1983).

As such, it was the intense class conflict in early postwar years—not unique Japanese cultural traits—that triggered the institutionalization of the Japanese employment system. Furthermore, whatever gains Japanese labor achieved from this employment system were a result of class struggle, not something voluntarily bestowed by the Japanese capitalist class. Nevertheless, after the Japanese working class was incorporated into enterprise unions in the 1950s, the intensity of class conflict subsided, and the Japanese antisystemic movement shifted to the student movement in the 1960s.

The Student Movement

The second contradiction in Japan's rise to the core was the Japan-United States link, which a growing number of Japanese objected to strongly. Formed in 1945, the National Federation of Students' Self-Governing Associations (the Zengakuren) adopted a militant platform regarding Japan's role in the Cold War. Throughout the 1960s, the Zengakuren played a leading role in the popular struggles against the renewal of the Mutual Security Treaty (AMPO) between Japan and the United States. Students took radical actions against the renewal, the most dramatic of which were the invasions of the Diet in November 1959 and June 1960. Apart from the treaty's renewal, the student movement also waged struggles against the normalization of relations between Seoul and Tokyo in 1965, the presence of American troops and nuclear weapons in Japan, as well as the remilitarization of Japan. Most of the students' struggles left behind no concrete achievements, and by 1970 both the student groups' internal fighting and state repression eventually led to a decline in student protests.

The Citizens' Movement

As the corization of Japan became more apparent in the early 1970s, the third contradiction of the growth-first strategy (also called "GNPism") began to assume the forefront. Because Japan channeled most resources to the promotion of corization projects, there was scant attention given to the undesirable consequences of industrialization, especially environmental pollution and the disruption of the livelihood of local communities. By 1970 as many as 3,000 local citizens' groups were protesting these environmental and community problems, constituting what was called the citizens' movement (*shimin undo*) (Eccleston, 1989, p. 220). For instance, the construction of the Narita Airport had led to the eviction of local farmers from their land. With the support of radical political organizations, student organizations, and trade unions, the farmers waged a community movement to oppose the airport construction. At first such peaceful tactics as petitions and disseminating leaflets were used, but violent confrontations later broke out between farmers and the police.

Due to pressures by the citizens' movement, 14 bills were passed, in 1970, to regulate the environmental impact of industries, leading to significant improvements in public control over industries. In addition, the citizens' movement heightened the level of local political mobilization, leading to the election of people with "progressive" leanings to local political offices. Litigation against polluting companies also secured compensation to victims and aroused widespread public attention to the problem of pollution.

However, the citizens' movement had its weaknesses. Its localized, ad hoc, and loose organizations could not been transformed into a long-standing and national progressive force against the state. Moreover, Smith (1986) points out that

> considering the scale of the problems and the extent of disaffection, citizens' movements may be said to have acted as a safety valve, confining popular disaffection at the level of local government and leaving central government and other institutions very largely untouched. (pp. 162-163)

CONCLUSION

This chapter traced Japan's postwar ascent to a core power. By 1970, Japan had done what it had failed to do with military power during the Second World War—achieve an equal status with the Western core states. We have emphasized the reverse course of U.S. Occupation, as well as the role of U.S. hegemony in Asia, in laying the foundation for the economic ascent of Japan. The Japanese developmental state and the Japanese capitalist class seized this excellent geopolitical opportunity to promote industrial and financial policies, to incorporate labor into enterprise unionism, to engage in transborder expansion of the subcontracting network, and to install an ideology of consensus, paternalism, and sexism to speed up the corization of Japan.

The corization of Japan, however, was not unproblematic. Its contradictions sparked the emergence of the labor movement in the 1950s, the student movement in the 1960s, and the citizens' movement in the 1970s. Moreover, Japan's rise to core status was yet incomplete by the early 1970s. Politically, it was still very much an appendage of American global strategy and had not articulated a clear vision of its own. Japanese culture also did not match the international hegemonic role played by American culture throughout the globe in the postwar era. As Chapter 10 will discuss, the continuous decline of the U.S economic and political hegemony in the world economy has created new uncertainties for Japan.

In addition, the corization of Japan has made a great impact on East Asian development. The transborder expansion of the Japanese subcontracting system has created the conditions for the spread of the Japanese economic miracle to the newly industrializing economies in East Asia. This topic will be the focus of the next chapter.

8. The Semiperipheralization of the Newly Industrializing Economies

The rise of the East Asian NIEs (Newly Industrializing Economies) in the postwar world economy, along with Japan's remarkable ascent to the core, has been dubbed the "East Asian miracle." Similar to Japan, the East Asian NIEs also experienced a turbulent period shortly after World War II, as they were confronted with serious political and economic problems. The changing dynamics in the world economy and in the East Asian region laid the foundation for the industrial takeoff of the East Asian NIEs. Nevertheless, this chapter shows that, given a similar opening in the world economy, different links between the state and the capitalist class in the East Asian NIEs have led to their divergent patterns of sociopolitical development in the past 3 decades.

DEVELOPMENTAL PROBLEMS IN THE EARLY POSTWAR YEARS

South Korea

The Allied forces defeated Japan on August 15, 1945, and brought Korea's colonial period to an end. The aftermath of World War II, as described by Henderson (1968, p. 69), was "an entire period of great flux, an era of mass participation virtually unprecedented in Korean history and unequaled since." A dizzying array of mass organizations of workers, peasants, youths, and women mushroomed, thanks to the unprecedented political freedom that accompanied independence. Amidst this atmosphere of exhilaration, the People's Republic of Korea was established in Seoul in late 1945; for a time, it was able to achieve de facto sovereignty throughout the country with the help of numerous local People's Committees.

The destiny of postwar Korea, however, had been determined even before Japan surrendered to the Allied forces. The nation was arbitrarily divided by the interests of two superpowers—the United States and the Soviet Union—thus setting the stage for divided and antagonistic state formation. The North, controlled by the Communists, formed its own government, the Democratic People's Republic of Korea, with Kim Il Sung as its prime minister. South Korea formed south of the 38th parallel under the auspices of the United Nations, which at the time was dominated by the United States.

As Koo (1993) points out, what followed in the South was a forceful demobilization of these mass organizations by the United States Army Military Government in Korea (USAMGIK). In early 1950, after the USAMGIK finally restored order through violent repression, it installed the conservative Syngnam Rhee regime, which was backed by businessmen and local elites, to replace the popular forces. With this development, both the Japanese colonial apparatus of coercion and the former Korean collaborators with the colonial government were revived. However, the Rhee regime was internally undermined by incessant factional fighting, Rhee's autocratic leadership, and his mismanagement of the economy.

In June 1950 North Korean troops crossed the 38th parallel and quickly occupied a large portion of the South. United Nations forces came to the South's rescue, and the Korean War broke out. After more than 6 million casualties, an armistice was finally achieved in July 1953. Koo (1993) remarks that no single event in modern Korean history influenced state formation in Korea more than the Korean War. The war bolstered Rhee's political authority, empowered him to eliminate radical elements and opposition groups, and led to the hyper-militarization of Korean society. The war also led to a firmer U.S. commitment to the security of South Korea as a bulwark against communism.

This U.S. intervention, however, introduced a new element of contradiction in South Korean politics. Although the United States installed a formal democratic government structure in the South, with a public commitment to democracy, in reality it had to support the conservative Rhee regime that blatantly violated such ideals in its daily practices. Had the United States not intervened in the political development of South Korea, the shape of politics in South Korea would have been very different. Rhee's regime would have fallen, and socialism would have become a viable option in the South.

Needless to say, the Korean War caused great damage to the South Korean economy. Vogel (1991) points out that about one fourth of the South Korean population became refugees without homes. Furthermore, when the country was divided, all the industrial facilities built during the Japanese colonial period went to North Korea. Thus, aside from being the nation's breadbasket, South Korea had little industry. In the early 1950s, enormous amounts of resources were spent on healing the wounds of this war.

In the mid-1950s the Rhee regime adopted the strategy of import-substitution. It tried to stimulate industrial production through installing protective tariffs against foreign imports and systems of multiple foreign exchange rates with overvalued *hwan*. The economy did recover, but its growth was relatively slow. By the late 1950s the Korean economy was besieged by a number of structural weaknesses, such as dependence on foreign aid, a chronic deficit in foreign trade, and exhaustion of the import-substitution industrialization strategy. In the early 1960s, the drop in foreign aid led to a crisis situation. After U.S. aid to South Korea was halved from US$383 million in 1957 to US$199 million in 1961, South Korea's real GNP growth rate quickly dropped from 7.7% to 1.9% in 1959, and wholesale prices increased at a annual rate of 15.6% from 1959 to 1961 (Cathie, 1989, p. 106; Mason et al., 1980, p. 98).

The Rhee regime finally collapsed in the face of a reduction in American aid, serious unemployment and inflation problems, and waves of student protest in the early 1960s (Koo & Kim, 1992). A new government, headed by opposition party politicians, proved unable to consolidate a durable regime and was quickly overthrown by a military coup led by Park Chung Hee.

Taiwan

After the Japanese surrendered in 1945, Taiwan was restored to Chinese sovereignty. Hostility soon developed between the indigenous society and the Guomindang (GMD) state apparatus. This was because Japanese colonialism had heightened the cultural differences between the indigenous Taiwanese and the mainland Chinese. Most Taiwanese spoke not Mandarin, but the Fujianese dialect and Japanese, making communication with the incoming GMD officials difficult and easily engendering misunderstanding (Lai, Myers, & Wou, 1991).

Moreover, there was the misgoverning of the GMD. The Taiwan government was run by mainland officials without any input from local Taiwanese people. Furthermore, the Taiwan government brought with it all the ills of the mainland GMD regime: lawlessness, corruption, nepotism, and inefficiency (Gold, 1986). Owing to wartime damages and GMD mismanagement, Taiwan's economy was in a crisis situation by 1946, with fallen production, high inflation, and serious shortages of food and other basic commodities.

Conflict eventually broke out in the "February 28 Incident." After a rebellion started in Taipei [Taibei] on February 28, 1947, it quickly spread to all the major cities on the island. It was quelled only after the GMD troops began a brutal crackdown on the Taiwanese resistance. The estimate was that at least 10,000 Taiwanese were killed. This February 28 Incident further widened the cleavage between the mainlanders and the Taiwanese (Meisner, 1964).

In 1949 the GMD retreated to Taiwan after defeat by the Communists on the mainland. The prospect of a resurgence of Taiwanese rebellion continued to haunt the GMD, prompting it to resort to authoritarian and restrictive policies. Stern measures were taken to crack down on anti-GMD movements, especially activities linked to Taiwanese independence. Martial law was declared in May 1949, and independence activists were forced to flee overseas. A two-tier (central and local) government was constructed. The head of state was the president, who enjoyed a wide range of power because of the state of emergency. Mainlanders continued to dominate at the top level of the government and the party; local Taiwanese were restricted to political participation at the local level.

In the early 1950s the GMD adopted the import-substitution strategy to stimulate industrial production. However, due to its small domestic market, there was a pronounced stagnation in the private-sector's real investment after 1954, even though investment by the government continued to grow. Between 1958 and 1960 a series of enterprise failures in the wake of the economic downturn caught public attention. These crises subsided only after the government came forth to rescue some of the enterprises.

More serious was the persistence of the balance-of-payment problem. In the 1950s Taiwan had huge trade deficits because it managed to export only 60% of its imports. Taiwan mostly exported agricultural and handicraft products, and the prospects for such exports were not promising. These trade deficits, therefore, had to be compensated for by a massive inflow of U.S. aid. What had alarmed the Taiwanese government was that it saw South Korea suffer from a deep cut in U.S. aid in the late 1950s. Subsequently, the Taiwanese government pondered what would happen to its economy in the event of complete termination of U.S. aid.

Hong Kong

Before World War II, the GMD government in Nanjing began to recover sovereignty over a number of foreign settlements and treaty ports in China. Hong Kong, however, remained a British colony. Britain was determined to hold on to this Far East colony because Britain conducted a prosperous entrepot trade with China and Southeast Asia through Hong Kong.

The Japanese wartime occupation disrupted the Hong Kong economy momentarily, but the rehabilitation process was swift enough to allow normal entrepot activities to recover in less than a year's time. In 1949, after the Chinese communists defeated the GMD and "liberated" the mainland, there was a sudden influx of refugees to Hong Kong. Subsequently, Hong Kong's population jumped from 1,600,000 in 1941 to more than 2,360,000 in 1950. Hambro (1955, p. 162) estimated that in 1954 there were about 667,000 mainland refugees who came to Hong Kong for political and economic reasons. This massive increase in population subsequently imposed a backbreaking burden on the colony in the early 1950s.

The Korean War dealt another blow to Hong Kong's entrepot economy. The war quickly prompted the United Nations to impose an embargo on Chinese trade, in June 1951. The embargo crippled the Hong Kong economy, because China was the colony's largest trading partner. In 1954 the total value of trade was a meager 60% of the 1948 level (Szczepanik, 1958, p. 45). Apart from the embargo, entrepot trade with China also declined in the 1950s because of the Communist regime's rigid control of foreign investments, imports, and exports. The Communist regime preferred to deal directly with foreign governments and investors, effectively bypassing the traders in Hong Kong. The immediate effects of the embargo and the decline in entrepot trade were disastrous. Taking together the direct loss of earnings from entrepot trade and of indirect earnings through providing warehouses, transport, banking, and insurance services, Hong Kong's real GDP fell by 5.5% in 1951 (Ho, 1979).

In sum, there were serious economic and political problems in South Korea, Taiwan, and Hong Kong in the postwar period. Yet in a short span of about 3 decades, these three states quickly transformed themselves into newly industrializing economies.

THE SEMIPERIPHERALIZATION OF THE NIEs

The post-World War II development of South Korea is described by Eckert (1992) as

> a tale whose drama is heightened by breathtaking contrasts: a per capita GNP of about US$ 100 in 1963 versus a figure of nearly US$ 5,000 as the year 1990 began; a war-ravaged Seoul of gutted buildings, rubble, beggars, and orphans in 1953 versus the proud, bustling city of the 1988 Summer Olympics with its skyscrapers, subways, plush restaurants, boutiques, first-class hotels, and prosperous middle class; a country abjectly dependent on foreign aid in the 1950s versus a 1980s economic powerhouse. (p. 289)

Furthermore, Vogel (1991, p. 1) points to the following achievements of East Asian NIEs in the late 1980s: Hong Kong, South Korea, and Taiwan are among the world's 17 top trading nations; South Korea is the second-largest shipbuilder in the world, as well as a formidable producer of steel and automobiles; Hong Kong joined New York and London as one of the great financial centers of the world; and the Taiwanese economy has one of the largest foreign currency holdings in the world.

The above vivid accounts aside, there are five indicators of the semi-peripheralization of Hong Kong, South Korea, and Taiwan. First, the East Asian NIEs had impressive growth rates during the past 3 decades. In the 1960s growth in GDP was 10% in Hong Kong, 8.6% in Korea, and

9.2% in Taiwan. In the 1970s, even when the Latin American NIEs' growth rates slowed down, the East Asian NIEs' GDP still grew at a respectable rate of 9.3% in Hong Kong, 9.5% in Korea, and 8% in Taiwan (Chiu, 1992).

Second, there was a tremendous expansion in NIEs' exports, which grew at an average rate of 23.7% in the 1960s. More significant, manufactured goods accounted for the lion's share of total merchandise exports. By 1970 about 76% of all exports from South Korea and Taiwan, and about 93% of all exports from Hong Kong, were manufactured goods (Chiu, 1992; Hirata & Osada, 1990).

Third, there was industrial upgrading among the East Asian NIEs. In the 1960s the NIEs' economies were dominated by traditional labor-intensive industries, such as textiles, apparel, and footwear. However, in the 1970s, there were "Heavy and Chemical Industrialization" programs that focused on steel, machinery, automobiles, shipbuilding, and petrochemicals. In the 1980s there was further upgrading toward skill-intensive, high value-added export industries, whose products ranged from computers and semiconductors to numerically controlled machine tools, televisions, videocassette recorders, and sporting goods (Gereffi, 1992).

Fourth, the NIEs largely escaped transnational domination. Whereas the labor-intensive industries of the Latin American NIEs were mostly owned by foreign transnationals, those of East Asian NIEs were owned by indigenous firms. As such, East Asian firms had more autonomy in promoting exports than their Latin American counterparts. East Asian firms could put their products up for sale to diversified buyers on the world market, and they were famous for finding export niches (Gereffi, 1992; Haggard, 1990).

Finally, as the East Asian NIEs became semiperipheries, they began to export capital to other East Asian states in order to strengthen their bargaining power in the world market. For instance, Hong Kong's investment in mainland China reached US$26,480 million in 1990; Taiwan's investment in mainland China, started only in the late 1980s, quickly jumped from US$437 million in 1989 to US$1,451 million in 1991; South Korea's investment expanded from nothing to US$269 million in 1991 (Kim, 1993).

What, then, explains the semiperipherization of the East Asian NIEs? How did geopolitics in East Asia in the 1950s lay the preconditions for the NIEs' industrial takeoff? What caused them to shift to export-led industrialization in the 1960s? And why were they able to sustain economic growth, upgrade industrial technology, capture export niches, and export capital in the 1970s and the 1980s? In order to answer these questions, the following sections will examine U.S. hegemony and world-system forces, as well as divergent paths of development among the East Asian NIEs.

U.S. HEGEMONY AND WORLD-SYSTEM FORCES

Geopolitical Preconditions in the 1950s

The global expansion in trade and the United States' free trade policy after World War II had provided an excellent opportunity for developing countries to strive for upward mobility in the world economy. Nevertheless, this favorable postwar environment would benefit any developing country. As such, why were the East Asian NIEs able to seize this favorable opportunity, when other developing countries failed to do so? As the following sections explain, Hong Kong, South Korea, and Taiwan were offered special advantages in promoting development as a result of their unique geopolitical positions in the East Asian interstate system.

To start with, the very existence of the East Asian NIEs was due to the Cold War. Without U.S. intervention and the Cold War, there would not be two Chinas (Communist China and the "Free China" of Taiwan) nor two Koreas (North Korea and South Korea). Though the resumption of Chinese sovereignty over Hong Kong was not yet on the agenda in the immediate postwar period, this would have occurred much more easily without the Cold War. In addition, the separation of Communist China from the capitalist world economy had closed off a more regionalist development trajectory in East Asia. The United Nations' embargo on Chinese trade caused the trade between mainland China and Hong Kong, South Korea, and Taiwan to come to an abrupt halt, pushing them away from links with the big Chinese hinterland.

Nevertheless, Hong Kong benefited incidentally from the Cold War climate in the 1950s. This was because the "windfall profit" from the Chinese Communist Revolution enabled Hong Kong to take advantage of refugee capital to start its industrial revolution. For example, the "liberation" of Shanghai prompted a large number of Shanghainese textile firms to divert their production to Hong Kong (Wong, 1988). In addition, the massive inflow of refugees from China, many of whom had industrial employment experience, created a pool of potential entrepreneurs. They were willing to work hard and take the risk of setting up manufacturing firms. The result was the mushrooming of small firms with low-level capital investment and technology. Once started, these firms were able to tap into the extensive commercial networks established throughout Hong Kong's entrepot history, as well as into the abundant supply of cheap and diligent refugee workers (Chiu & Lui, unpublished).

The intensive Cold War climate benefited South Korea and Taiwan as well. U.S. interests in East Asia, from the late 1940s to the 1970s, had been political and strategic rather than economic. In order to prevent East Asian states from leaning toward Communist China, the United States provided huge amounts of aid to South Korea and Taiwan to help their military regimes stay in power. From 1946 to 1977, military and economic aid to these two countries (US$18.5 billion) accounted for 10.5% of all American foreign aid, exceeding the totals for all of Africa or Latin America. In both South Korea and Taiwan, foreign economic assistance figured heavily in alleviating huge government budget deficits, financing investment, and paying for imports. In South Korea, foreign aid averaged 9.4% of the GNP, 39.7% of the government budget, 65% of total investment, 70% of imports, and nearly 80% of total fixed capital formation during the period from 1953 to 1961. In Taiwan, U.S. aid financed 95% of its trade deficit in the 1950s; and, through foreign savings, it almost totaled 40% of gross domestic capital formation. Nearly all U.S. aid before 1964 was provided on a grant basis, thus making it possible for South Korea and Taiwan to begin their export-led growth in the 1960s without a backlog of debt (Bello & Rosenfeld, 1990, p. 438; Cumings, 1987, p. 67; Eckert, 1992, p. 295; Kurian, 1979, pp. 64, 79).

If the favorable postwar economy, the huge amount of U.S. aid, and the influx of refugee capital laid the preconditions for the industrial takeoff of East Asian NIEs, what explains the shift of their developmental strategy from import-substitution in the 1950s to export-led industrialization in the 1960s?

Export-Led Industrialization in the 1960s

While Hong Kong pursued export-led industrialization early in the 1950s, the United States still had to take an active role to induce the South Korean and Taiwanese states to adopt such a strategy. In the late 1950s, after making it clear that U.S. aid would not be continued by the mid-1960s, the U.S. AID Mission in Taiwan prodded the Taiwanese state to liberalize its trade regime and reduce its interference in the market. The AID Mission listed areas of economic and financial policies that needed reform, including privatization of public enterprises, liberalization of trade, unification and devaluation of the New Taiwan Dollar, stabilization of the monetary supply, and encouragement of private investment. Upon the proposal of the AID Mission, the Taiwanese planning agencies formulated a 19-Point Program of Reform, encompassing every major aspect of the island's economic, fiscal, monetary, and trade policies (Jacoby, 1966, p. 134; Lin, 1973, p. 83).

South Korea's export-led program was also decided by the United States. Eckert (1992) points out that the U.S. AID Mission

> officials had full access to South Korean government information and personnel. American experts spoke of tutoring President Park in economics and did not hesitate to use aid funds as leverage to force the South Korean government into compliance with their economic suggestions. (p. 295)

Coaxed by U.S. aid officials, the Korean state implemented a series of reforms to promote exports, most notably the currency devaluation in 1964 and the provision of export subsidies (Lim, 1985).

In order to provide more incentives for East Asian NIEs to adopt export-led industrialization, the United States was willing to open its own market to them. Eckes (1992, p. 139) remarks that it was "in the interests of global economic recovery and containment [that] the United States would lower its duties on imported goods while tolerating continued discrimination against dollar exports." That explains why, despite the notorious closed domestic markets of South Korea and Taiwan, their exports still enjoyed unrestricted access to the American market for so long. The U.S. market was critical to the NIEs' economic growth, because it was their largest single market throughout the 1960s and 1970s. Exports to the United States accounted for 30.5% of Hong Kong's exports and 39.5% of Taiwan's exports, respectively (Chiu, in press).

In the late 1960s the East Asian NIEs also reaped important economic benefits from their role as America's chief allies in the Vietnam War. For the NIEs as a whole, their fledgling electronics industry had greatly benefited from the American orders for military radios and radar during the Vietnam War. For Hong Kong, the tourist industry started during the Vietnam War. Wanchi district was a favorite recreational spot for Vietnam soldiers on leave, bringing a huge number of U.S. dollars to the Hong Kong economy. For Taiwan, the war gave an incalculable boost to its economy in the form of U.S. purchases of agricultural and industrial commodities, American spending on "rest and recreation" in Taipei, and U.S. contracts awarded to Taiwanese firms for work performed in Vietnam. For South Korea, the United States not only agreed to equip, train, supply, and pay all the South Korean forces used in Vietnam, but also agreed to modernize its military through new loans and aid in return for South Korea's dispatching 300,000 troops to Vietnam between 1965 and 1973. In 1966 the war accounted for 40% of South Korea's crucial foreign-exchange receipts. Indeed, in the late 1960s, Vietnam War-related revenues accounted for about 4% of South Korea's GNP and up to 58% of total exports in 1967 (Lie, 1992b). By 1970 U.S. payments to South Korea totaled nearly US$1 billion. Many South Korean business firms got their first big economic boost from the war. For example, Hanjin established an air and sea transport firm in South Korea, mainly to carry South Korean products and workers to Vietnam (Eckert, 1992).

In sum, the Vietnam War provided a further influx of U.S. money to the East Asian NIEs, and the U.S. market and U.S. planners induced the East Asian NIEs to pursue the strategy of export-led industrialization. Nevertheless, most industries of the NIEs pursued the pattern that Landsberg (1979) labels "international subcontracting." Under such an arrangement, foreign buyers supplied the designs and specifications of the products they wanted to firms of the NIEs, and often supplied the machinery and raw materials as well. Products were then marketed in overseas markets by buyers under a label or brand name owned by the buyers. The manufacturers of the NIEs thus served as no more than subcontractors in the process, responsible for low-skilled assembly work, because they had no direct access to the market and were technologically dependent on the transnationals.

Moreover, the golden era of postwar economic expansion came to an end in the early 1970s. After the oil crisis broke out in 1973, inflation soared and protectionism was on the rise. As a result, many developing countries—including many Latin American NIEs—slipped into recessions by the end of the 1970s. What, then, explains the continuation of economic growth and industrial upgrading among the East Asian NIEs during this period?

Continued Economic Growth in the 1970s

First of all, many South Korean construction companies made use of their Vietnam War contacts and experience to expand into the international construction business, most notably in the Middle East. Eckert (1992) reports that between 1974 and 1979, South Korea's corporations built roads, harbors, and industrial complexes during the oil boom in the Middle East, taking home nearly US$22 billion in construction sales.

Moreover, as a result of the Middle East oil boom in the 1970s, there was a massive increase in the supply of cheap credit and monetary instruments by Western core countries to the East Asian NIEs. As Arrighi et al. (1993) suggest, the inflation of "oil rents" boosted the already overabundant liquidity of these Western financial institutions, so they began outcompeting one another in recycling this liquidity to the NIEs. For example, most of South Korea's foreign loans were made either in the form of supplier's credit or used to finance imports of foreign capital goods, dovetailing with the advanced countries' desire to expand their exports of surplus capital goods. Given a substantially lower nominal interest rate for foreign loans, and also given domestic inflation, the cost for borrowing from abroad was minimal. Subsequently, as the volume of foreign aid inflows declined by the late 1960s, the East Asian NIEs, especially South Korea, came to enjoy a practically unlimited supply of hard currencies and cheap credit to sustain their economic growth in the 1970s.

Furthermore, there was what Bello and Rosenfeld (1990) call "the Japan factor." In the early 1970s, due to the sharp rise of the yen and the rising cost of production in Japan, there was a transborder expansion of Japanese trading companies and small and medium-sized firms to the NIEs. Arrighi et al. (1993) report that only 54 investment projects in the NIEs were authorized by the Japanese government through 1964. But in the early 1970s a total of 1,171 projects were authorized: 581 for South Korea, 400 for Taiwan, 111 for Singapore, and 79 for Hong Kong. Unlike the U.S. transnationals, the Japanese firms preferred minority ownership of these projects, because this approach combined the reach and flexibility of Japanese trading companies and small and medium-sized firms. Moreover, Japanese firms provided a significant portion of the machinery and components that enterprises of the NIEs needed to turn out toys, bicycles, radios, television sets, and personal computer monitors.

What emerged in East Asia, therefore, was an "organic division of labor" between Japan and the NIEs that married Japanese capital and technology to the cheap, relatively docile labor in Hong Kong, South Korea, and Taiwan (Cumings, 1987). The East Asian NIEs became a base for the relocation of Japan's labor-intensive industries as they moved upward through each product cycle and progressively toward high-tech production. In addition, Japan and the NIEs had benefited from their privileged access to the huge U.S. market. Their products were capturing an increasing market share in the United States in the 1970s because of the high U.S. dollar and the high interest rate policy in the United States.

In short, the cheap credit in the 1970s, the arrival of Japanese capital in East Asia, and the access to the U.S. market in this region provided a new space for the states of the NIEs to intervene actively in the industrialization process. Nevertheless, the mode of state intervention and the societal responses to such intervention were quite different in Hong Kong, South Korea, and Taiwan, reflecting divergent paths toward semi-peripheralization. The following sections will discuss the authoritarian developmentalism of South Korea and Taiwan, as well as the positive noninterventionist policy of Hong Kong.

SOUTH KOREA: *CHAEBOL* AND AUTHORITARIAN DEVELOPMENTALISM

The Developmental State and *Chaebol*

In South Korea, economic development (in terms of growth, productivity, and competitiveness) was the foremost priority of state action. The state was single-mindedly adherent to economic development, even at the expense of other objectives such as equality and social welfare.

As such, how did the South Korean state upgrade and sustain its industrialization processes in the 1970s? Amsden's (1989) study points to the dual policies of "subsidies" and "discipline." The allocation of subsidies rendered the South Korean government not merely a banker but an entrepreneur, using subsidies to influence what, when, how much to produce, and which strategic industries should be favored. Subsidies were necessary because the long gestation periods and relatively low profitability through adolescence made capital-intensive industries less desirable investments to South Korean firms. Nevertheless, the South Korean government also specified stringent performance requirements (notably in the field of exports) in return for the subsidies it provided. The discipline exercised over private firms involved both rewarding good performers and penalizing poor ones. This carrot-and-stick policy took the form of granting or withholding industrial licensing, government bank loans, advanced technology acquired through government investment in foreign licensing and technical assistance, and so on.

The South Korean state was unusual because it experienced both bureaucratic autonomy and public-private cooperation. On one hand, there was a high degree of bureaucratic autonomy and capacity because of the meritocratic recruitment and a sense of unity and mission among state managers. There was also a strong central planning agency, similar to Japan's MITI, to develop national strategic developmental policies independent of the powerful groups in Korean society.

On the other, there were close institutional links between the developmental state and private-sector conglomerates (*chaebols*) that dominated strategic sectors of the economy. Park (1986) describes the relationship between the postwar Rhee regime and the nascent big capitalist class as one of "alliance for profit." Using this alliance, the Rhee group developed clientele ties with a small number of big capitalists, supported their economic monopolies in exchange for a steady supply of political funding, and prevented the development of anti-Rhee business groups. With the backing from the Rhee regime, the *chaebols* quickly emerged from the ruins of World War II and the Korean War. Then the *chaebols* took advantage of the export-led industrialization programs of the Park regime in the 1960s and the 1970s (Kim, 1979). Having privileged access to bank credit and foreign loan guarantees, the *chaebols* accumulated capital at a rapid rate and achieved dominance in such key sectors as import-export trading, textiles, and electronics industries. Their economic strength can be seen from the fact that top 46 *chaebols* accounted for some 13.4% of South Korea's GDP, and 36.7% of value-added manufacturing by 1975 (Jones & Sakong, 1980, p. 266). Relying heavily upon the state for credits and resources, the *chaebols* were thus highly cooperative with the state's developmental policies.

The developmental state in South Korea, no doubt, played an important role in industrialization. Still, researchers want to know: How could this developmental state emerge within South Korea in the first place? Why was it so autonomous from the private sector and civil society?

Colonial Origins

As Koo (1993) remarks, it is impossible to understand the processes of modern state formation in South Korea apart from its Japanese colonial legacy. In South Korea, the Japanese colonial state possessed a comprehensive, autonomous, and penetrating quality that no previous Korean state could muster. The colonial state modernized the government bureaucracy, built a vast network of police and security forces, introduced modern land taxation, and improved the infrastructure. Subsequently, the Japanese colonial era left behind an "overdeveloped state" and a weak civil society. Moreover, because the indigenous bourgeoisie in South Korea were tightly controlled by the Japanese colonial state, they remained highly undeveloped and failed to form any strong class organization to protect their interests. Hence, they were too weak to carry out the industrialization projects on their own in the postcolonial era, allowing the state considerable autonomy in planning and implementing its industrial strategies.

In addition, personal relationships formed by Koreans with Japanese during the colonial period were by no means entirely severed after 1945. For many Korean elites who received an education during the colonial period, Japanese newspapers and magazines continued to be a source of the latest information on economic, industrial, and political trends in East Asia. For example, Korean President Park Chung Hee, who was himself an elite product of the colonial military system and was fluent in Japanese and deeply influenced by his training during Japan's period of Asian military industrial supremacy, naturally pushed for a cooperative relationship with Japan and adopted the Japanese developmental state as a model for Korean modernization (Eckert, 1992).

Furthermore, the massive inflow of U.S. aid also buttressed the capacity of the state in South Korea. Foreign aid not only helped solve South

Korea's economic problems in the 1950s, but it also presented the state with powerful tools with which to intervene in the economy, enforce compliance in the private sector, and build up a strong military for defense.

Authoritarianism and Ideology

Even so, the developmental state in South Korea still required a strong dose of authoritarianism in order to maintain its control over the civil society. In South Korea, state repression operated to dampen labor militancy (Choi, 1989). In Park's regime, strikes were banned, existing unions were outlawed, and activists were arrested. Under the Yushin Constitution, the terms under which unions could function were restrictive enough to eliminate the possibility of any genuine independent organizing. For example, there was the Korean Labor Union Law, as Bello and Rosenfeld (1992, p. 31) point out, which worked to prevent "unions from cooperating, forming, or contributing to a political party; and another [law] that banned collective bargaining beyond the union local, thus preempting the solidarity, technical cooperation, and strength in numbers that could emerge with industrywide associations." Lie (1991, p. 71) further emphasizes that "the Korean Central Intelligence Agency and the police, aided by goon squads hired by management, intimidated and harassed union organizers and labor leaders." This labor repression served to depress workers' wages, so that the South Korean labor-intensive industries could remain competitive in the world market.

Aside from labor repression, however, the state also promoted the ideologies of anticommunism, GNPism, and sexism to maintain social control in the South Korean society. Koo (1993) points out that the Korean War helped establish anticommunism as a hegemonic ideology in South Korea. The Korean War experience brought the Cold War's broader ideological conflict down to the level of daily experiences, individual psyches, and social relationships. Because the Korean War never officially ended, the people of South Korea are still subject to a sense of the "constant military threat" from Communist North Korea, making the impact of the war particularly penetrating and enduring.

In addition, there was GNPism. When Park rose to power in the early 1960s, he justified the coup in terms of the urgent need to "rescue the nation from the brink of starvation" as well as defend it from the

Communist threat (Koo & Kim, 1992). Export-led industrialization strategy, therefore, was not only a response to the demands of U.S. advisers, but also a means for Park's military regime to establish its political legitimacy and consolidate its power. As a result of this GNPism, social spending by the South Korean government was minimal. In 1973 expenditures on social insurance, public health, public assistance, welfare, and veterans' relief represented only 0.97% of the GNP in South Korea (Cumings, 1987, p. 74).

Furthermore, the enterprise level was infused with the ideology of sexism to exploit and control female workers. Bello and Rosenfeld (1992) argue that the centrality of cheap labor in global competition led South Korean capitalists to prefer women workers in the early years of the industrialization process. The target group was unmarried women aged 16 to 25, with some high school education. In the social organization of these enterprises, patriarchal authority was used as a means of discipline, with few female workers promoted to supervisory positions.

The state structure, the state-capitalist class relationship, and the ideologies in South Korea, however, were quite different from those in Taiwan and Hong Kong.

TAIWAN: SMALL BUSINESSES
AND AUTHORITARIAN DEVELOPMENTALISM

The Developmental State and Small Businesses

Like the South Korean state, the state in Taiwan was highly developmentally oriented. The GMD set up a complex trade regime—such as import quotas, tariff barriers, and export subsidies—to regulate foreign trade. Basic and strategic industries in Taiwan were protected from foreign competition, and export-oriented industries were provided incentives. There were the ingenious tariff and tax rebate systems, through which exporters were qualified to gain refunds on customs duties and other taxes for inputs they imported. In addition, through the control of the financial system, selective credit controls were employed to foster the development of preferred sectors, such as heavy industry, in the 1960s and the 1970s.

However, Taiwan's state-capital link was quite different from its South Korean counterpart in the following aspects. First, the state sector in Taiwan was larger than that in South Korea (Chiu, 1992). The average share of public enterprises in Taiwan's GDP was 15.9% during 1971-1975, which was almost twice the 8.4% share in South Korea (Short, 1984). Whereas South Korean public enterprises mainly served as absorbers of the risk involved in establishing new sectors so private investment could later take over, Taiwan's public enterprises tended to be monopolistic and exclude private participation.

Second, although a few dozen *chaebols* monopolized the South Korean economy and dominated the export sector, it was the small and medium-sized (hereafter abbreviated as SM) firms in Taiwan that filled up the export sector (Shieh, 1992). Of the 260,000 business enterprises in Taiwan, 98% are considered SM firms, and they employ 70% of all employees and account for 65% of exports (Bello & Rosenfeld, 1992, p. 241).

Third, whereas South Korean *chaebols* relied heavily on state credits for export promotions, the SM firms in Taiwan had to rely upon self-financing or informal money markets. The small businessmen in Taiwan complained about the inability to obtain credit from the state, because most credit went to the big enterprises. They also complained that the state failed to supply them with information on trends in international trade, and that they had to pay more than the bigger firms to buy materials from big or state-run companies (Bello & Rosenfeld, 1992).

What, then, made the GMD regime reluctant to fully support SM enterprises in Taiwan?

Ethnic Divisions, Authoritarianism, and Ideology

The GMD regime and the small capitalists in Taiwan were divided by quasi-ethnic schisms and mutual apprehensions after the tragic February 28 Incident. The GMD feared the Taiwanese ambitions for self-sufficiency and independence. As such, the GMD regime maintained a large state sector in order to keep the reins of power in the hands of the mainlanders, and it discouraged the concentration of economic power among the local Taiwanese. Subsequently, after the GMD took over the enterprises belonging to the Japanese colonial government, it staffed the enterprises primarily by mainlanders, especially in the area of management. In this respect, the state sector had safeguarded the GMD's political domination by serving as an economic preserve for the 1.5-million-member retinue of soldiers, bureaucrats, party faithfuls, business people, and family dependents from the mainland. This state sector was used to counter and control the SM sector, which, for the most part, was dominated by indigenous Taiwanese.

Bello and Rosenfeld (1992) suggest that the pattern of state intervention in the economy was influenced by the struggle between mainlander and indigenous Taiwanese economic interests. Power was apparently a major consideration when the GMD government promoted industrial upgrading in the 1970s, which saw the launching of 10 industrial projects, including the state-owned Gao Xiong Shipyards, the government-owned China Steel integrated cold rolling mill, and the state-owned China Petroleum petrochemical project. State control was partly a front for the mainlanders' efforts to continue exercising strategic direction over the economy vis-à-vis the up-and-coming Taiwanese capitalist class.

In order to exercise social control over Taiwan, the GMD's Leninist party deeply penetrated into civil society, so it could curb the development of any organized oppositional forces. Due to martial law, civil liberties—such as freedom of assembly—were severely limited and there was strict censorship of the mass media. Moreover, government surveillance and the strong threat of repression were central mechanisms for GMD's labor control. Its Labor Union Law prohibited unions in workplaces with fewer than 30 employees—or almost 80% of the workforce. For large enterprises, formation of a union had to have the approval of both local government and local GMD committees. Needless to say, strikes were made illegal and banned before the 1980s.

As in South Korea, the GMD promoted the ideologies of anticommunism, GNPism, and sexism. For example, capitalists in Taiwan preferred to hire women workers because they believed "that women were more temperamentally suited to tedious, repetitive work than men; that women had the manual dexterity or nimble fingers required for textile work and electronics assembly; and that women were less likely to rebel than men" (Bello & Rosenfeld, 1992, p. 216). In addition, the GMD promoted the "Three People's Principle" as its state ideology. The Principle of the People's Livelihood, for instance, was used to justify the large state sector in Taiwan, because it ostensibly aimed at establishing a developmental state capable of initiating economic development and preventing capitalist domination.

HONG KONG: SMALL BUSINESSES
AND POSITIVE NONINTERVENTIONISM

Small Businesses and Positive Noninterventionism

There were several distinguishing features that characterized the Hong Kong state and its links with capital. First, it was a liberal colonial state. Because it was a colonial state, the governor of Hong Kong was appointed by the British Parliament and was responsible to the British state. The governor ruled Hong Kong with the help of major British banking capitalists, who were appointed into the Executive Council and the Legislative Council. But unlike other authoritarian states, the state of Hong Kong showed a high degree of political tolerance toward dissent. It is often pointed out that Hong Kong is a free society—its citizens are free to express political opinions, free to criticize the Hong Kong state, free to form political organizations, free to protest, free to travel, and so on (So & Kwitko, 1990).

Second, the Hong Kong state adopted a positive nonintervention policy toward the economy. Although the state in South Korea and in Taiwan intervened extensively in the marketplace to direct industrialization according to state priorities, the colonial state in Hong Kong left investment decisions to the private sector. Certainly the state in Hong Kong has assisted private capital accumulation in a variety of ways, most notably in infrastructure provisions, such as the maintenance of a low-tax business environment, the expansion of the public education system, and the massive public housing program (which houses more than 40% of Hong Kong's population). The public housing program, in particular, had the effect of subsidizing the earnings of low-wage, working-class families, thus socializing the cost of reproduction of labor, keeping down the pressures for wage increases, and increasing the competitive power of Hong Kong products in the world market (Castells, Goh, & Kwok, 1990).

Nevertheless, Hong Kong is still a far cry from the developmental states portrayed in statist literature. In the postwar era, the colonial state deliberately refrained from interfering with the distribution of resources across different sectors, as well as from providing any directions for industrial development. For example, the colonial state failed to support technological innovations, to assist industrial upgrading, to provide bank credits to strategic industries, to promote exports, and to protect domestic markets. Haddon-Cave (1984) thus describes Hong Kong's state-industry relationship as "positive noninterventionism."

Third, like Taiwan, Hong Kong's export sector was composed of predominantly small, local firms which received little help from the colonial government. The Hong Kong SM firms had to rely upon themselves for self-financing, technological innovation, and securing links to transnational corporations (Chiu & Lui, unpublished).

What, then, explains the emergence of this liberal, laissez-faire state in Hong Kong after World War II?

Colonialism and Communist Origins

First, the Hong Kong state was constrained from pursuing an active developmental strategy or embarking on financially risky intervention because, as a colony, it needed to remain financially solvent and balance its budget or see the British home government step in. In addition, the Hong Kong state also had not benefited from the same sort of geopolitical links with the United States that had endowed the state in South Korea and in Taiwan with large amounts of aid and loans (Chiu, 1992).

Second, the long-standing alliance between the colonial state and the financial-commercial capitalists in Hong Kong, which had evolved during the previous century of entrepot history, served as a social basis for the nonintervention policy. These financial and commercial bourgeoisie were inclined to support the state's hands-off policy in the manufacturing sector. Bankers, for example, opposed the proposal to establish an industrial bank in the late 1950s, because they were afraid that this would cause the state to shift resources away from the commercial and financial sectors to the manufacturing sector.

Third, heightened hostility with the United States during the Cold War explained why socialist China did not take back control of Hong Kong right after the Communist Revolution. Hong Kong was the only port where China could gain the foreign currency to buy necessary foreign equipment. As a result, China was very willing to supply food products, raw materials, and even drinking water to Hong Kong in exchange for much-needed foreign currency. This unequal exchange between cheap Chinese products and Hong Kong currency subsidized the Hong Kong economy, lowered the cost of living, strengthened Hong

Kong's competitiveness in the world market, and made the direct inter-vention of the colonial state less necessary.

Finally, the classic ethnic struggles between the British and the Chi-nese in Hong Kong were not acute in the late 1970s. The sudden influx of Chinese refugees after World War II did not arouse any tension between the Chinese population and the British ruling class in Hong Kong. Because these refugees were fleeing Communist rule, their refugee mentality made them endure the British monopoly of the colonial gov-ernment so as not to "rock the boat" (So, 1986a).

The Liberal State and Its Ideology

In sum, Hong Kong's financial constraints as a British colony, the strong links between financial capitalists and the colonial state, the support from the Communist regime in China, and the lack of ethnic struggles against the British help to explain the liberal and noninterven-tionist policies of the Hong Kong state. Unlike the South Korean and Taiwanese states, the Hong Kong state did not need to militarize in order to stop the spread of communism, or strengthen its police force to suppress local opposition. The Hong Kong state also did not have to involve itself with the promotion of industrialization, because the Hong Kong Chinese capitalists were already getting a head start in exports in the early 1950s, due to their previous experience in conducting entrepot trade.

As a noninterventionist state, the Hong Kong government had not promoted any ideology to enhance its political legitimacy. At the enter-prise level, however, the same sexist ideology prevailed in Hong Kong as in South Korea and Taiwan. Salaff's (1981) study of "working daughters" in Hong Kong shows how a traditional sexist ideology compelled young women to leave school early and take up low-paying, unskilled jobs in the fast-expanding manufacturing sector. While forgoing the opportu-nity to be educated, and hence any hope of upward mobility, these working daughters took home most of their wages. This extra income from the working daughters often enabled the sons in these families to continue their education, in the hope that the status of the family might improve. Therefore, as in South Korea and Taiwan, a sexist ideology was mobilized in Hong Kong to promote the competitiveness of domestic labor-intensive industries in the world market.

ANTISYSTEMIC MOVEMENTS

Due to the different state structures and state-capitalist class relation-ships, there were also different forms of antisystemic movements in South Korea, Taiwan, and Hong Kong.

South Korea

Despite strong state repression, there were robust antisystemic move-ments in South Korea. The origins of this "contentious society" in South Korea, as Koo (1993) explains, emerged during the colonial period. As a result of the extreme coercive nature of Japanese rule in Korea and the intensive anti-Japanese nationalist struggle among Koreans, civil society became highly politicized and antistatism became a deeply ingrained Korean intellectual orientation during the colonial period, and this antistatist tradition continued in the postwar period. In addition, the intellectuals did not forgive the "original sin" of the Rhee and Park regimes: their secret deals with the *chaebols*, their revival of the colonial coercive apparatus, and their overreliance on the United States for power maintenance. The students and the intellectuals were particularly of-fended by the contradiction between the ideal of democracy and a mili-tary regime that blatantly violated such an ideal in its daily practices, the contradiction between rapid economic growth and the widening gap between the rich and the poor, and the corruption and the conspicuous consumption of the *chaebols*.

Besides students and intellectuals, workers were also getting restless. Despite labor repression, the high concentration of workers in the *chae-bols'* large-scale heavy industries provided favorable conditions for a militant labor movement. In the 1970s the Chonggye Garment Workers' Union (CGWU) struggle was marked by a creative combination of tenacity, self-sacrifice, and confrontational tactics that made it the sym-bolic center of the nascent South Korean labor movement (Bello & Rosenfeld, 1992). Later, the labor movement became explosive when "it developed close linkages with political conflicts outside industry, sup-ported organizationally and ideologically by the larger *minjung* (the people's or the masses') movement, while supplying a major social base and an arena for democratization struggles among students" (Koo, 1993,

p. 7). It was this merge between the labor movement and the democratic movement that finally led to the downfall of the Chun regime in 1987.

Taiwan

What distinguished Taiwan from South Korea, however, was the weakness of its labor movement. Whereas South Korea had a robust labor movement that could challenge the military Park regime, the labor movement in Taiwan was weak. First, the GMD was equipped with an elaborate "Three People's Principle" state ideology, and the Leninist party organization was quite effective in controlling labor at the shop-floor level. Second, the docility of the labor force in Taiwan can be explained by its part-time nature. According to Gates (1979), in Taiwan's early phase of industrialization, workers often went from villages to cities to seek work in seasons when their labor was not required in the field. They were willing to accept low wages because they were only temporarily in the cities. Thus, the transient character of the proletariat prevented the growth of a stable working-class community that could buttress collective action. Third, because SM factories accounted for the majority of the manufacturing establishments, the result was a greater organizational dispersion of Taiwan's industrial proletariat (Deyo, 1989). Small firm size has long been regarded as inimical to labor organization because it increases the cost of organizing. Fourth, although women workers cherished few hopes of upward mobility, male workers often saw their factory work as a stepping-stone to entrepreneurship (Stites, 1982). As a result, male factory workers, mainly skilled workers and supervisors, often identified with their employers and served as disciplinary agents over their female coworkers. The weak labor movement in Taiwan had considerably enhanced the competitiveness of its labor-intensive industries in the world market.

Without a workforce amenable to managerial directives, without workers willing to do boring, repetitive, and exhaustive jobs, and without workers willing to work overtime when necessary and to shift to another product at short notice, the export firms of Taiwan would not be so prompt in their delivery of products to, and so flexible in meeting the deadlines of, transnational corporations.

Nevertheless, despite the peacefulness of industrial relations, there emerged a reform movement among Taiwanese intellectuals in the early

1970s (Chen, 1982). Sparked by the expulsion of Taiwan from the United
Nations and the overseas Diaoyutai movement (over the Japanese occupation of the Senkaku Islands), a new generation of indigenous Taiwanese intellectuals began to demand their rights to political participation
and representation in the state, freedom of speech, and the lifting of
martial law. They complained about violations of human rights by the
GMD; they used such new magazines as *China Tide* to resurrect struggles
against despotism during the Japanese occupation of Taiwan; they started
a native literature focusing upon the lives of indigenous Taiwanese
people; and they organized a Dangwai (non-GMD) political group to
challenge the GMD in elections. United through their Taiwanese language and culture, this new generation of intellectuals laid the foundation for a middle class and a strong democratic movement in the late
1980s.

Hong Kong

Like Taiwan, Hong Kong also did not possess a strong labor movement. Due to expanding job opportunities and the rise of real income,
the Hong Kong working class was fairly satisfied with its existing situation and did not press for structural changes. Whereas Western Marxist
critics observed terrible working conditions, immigrant laborers in
Hong Kong perceived instead their relatively improved status as compared to their previous work situation in mainland China. Of course,
there were unions and there were strikes. But unions tended to be small
and ideologically divided between pro-Communist and pro-Nationalist
factions, and China was reported to have held back the radical demands
of the pro-Communist trade unions so as not to risk any disturbances of
its substantial foreign exchange earnings in Hong Kong. Consequently,
strikes were few in number, and serious strikes were almost unknown in
the 1970s (Levin & Chiu, 1993; Turner et al., 1981).

Instead, the political struggles in Hong Kong in the late 1970s revolved
around the new middle class. In the early 1970s many college students
participated in pro-China movements, such as the patriotic Diaoyutai
protest and the China Week Exhibitions. In the mid-1970s, after the
"China heat" died down, this new middle class shifted its attention to the
social problems in Hong Kong. Many college students and young professionals formed "pressure groups" to criticize the policies of the Hong

Kong state. Through newspaper articles, social protests, and political pressure, they complained about police abuse of power, bureaucratic arrogance, the lack of localization, inadequate services for squatter residents, and so on (Lui & Gong, 1985). These "urban movements," needless to say, proved to be a training ground for new leaders and prepared the new middle class for its forthcoming democratic struggles in the early 1980s (So & Kwitko, 1992).

CONCLUSION

In the aftermath of World War II, there were serious economic and political problems in South Korea, Taiwan, and Hong Kong. Yet, in a short span of about 3 decades, these three states quickly transformed themselves into newly industrializing economies. This chapter shows that the favorable postwar capitalist world economy, huge amounts of U.S. aid, and influxes of refugee capital in the 1950s laid the groundwork for the industrial takeoff of the East Asian NIEs. Then, the Vietnam War provided a further influx of U.S. money, and the U.S. market and U.S. planners induced the East Asian NIEs to pursue the strategy of export-led industrialization in the 1960s. Finally, cheap credit in the 1970s, the arrival of Japanese capital in East Asia, and the relative decline of U.S. hegemony in this region provided more space for the NIEs' states to intervene actively in the industrialization process.

However, there were divergent paths of development among the East Asian NIEs. In South Korea, there was a close alliance between the developmental state and a small number of *chaebol* monopolist capitalists. In response to the authoritarianism imposed upon the Korean civil society, there was a robust *minjung* movement by workers and students challenging the military Park regime. In Taiwan, there was an ethnic division between the mainlander-run developmental state and the local Taiwanese small capitalists, who dominated the export sector. Although the GMD was highly effective in exercising authoritarianism over labor, the 1970s saw a new generation of Taiwanese intellectuals rising up to challenge mainland domination. In Hong Kong, because the colonial state adopted a nonintervention policy, small Chinese capitalist firms had to rely upon themselves for survival. Despite the lack of authoritarian control, the labor movement in Hong Kong was weak. Only in the

1970s did a new middle-class generation emerge to challenge colonial rule through urban movements.

These divergent patterns of development among the NIEs, this chapter has argued, resulted from complex interactions among the following factors: colonial heritage (Japanese authoritarianism and nationalist movements in Korea versus British laissez-faire in Hong Kong), historical experiences in the aftermath of World War II (the "original sin" of the Park and Rhee regime, the February 27 Incident in Taiwan, and the influx of refugees in Hong Kong), the general Cold War ideological climate (anticommunism and GNPism in South Korea and Taiwan versus a refugee mentality in Hong Kong), as well as their different industrial structures (concentration of workers in *chaebols* versus organizational dispersion in Taiwan and Hong Kong).

Since the 1980s, the East Asian region has begun to play a more central role in global capital accumulation than before. The next section will examine the national reunification project among mainland China, Taiwan, and Hong Kong, as well as the hegemonic rivalry between Japan and the United States.

PART V

Centrality

The golden era of postwar economic expansion came to an end in the 1970s. After the oil crisis in 1973, the world economy entered into a downward phase. In addition, the United States became a declining hegemon, as its industrial, commercial, and financial supremacy were increasingly challenged by rival core powers. In order to overcome economic stagnation, core states formed regional blocs to enlarge their trading networks and to protect themselves from competitors. Nevertheless, the Communist states did no better than the United States, as they were either overthrown by popular rebellions or forced to adopt market policies to promote their economies.

It is through these global dynamics that the East Asia region has become a new epicenter of capital accumulation in the world economy. One by one, East Asia states came out of the United States' shadow and began to assert their own economic, political, and cultural initiatives. As Arrighi (1994b) points out, there is an "Asianization of the Asian economies" in the last 2 decades of the 20th century. In 1980 trans-Pacific trade began to surpass in value trans-Atlantic trade. By the end of the decade, it was one and one-half times greater. At the same time, trade among countries on the Asian side of the Pacific Rim was about to surpass in

213

value trade across the Pacific. In 1991 Asia surpassed the United States as Japan's largest export destination, and 2 years later Japan's trade surplus with the region surpassed its trade surplus with the United States (Friedland, 1994; Ozawa, 1993).

Subsequently, Japan gradually evolved from a regional to a global economic power, challenging the hegemony of the United States. Technologically, Japan's high-tech sectors were closing up their gaps with the United States, while Japanese manufacturers outsold their American competitors. As a result, Japan accumulated a sizable trade surplus and became the largest creditor of the world. Japan also started to play a leadership role in global affairs, and its "flying geese" model of development began to attract followers from the peripheries. In response, the United States imposed protectionist measures against Japanese imports, sought to open up the Japanese market for U.S. imports, and forced the Japanese yen to appreciate, and the U.S. mass media started Japan-bashing. Chapter 9 examines the origins, the development, and the future prospects for this U.S.-Japanese hegemonic rivalry in the capitalist world economy. Should Japan's economic growth continued, it will certainly become an economic powerhouse for the world economy in the 21st century.

In addition, when the Cold War mentality faded away in the 1980s, mainland China, Taiwan, and Hong Kong began to develop a project of national reunification to solve their developmental problems. As the world economy began its downward phase and the global market contracted in the 1970s, the semiperipheral economies of mainland China, Taiwan, and Hong Kong were squeezed in the middle, by both the protectionism in the core and the stiff competition from the peripheries; their previous developmental policies—Maoist socialism, developmental authoritarianism, and positive noninterventionist policy—had run into difficulties. In this respect, economic integration with mainland China helped solve the developmental problems of Taiwan and Hong Kong by providing them with cheap labor, resources, and investment opportunities. On the other hand, economic integration with Taiwan and Hong Kong have contributed to mainland China's development by providing employment opportunities, market stimuli to local enterprises, and vital information and contacts for reentering the world market. Chapter 10 focuses upon the actors who formulated the national integration strategy, the economic and political complexities of integration, and the profound impact of integration strategy on mainland China, Taiwan, and Hong Kong development. Should this Chinese national integration project succeed, it will provide another strong impetus to propel East Asia to become an epicenter of global capital accumulation in the next century.

9. United States-Japan Hegemonic Rivalry

By the 1980s, as Japan had grown from a regional to a global economic power, it became a center of capital accumulation in the world economy. Conversely, the decline of U.S. hegemony also became apparent. The simultaneous decline of the United States and the rise of Japan at the economic level brought the two countries into intense rivalry. This chapter will examine the origins and the development of this United States-Japan rivalry in the economic, political, and cultural fronts. In particular, it will discuss whether Japan will displace the United States as the next hegemon in the world economy by the turn of this century.

THE HEGEMONIC DECLINE OF THE UNITED STATES

In Wallerstein's (1984) formulation,

> hegemony in the interstate system refers to that situation in which the on-going rivalry between the so-called 'great powers' is so unbalanced that one power is truly *primus inter pares*; that is, one power can largely imposed its rules and its wishes (at the very least by effective veto power) in the economic, political, military, diplomatic, and even cultural arenas. (p. 38)

Hegemony, in this sense, thus only refers to situations in which the edge is so significant that allied major powers are de facto client states, and the opposed major powers feel relatively frustrated and highly defensive vis-à-vis the hegemonic power.

Using this restrictive definition, Wallerstein (1984) further contends that there were, so far, only three instances of hegemony since the emergence of the capitalist world economy in the 16th century—the United Provinces from 1620 to 1672, the United Kingdom from 1815 to 1873, and the United States from 1945 to 1967.

In the third hegemonic instance, Wallerstein (1992) explains that U.S. enterprises achieved an economic edge first in industrial production, then in trade and commerce, and then in finance. American economic hegemony thus refers to that period in which the United States has a simultaneous advantage in all of the above economic domains. Then, through its victory in World War II, the United States further built up a global military force and achieved political hegemony, controlling virtually all significant decisions in global political affairs for the next 25 years. At the height of its political and economic power in the postwar decades, the United States advocated liberalism, both at the global level (free trade and investment throughout the world economy) and on the home front (welfare state). In doing so, this liberal ideology guaranteed political satisfaction both at home and in the world market for U.S. enterprises.

Nevertheless, Wallerstein (1993) argues that American liberalism and militarism bred its own hegemonic demise. First, the U.S. domestic welfare state led to the rise in real income of workers, middle managers, bureaucrats, and professionals—which meant that, directly and indirectly, costs rose for U.S.-based production relative to costs in Western Europe and Japan. This higher cost of production eventually reduced the competitiveness of U.S. enterprises in the world market.

Second, American global liberalism made it more difficult to retard the spread of technological expertise of the hegemonic contenders. Over time it was the latecomers, such as Japan and Germany, that gained the advantage of newer machinery and a cheaper labor force, thus eating into the material base of the productivity edge of U.S. economic hegemony. Furthermore, global liberalism made the United States lay its markets open to trade invasions by these latecomers.

Third, global militarism also had its costs for the United States. In order to defend its hegemonic position from the "contenders for the succession" (Wallerstein, 1984, p. 42), the United States had to foot a large politico-military bill, both for itself and for its allies. American

TABLE 9.1 Indicators of U.S. Decline in the 1970s

	1970	1975	1980	1970-1980 Gain
GNP PER CAPITA (in US$)				
United States	4,970	7,400	12,040	242%
Japan	1,950	4,530	9,840	505%
OECD Countries	3,110	5,680	10,430	335%
LABOR PRODUCTIVITY IN MANUFACTURING (US$1,000)				
United States	29.6	32.9	33.6	114%
Japan	8.4	13.1	23.1	275%
West Germany	11.5	16.3	34.3	298%
Great Britain	3.8	4.8	4.8	126%

SOURCE: Economic Planning Bureau, Ministry of Finance, Japan (1994); World Bank (1992, 1994).

involvement in the Korean and Vietnam wars further aggravated the problem. By the 1980s the U.S. balance of payments and federal budget deficit were becoming too large to ignore. In addition, the large defense budget sucked money and resources from research and development, which further weakened the productivity of U.S. enterprises.

The decline of U.S. economic hegemony can be seen through the following indicators (See Table 9.1). First, the United States' GNP per capita increased only by 242% in the 1970s (from US$4,970 in 1970 to US$12,040 in 1980), whereas Japan's GNP per capita increased by 505% in the same period (from US$1,950 in 1970 to US$9,840 in 1980). Second, the United States experienced a much slower rate of increase in labor productivity during the 1970s. Labor productivity of U.S. manufacturing industries increased by only 114% between 1970 and 1980, whereas Japan's and Germany's labor productivity increased by 275% and 298%, respectively, in the same period. Consequently, U.S. productivity improvements lagged behind those of most industrialized countries. In the period from 1960 to 1973, the United States ranked last among 11 industrialized countries in productivity improvements (Magaziner & Reich, 1982, pp. 12, 30). Third, subsequently, the U.S. overall trade deficit jumped from US$9.3 billion to US$108.3 billion between 1976 and 1984, and the U.S. trade balance for manufactured goods turned from a surplus in 1976 to a deficit of US$96.5 billion in

1984 (Gilpin, 1987, p. 157). Finally, Krause (1989, p. 103) points out that "in order to finance this deficit, the U.S. annually has to borrow large amounts abroad. The culmination of this borrowing has quickly turned the U.S. into the world's largest debtor where previously it was the largest creditor."

Aside from its decline in economic hegemony, there was also a decline in U.S. political hegemony. In the 1980s the U.S. military and political power edge was no longer overwhelming; Wallerstein (1984) remarks that the United States' ability to dictate to its allies (Western Europe and Japan), intimidate its foes (North Korea, Cuba, Iran, and Iraq), and overwhelm the weak (compare the Dominican Republic in 1965 with El Salvador in the 1980s) were vastly impaired. Even in the 1990s, after the collapse of the Soviet communist bloc (which eliminated a major challenger to American military supremacy), the readiness of the United States to exercise its military prowess is still quite limited, as events in Somali, Bosnia, and Haiti testify. The dynamics of American hegemonic decline have led to an erosion of the alliance network the United States patiently created in the postwar years. This hegemonic decline ultimately led to a redefinition of the United States-Japan relationship in East Asia as well as in the global arena.

JAPAN AS A REGIONAL
ECONOMIC POWER IN EAST ASIA

After the triumph of the Chinese Communist Revolution and the spread of communism to Korea and Vietnam in the late 1940s, Japan was chosen as a junior partner by the United States to assist in hegemonic domination over communism in the East Asian region. On one hand, Japan was repositioned from a wartime enemy to a friendly ally, granted privileged access to U.S. markets, and awarded lucrative Korean wartime procurement in the early 1950s. On the other, the United States kept Japan in a defense dependency and shaped the flow of essential resources (such as oil) to it, in order to exercise a diffuse leverage over all its policies (Cumings, 1993).

Nevertheless, as the rapid Japanese economic growth continued, Japan emerged as a regional economic power in East Asia in the 1980s.

The power of Japan over the East Asian economies can be seen through the following indicators in trade, investment, and foreign aid.

Trade

First, Japan is now the center of international trade in East and Southeast Asia, overshadowing the United States. As Nester (1992) observes, by the late 1980s:

> Of the nine countries in the region, three—China, Malaysia and Indonesia— are both export- and import-dependent on Japan. Five countries—South Korea, Taiwan, Hong Kong, Singapore and Thailand—are import-dependent on Japan and export-dependent on the United States. Only the Philippines is both export-and import-dependent on the United States. (pp. 89-90)

Because Japan is the largest source of imports for most states in East and Southeast Asia, the high-speed industrial growth of this region is dependent on the supply of Japanese industrial raw materials and technology. In addition, due to the high volume of Japanese imports into the region, Japan continues to run sizable trade surpluses with these East Asian countries. By the late 1980s, while the United States still remained an important trading partner of East Asia, Japan's trade surplus with the NIEs came to match that of the United States (MITI, 1992, p. 6).

Nevertheless, Japan has gradually emerged as an important market for the East and Southeast Asian economies in recent years. South Korea showed the highest export dependence on Japan among the NIEs; some 21.6% of its exports went to Japan in 1989. Among the Southeast Asian countries, Indonesia shipped more than 40% of its exports to Japan in the same year (Moon, 1991, p. 27). Due to increasing labor costs at home, Japan came to import more manufactured consumer goods from the NIEs. In 1980 some 50% of Japan's imports from the NIEs were manufactured consumer goods. In 1990 this share grew to more than 77% (Cronin, 1992, p. 53). Although Japanese trade with the East and Southeast Asian states in general was very important to Japan, Japan's reliance on any one of these states was relatively low. This was because trade the with individual Asian economies constitutes only a small share of Japan's total foreign trade (Nester, 1992, p. 113).

Furthermore, in terms of power, it is the Japanese companies who actually dominate the movement of exports from the East Asian economies to Japan. Most manufactured goods exported to Japan are manufactured either by Japanese overseas affiliates or under contract with Japanese manufacturers. Japanese trading companies also handle much of the foreign trade leaving East Asia. For example, about half of Taiwan's and one third of South Korea's foreign export and import trade is handled by Japanese trading companies. Without the intermediation of Japanese companies, East Asian exporters find it difficult to enter the Japanese market (Cronin, 1992, p. 52; Nester, 1992, p. 86).

Investment

Japan's huge trade surpluses and its yen appreciation in the 1980s stimulated a dramatic expansion of Japanese foreign direct investment abroad. Subsequently, Japan emerged as both the largest source of new foreign direct investment and the largest investor in terms of cumulative investment in East and Southeast Asia. In 1990 Japanese corporate investment in the Asia-Pacific region amounted to nearly twice the investment of American companies. Between 1951 and 1990 the cumulative total of Japanese investment in Asia was US$47.5 billion, compared with the United States' US$24.5 billion (Cronin, 1992, pp. 10-11; Nester, 1992, p. 93).

In terms of types of investment, by the 1990s, Japanese companies had made extensive inroads in investing in manufacturing industries all over East and Southeast Asia. Although U.S. companies relocated many labor-intensive production processes to Asia in the 1970s, they were largely overshadowed by their Japanese counterparts in the late 1980s. For instance, the total sales generated by Japanese subsidiaries in Asia in 1988 (US$85.5 billion) were about one third higher than the total sales of U.S. subsidiaries in Asia in the same year (US$65.9 billion). Nevertheless, the NIEs and the Southeast Asian states were critical of Japanese investment, because the latter had brought little linkage effects to their local economies. The Japanese companies' practice of shipping inputs from Japan, and Japanese reluctance to hire local managers and engineers, for example, limited the technological diffusion effect of Japanese investment (Encarnation, 1992, p. 179; *Far Eastern Economic Review* [FEER], 1991, pp. 102-103, 122).

Because Japanese overseas subsidiaries tended to source their inputs from Japan instead of from the NIEs or the Southeast Asian economies, the presence of Japanese overseas investment in these economies effectively increased Japan's exports to Asia. In this respect, Japan's foreign investment is said to have a "market penetration" orientation in Asia. As a result, its strategic position as the largest investor in Asia benefits Japan tremendously in the long run, given the rapid economic growth of the Asian region in the late 20th century.

Furthermore, Japanese companies also gained an edge over American ones by seizing new investment opportunities in Asia. In general, U.S. companies failed to capitalize on the rapid growth of the East and Southeast Asian economies in the 1980s to the same degree as Japanese companies. For example, Japan's investments in China far exceeded those from the United States; Japan was able to take advantage of the tremendous potential of the huge Chinese market when it was gradually opened to foreign imports in the late 1980s. Japanese investors also returned to China much more quickly than other investors in the wake of the Tiananmen Incident in June 1989. In addition, Japan became North Korea's biggest capitalist trading partner. Indeed, Cumings (1993, p. 33) points out that "Japanese experts have been asked to come back and renovate industrial technology in Manchuria and even to revive big gold mines in North Korea that were formerly owned by Japanese and American firms." In Southeast Asia, Japanese investors had already established a strong foothold in the Vietnamese economy in the early 1990s, but American companies were still prohibited by their government's investment embargo.

Foreign Aid

By Cronin's (1992, p. 16) account, the foreign aid that Japan's official development assistance (ODA) gave to "the Asia-Pacific region totalled about US\$ 4.1 billion in 1990, more than twice that of the United States. Japan is the single largest aid donor to some twenty-five Asia-Pacific countries, and Asian countries constituted nine of Japan's ten top aid recipients during the period 1985-89."

Japan's foreign aid worked to consolidate its economic dominance over the Asian region. Its aid policy has been described as "neo-mercantilism": aiming at expanding Japanese economic influence over aid recipients, promoting Japanese exports, and advancing Japan's international prestige and geopolitical ascendance (Nester, 1992, p. 104). The early manifestation of the neo-mercantilist nature of Japan's foreign aid was Japan's war reparations to Asian countries in the early postwar period. Such war reparations were designed largely to gain diplomatic recognition for Japan and normalize Japan's economic and political relationships with its neighbors. Its war reparation negotiations with South Korea, for example, were instrumental to the normalization of the Japan-Korea relationship and helped Japanese companies reenter the Korean market.

In the 1980s Japan went on to formulate the New Aid Plan, which represented a joint public-private aid program to promote Asian industrialization. This new plan concentrated in programs around economic infrastructure construction. For example, about half of Japanese aid to Asia in 1988 was allocated to economic infrastructure projects (Yanagihara & Emig, 1991, p. 46). Due to Japan's expertise in engineering and construction, the bulk of the aid-financed infrastructure projects naturally went to Japanese companies.

The advantage Japanese companies enjoyed because of Japanese foreign aid projects was further enhanced as many Japanese loans became tied to the procurement of Japanese products (Nester, 1992, p. 104). Although not all Japanese aid programs were officially tied to the purchase of Japanese goods, the engagement of Japanese consultants to conduct feasibility studies and provide engineering services often resulted in a more subtle way of tying projects to Japanese suppliers and construction firms (Yanagihara & Emig, 1991, pp. 51-52).

After becoming a regional economic powerhouse in East Asia, Japan also began to emerge as a global economic power.

JAPAN'S RISING GLOBAL ECONOMIC POWER

By the late 1980s there was a relative economic ascendance of Japan in the capitalist world system at the expense of the United States. In some economic areas, Japan replaced the previous American monopoly on leadership positions. In others, it significantly closed the gap between itself and the United States.

Technological Ascendancy

Technological innovation and productivity growth have always been the hallmarks of Japan's economic ascendancy. In one product area after another, Japanese manufacturers acquired technical expertise, perfected the production systems, and outsold their American competitors in such areas as TVs, steel, and autos.

Even so, it was a great shock when Fujitsu offered to buy Fairchild, the American multinational semiconductor maker, in 1986. This Fairchild event was symbolic of the decline of American technological hegemony and Japan's ascent. When Americans lost out to the Japanese in industry after industry, they still consoled themselves with the thought that those were old and dirty industries, no longer suitable for Americans whose future lay in high-technology industries spearheaded by the semiconductor revolution. But when news of the Fujitsu offer emerged, Americans came to realize that even this last line of defense had been breached. As Prestowitz (1988) remarks:

> The story [of Fujitsu's offer] was much bigger than Fairchild, however, or even than semiconductors. It encompassed virtually all the high-technology industries. Whether in disk drives, robots, printers, optical fiber electronics, satellite ground stations, or advanced industrial ceramics, the Japanese have come to dominate. New consumer products such as digital-audio tape recorders appear first in Japan. . . . Even the U.S. lead in such areas as aircraft and biotechnology is rapidly being whittled away. (p. 99)

With their technological and productivity lead, Japanese manufacturers controlled a sizable share of the American and European markets in many important products. As Table 9.2 shows, in automobiles the Japanese manufacturers' share of the U.S. market (including cars made by Japanese subsidiaries in the United States) has jumped from 20% in 1980 to 30% in 1992. For machine tools, the Japanese manufacturers had 30% of the U.S. market and 10% to 20% of the EC market in the early 1990s. In the semiconductor industry, 22% of the U.S. market and 42% of the world market in 1992 were controled by Japanese manufacturers. Furthermore, Japan's share of sales of large computer systems by the world's top 15 vendors was 44% in 1991. Japan also had come to acquire about 16% of software sales, 21% of personal computers, and 38% of data communications (Rowley & Sakamaki, 1992, p. 53).

TABLE 9.2 Economic Indicators of Japan and the United States in the 1980s and the Early 1990s

	Japan		United States	
TRADE (In billion US$ balance-of-payment basis)	1980	1992	1980	1992
Export of goods & services	158	525	344	730
Import of goods & services	168	403	334	764
Export to United States	37	96		
Import from United States	24	52		
Trade surplus against the United States	13	44		
FINANCE	1980	1992	mid-94	
Currency (Yen per US$)	227	127	100	
	1985	1993	1985	1993
Number of banks in top 10	5	6	2	0
Foreign direct investment (in billion US$)	6	34	6	26
Cumulative *bilateral* FDI (in billion US$)		162		26
INDUSTRIAL PRODUCTION	1980	1992	1980	1992
Automobile production (in 10,000 vehicles)	1,104	1,250	801	973
Share of U.S. personal vehicle market	20%	30%	74%	65%
Share of world semiconductor production	27%	42%	57%	42%
	1987	1992	1987	1992
Production of machine tools (in billion US$)	5	7	2	2
FOREIGN AID	1980	1992	1980	1992
ODA as percentage of GNP	0.3%	0.3%	0.3%	0.2%
In billion US$	4	11	7	11

SOURCE: Das (1993); Economic Planning Bureau, Ministry of Finance, Japan (1994); Japan External Trade Organization (JETRO, 1994).

Trade

As a result, Japan's exports to the United States increased steadily in the 1980s, from US$37 billion in 1980 to US$96 billion in 1992 (see Table 9.2). The annual rate of growth of Japanese exports to the United States was 81.6% in 1983. In 1985 the core states reached the Plaza Accord for the appreciation of the yen, and the average exchange rate of the yen against the dollar skidded from 238.54 yen in 1985 to 137.96 yen in 1989, almost 100%. The surge of the yen continued unabated in the 1990s, reaching 100 yen against the dollar in mid-1994 (see Table 9.2). The appreciation of the yen, however, failed to produce an absolute decline in Japan's export value measured in dollar terms (Das 1993, p. 46). This is because American imports of Japanese goods, like automobiles, semi-conductors, VCRs, machinery, and other electronic goods and parts, were relatively insensitive to dollar-yen exchange-based price fluctuations, but American exports to Japan, like food, timber, and other raw materials, were adversely affected by the Japanese recession in the late 1980s. Therefore, although the growth of the American trade surplus slowed down, it did not stop. In 1991 Japan's trade surplus with the United States still amounted to US$38.2 billion (MITI, 1992, p. 4). Even with the expansion of imports after the yen's appreciation, Japan consistently imported about half as much as it exported to the United States.

In the contemporary world economy, however, it would be misleading to gauge a nation's global economic position through international trade alone. With the tremendous growth of foreign direct investment and expansion of the activities of transnational corporations, trade balance has become only a partial indicator of its success or failure in the world economy. Other international transactions, such as foreign direct and portfolio investments, must be taken into account.

International Finance

In the 1980s Japan emerged as a superpower in the global financial system. As Das (1993, p. 71) points out, "riding on the domestic economy's long-running expansion, current account surpluses and an appreciating yen, and assisted by deregulation of the domestic banking and financial markets, Japan turned into the most solvent nation and the leading financial power of the 1980s."

There are several indicators to show Japan's global financial power. First, in terms of international assets, the share of Japanese banks in international assets (25.7%) exceeded that of the United States (23.3%) by 1985. Then, in 1990, Japan further increased its share of international assets to 36%, and those of the United States waned to 11.9% (Das, 1993, p. 73).

Second, in terms of position in the international financial market, five Japanese banks entered the top 10 by 1985, compared to only two U.S. banks in the same category. In 1993, the six largest banks in the world were Japanese, but no American bank remained in the top 10 category (see Table 9.2).

Third, during the past decade, after Japan dominated international commercial banking, it became the largest creditor in the world. For example, Japanese investors became the major buyers of U.S. Treasury bonds in this period.

Fourth, Japan has overtaken the United States as the largest foreign investor in the world. Japan's net foreign direct investment was US$6 billion in 1985, which was equal to that of the United States. However, in 1993, Japan's net foreign direct investment reached US$34 billion, whereas that of the United States was merely US$26 billion (see Table 9.2).

Finally, Japan has emerged as the largest foreign investor within the United States itself. Japanese cumulative foreign direct investment in the United States at the end of 1992 reached US$162 billion, but the cumulative figure for the United States in Japan was only US$26 billion (Table 9.2). As a result, Japanese subsidiaries "every week sell over $1 billion more in the U.S. than the Americans sell in Japan" (Encarnation, 1992, p. 3). Indeed, Japanese investment in the United States generated twice as much in Japanese sales in America as the amount of Japanese exports sold in the United States.

After Japan became a global economic power in the 1980s, it gradually grew quite active in international affairs.

JAPAN'S POLITICAL ACTIVISM
AND GROWING CULTURAL INFLUENCE

Political Activism

From the 1950s to the 1970s, the "Yoshida Doctrine" was the central pillar of Japan's foreign policy. As Pyle (1987, p. 9) remarks, this doctrine espoused the following tenets:

1. Japan's economic growth should be the prime national goal. Political-economic cooperation with the United States was necessary for this purpose.
2. Japan should remain lightly armed and avoid involvement in international political-strategic issues.
3. In order to gain a long-term guarantee for its own security, Japan would provide bases for the U.S. Army, Navy and Air Force.

This "growth-first" approach to Japan's international affairs gradually worked well for Japan throughout the postwar years, helping to free energies and resources for Japan's economic development.

In the early 1980s, however, in response to Japan's economic ascent and United States's hegemonic decline, Japan began to alter its foreign policy. According to the so-called Comprehensive National Security principle, the definition of security was broadened from purely military aspects to economic and political issues. Although military and diplomatic cooperation with the United States was still deemed necessary, greater military self-reliance and a more autonomous diplomatic relationship with the Soviet Union and China were pursued. Furthermore, the scope of Japan's national security also began to include energy and food supplies, which were maintained by greater economic cooperation with producer nations. Japanese foreign direct investment cemented the ties between Japan and foreign suppliers by vertical as well as horizontal divisions of labor. Japan would also diversify the markets for its exports and diversify the supply of critical resources and raw materials.

In the mid-1980s, Japan's new conception of its international role was even more explicit in Nakasone Yasuhiro's "Grand Design." Nakasone declared that Japan should no longer play the part of a follower nation, and it should assume more responsibilities as a leader of the world. Hence, in order to assume global leadership, Japan should develop a new liberal nationalism, with "an appreciation of Japan's special strengths and abilities within an international framework that combined national pride with appreciation for the cultures and traditions of other nations" (Pyle, 1987, p. 23).

The 1986 Maekawa report, submitted by a private study group appointed by Nakasone, also spelled out the future role of Japan in the world economy. The report urged Japan to internationalize its economy and harmonize the Japanese economy with others:

> In order to create an internationally cooperative economy and for Japan to become a truly international state, it is essential that Japan endeavor to achieve economic growth, led principally by its domestic demand, as well as to promote fundamental changes in its trading pattern and industrial structure. (Quoted in Yamamura, 1987, p. 36)

Through liberalization of imports and financial markets, reforms in fiscal and monetary policies, and multilateral coordinations in exchange rates, the report said, Japan should become more like a leader, rather than a follower, in the world economy. The report also stressed the need for expansion of official development assistance to developing countries and an increase in imports from these countries.

In the early 1990s, following the dissolution of the Soviet empire, Japanese leaders began to articulate their own visions of the international order. Prime Minister Kaifu Toshiki argued that Japan had to play a more active role in world affairs so as to bring about a democratic and stable international order. Thus, the United States, Europe, and Japan would become equal partners in exercising global leadership (Kaifu, 1990).

There were also signs that Japan was willing to shoulder the cost of leadership. After heated debate at home, Japan sent a peacekeeping force to Cambodia, under the auspices of the United Nations. In the Gulf War, Japan was also one of the largest underwriters of the American military campaign, contributing some US$13 billion (Kumao, 1993). Japan also actively extended aid to Russia for its reconstruction and market reforms. Meanwhile, Japan strove to become a standing member of the United Nations Security Council, an indication of Japan's willingness to employ multilateral means to achieve its foreign policy goals and construct the new international order.

A testament to Japan's new activism in international affairs was its contribution to foreign aid programs. In the 1980s Japanese foreign aid (the total financial flow), measured in U.S. dollars, to developing countries increased more than threefold. In 1988 Japan's share of total financial flows to developing countries was 31% of all Development Assistance Committee (DAC) members, but the share of the United States was merely 25% of the DAC total. While the United States's foreign aid as a percentage of its GNP shrunk from 0.3% in 1980 to 0.2% in 1992, Japan's foreign aid as a percentage of its GNP maintained the same 0.3% during the same period (see Table 9.2). This clearly reveals that while U.S.

international commitments contracted parallel to its decline in the world economy, Japan stepped up to become the largest aid donor in the world.

Furthermore, Japan was instrumental in the formation of the Asian Development Bank (ADB), taking a very active role in its operation. The president of the ADB has always been Japanese. In the 1980s Japan's contributions to the World Bank increased tremendously, making it the second-largest donor after the United States (Yanagihara & Emig, 1991).

Following the rise of Japan's global economic power and new political activism, Japanese culture also seemed to enjoy a growing influence in the world system.

Cultural Influence

The 1945-1967 period saw an incredible expansion of U.S. cultural influence worldwide, which can be observed through such phenomena as the universal adoption of the ideology of developmentalism, U.S. leadership in the contemporary social sciences and the arts, and the successful imposition of English as the sole lingua franca of the world system. Therefore, such American cultural constructs as free trade, democracy, individualism, and consumerism spread around the world, along with Hollywood movies, American popular music, McDonald's, and Coca-Cola. As Russett (1988, p. 102) states, "in longer-term ways, it [American culture] shaped people's desires and perceptions of alternatives, so that their preferences for international politics and economics were concordant with those of Americans."

However, the erosion of U.S. economic hegemony also began to weaken the foundations of U.S. cultural hegemony. By the 1980s there were several signs to suggest that Japan and East Asia were having more cultural influence in the capitalist world economy.

First, certain facets of the Japanese and East Asian cultures were subsumed under the general rubrics of Confucianism and brought to the forefront as a countervailing Asian ideology to compete with the U.S. ideology of developmentalism. Where American developmentalism stresses the role of the individual, Confucianism emphasizes the subordination of the individual to group harmony. Where American developmentalism endorses liberty and democracy, Confucianism supports enlightened authoritarian rule by a centralized bureaucracy. Where American developmentalism promotes consumerism, Confucianism values frugality, saving, discipline, and hard work. From the ideological framework of Confucianism, Japan's economic success owed more to its cultural ethos of paternalism, company loyalty, the work ethic, and the interventionist state than to the American ethos of democracy, individualism, consumerism, and free trade.

Second, there is a new "flying geese" ideology to highlight Japanese, rather than American, leadership in East Asian development (Awanohara, 1989). In this flying geese model, Japan played the lead position in the East Asian region, because it had the most advanced level of technology sophistication. Ranked behind Japan in a spreading "V" of decreasing levels of technical sophistication are first the NIEs (Hong Kong, Singapore, South Korea, and Taiwan) and then the Southeast Asian states (Malaysia, Thailand, Indonesia, and the Philippines). The "geese" behind Japan, it is argued, will learn from the progress of those up ahead, move into their positions, and eventually close the technological gap. This model predicts that the NIEs will follow the Japanese pattern, and the Southeast Asian states will follow the NIEs. As a result, every player can supposedly improve its position in following the Japanese leadership in East Asia. As such, the ideological implication of this model is that Japan has replaced the United States as a new model for Third World development.

Finally, another feature of Japan's cultural influence has been the overseas success of its popular culture industry ("The Southward Invasion,", 1994). Japanese popular music and TV programs (e.g., the drama series of Oshin) have begun to conquer the hearts and minds of East Asian audiences. Many Japanese pop singers are much adored in Hong Kong, Taiwan, and South Korea. The Japanese comics industry, another pillar of Japan's popular culture industry, has already conquered the East Asian markets (especially Hong Kong and Taiwan) and is beginning to gain a foothold in the United States and Britain. In addition, there is Japan's control over the world computer-game industry and the worldwide popularity of karaoke as an entertainment pastime. The Japanese language is also being heard more often all over the world because of the large number of Japanese tourists since the 1980s.

Needless to say, many Americans became irritated by Japan's dominance over the East Asian economies, global economic power, new political activism, and growing cultural influence. Subsequently, there began a rivalry between the United States and Japan in the 1980s.

UNITED STATES-JAPAN RIVALRY

Economic Rivalry

Throughout most of the postwar decades, the United States sacrificed commercial interests in favor of geopolitical advantages. In order to sustain the containment policy toward the Communist bloc, the United States "traded access to the American market for foreign policy favors" (Eckes, 1992, p. 135). As the United States fell from its undisputed hegemonic position in the world system in the 1980s, such an approach to trade became difficult to maintain.

When Japan's merchandise trade surplus began to swell from US $7 billion in 1980 to more than US $30 billion in 1984, there were pressures to push the U.S. government to reorient its policy toward United States-Japan trade (Higashi & Lauter, 1990, p. 76). As Bhagwati (1991, p. 48) observes, "the overall ethos favorable to protectionism came from the national psychology produced by America's relative decline in the world economy." Protectionism was part and parcel of the American "diminished giant syndrome."

Seeking to contain protectionist sentiments at home, the Reagan administration championed the idea of fair-trade and sought to open up the supposedly closed Japanese market to American exports. The rationale behind this approach was that the closed nature of Japan's domestic market and the distortions in its market mechanism posed undue barriers for American exports and were therefore the root of persistent trade surpluses. In numerous negotiations, American trade negotiators tried to force concessions from Japan in a wide range of areas, including reduction of import quotas, relaxation of import certification rules, abolition of the tobacco monopoly, and admission of American lawyers (Prestowitz, 1988, p. 451). From the American point of view, progress was painfully slow.

In 1985 the meeting between Reagan and Nakasone in the United States unveiled the Market-Oriented, Sector-Specific (MOSS) approach to addressing specific barriers in specific markets, such as telecommunications, medical equipment and pharmaceuticals, electronics, and forest products (Higashi & Lauter, 1990, p. 77). Later on, the American agenda widened to include new issues such as services, the protection of intellectual property, and trade-distorting investment measures. By the late

1980s such efforts were intensified with the passage by the U.S. Congress of the Omnibus Trade and Competitiveness Act, in 1988. In particular, the so-called Super-301 provisions in the act gave "legitimacy to unilateralism in defining America's trade rights, in determining their violations, and in meting out punishment to secure satisfaction," thus it departing fundamentally from the multilateral principles of GATT (Bhagwati, 1991, p. 36). After the Omnibus Act, the United States and Japan engaged in what was called the Structural Impediment Initiatives (SII) talks, which focused on "distortions" in the Japanese distribution and retailing system.

Apart from its foreign trade policy, the American offensive against Japan also extended to the broader area of macroeconomic management, mainly in the form of coaxing Japan to appreciate the yen. In the Reagan era, unprecedented budget deficits drove up U.S. interest rates, which in turn pushed up the exchange rate of the dollar. The resultant overvalued dollar reduced the competitiveness of American exports and incurred substantial trade deficits. The U.S. administration believed, on the other hand, that the yen was kept undervalued by the Japanese government in order to maintain Japan's export market shares. Hence, in September 1985, the Plaza Accord was reached between the United States and the other major industrial powers (the Group of Five) to engineer a devaluation of the dollar in order to reduce the growing U.S. trade deficit. After the concerted action of the Group of Five, the yen dropped sharply from 237 yen to the dollar before the 1985 Plaza Accord to 128 yen to the dollar in 1988.

Besides American attempts to dismantle the "structural impediments" to American exports to Japan, the United States also applied pressure on Japan to stimulate its domestic demand. From the American point of view, an expansion of Japanese domestic demand would increase Japanese imports and reduce Japanese exports. It would also make Japan less productive and hence less competitive—if Japanese corporations reduced working hours and paid higher wages, and if the Japanese government stopped encouraging a high rate of savings through tax incentives to spend. In the mid-1980s American trade negotiators began to criticize Japan's uniquely high savings rate and weak domestic demand as other reasons for its low appetite for imports. For instance, Secretary of State George Schultz, in 1985, called for Japan to save less and spend more, so as to reduce trade imbalances with other countries (Higashi & Lauter, 1990, p. 81; Yamamura, 1987, p. 33).

Apart from attempts to change Japan, the United States also sought to transform its own industries and state-industry relationship in order to compete more effectively in the world economy. The American state steered away from its traditional aversion to industrial policy and toward a more active approach to promoting American industrial development. For example, after the initial United States-Japan trade dispute over semiconductors in 1985-1987, the U.S. Department of Defense decided to support the Sematech project, a joint venture involving 13 U.S. companies. The objective of the Sematech project was to boost the development of semiconductor production facilities and the diffusion of technology in the United States. At about the same time, the Reagan administration announced a program aimed at assisting the commercialization of superconductivity and keeping this technology in the United States. According to Prestowitz (1988), in spite of their inadequacies, these two programs were a milestone in American economic policy:

> By reversing the administration's own arguments against government intervention, it establishes the legitimacy of cooperation between government and business to reach specific industrial goals. It asserts that because we know superconductivity is a key technology promising great economic benefits, and because our power as a nation rests on industrial and economic strength, we should not balk at enhancing it just as we would not balk at developing weapons technology. And if this logic holds for superconductivity or semiconductors, it should hold for other areas as well. (p. 508)

The coming of the Clinton administration further accentuated the willingness of the American state to assume a more active role in promoting the U.S. economy. The appointment of Laura D'Andrea Tyson, a member of the "manufacturing matters" school and a proponent of an active industrial policy to rejuvenate American industry, as the President's Chief Economic Advisor signals the depth of the changing mood in Washington.

Ideological Rivalry

Japan-bashing emerged at the height of the United States-Japan economic rivalry. Myriad American popular literature—including the writings of Prestowitz (1988), van Wolferen (1989); James Fallows' dispatches for *The Atlantic Monthly*; and movies such as *Rising Sun*—attempted to reveal the dark side of Japanese success (Awanohara, 1991). In addition, this popular literature attempted to convey the belief that the Japanese rise to economic power in the world was achieved and is being maintained unfairly. They suggest that Japan has retained many features of an authoritarian structure, that Japan pursues "adversary" trading policies, that Japan has targeted and destroyed sectors of American industry such as semiconductors, and that Japan might, after all, be "the only Communist nation that works" (McCormack, 1990, p. 5).

Furthermore, this Japan-bashing literature insinuated a picture of an all-powerful Japan that would eventually colonize the United States and the world. In the *Times Literary Supplement*, Murray Sayle articulated a vision of the future in which:

> Britain and Ireland could respectively be Japan's Hong Kong and Macao, well-placed for the European entrepot trade, the United States will be Japan's fabulously wealthy India, *terre des merveilles*, while Australia can be Japan's Australia, land of rugged adventure and heavy drinking, the appropriate place of exile for Japanese dissidents and remittance men. (Quoted by McCormack, 1990, p. 2)

Due to this Japan-bashing literature, the public image of Japan in the United States began to worsen significantly by the late 1980s. In 1991, 77% of Americans polled in an *Asahi Shimbun* survey viewed the mutual relationship between the United States and Japan as prominently one of rivalry rather than partnership (Calder, 1992, p. 129).

In response, the Japanese opinion of America has similarly deteriorated. From the Japanese viewpoint, Americans mask their own societal and policy failures with bullying and complaints against Japan. Borthwick (1992) points out that:

> A $13 billion contribution from Japan to the cost of the Persian Gulf received scant praise from the U.S. where the focus seemed to be instead on Japan's lukewarm enthusiasm for the cause. . . . As a result, a new Japanese word has come into more frequent use: *kenbei*, meaning "dislike of the U.S." Equally irritating to Japan is what seems an American tendency to view it as a banker and passive partner in funding U.S. foreign policy initiatives. (p. 544)

In the midst of the *kenbei* sentiment, Sony Chairman Morita Akio and maverick LPD Diet member Ishihara Shintaro, in a coauthored bestseller titled *The Japan That Can Say "No"*, argued that Japan could indeed become a powerful nation in the world.

However, despite the above economic and ideological rivalries, there were also economic and geopolitical conditions that called for the continuation of a United States-Japan partnership.

UNITED STATES-JAPAN PARTNERSHIP

Economic Interdependence

The United States-Japan trade deficit surged above US$50 billion in 1985, yet during this period the American and Japanese leaders were on friendly first-name terms, and their overall trans-Pacific ties remained remarkably smooth. Although the United States adopted a patchwork of voluntary export restraint agreements, in sectors ranging from automobiles and color televisions to steel, these agreements were hardly onerous to Japanese producers and very often enhanced their profitability. Despite the much-dramatized Super 301 provisions of the 1988 Omnibus Trade Law, the law inspired only a brief tempest in United States-Japan relations: three short investigations and no actual trade retaliation. Other more threatening legislation than the Omnibus Trade Bill was decisively rejected in the late 1980s and has not been seriously reconsidered. In short, the warning of a full-scale trade war has not materialized, despite the persistent U.S. trade deficit against Japan into the 1990s. What, then, explains this remarkable resistance of the American political economy to protectionism in the midst of large-scale trade imbalances with Japan?

According to Calder (1992), this is because of the rising economic interdependence between the United States and Japan. In fact, the United States-Japan economic relationship has been the principal support of American global political-economic preeminence since World War II. In 1990, United States-Japan trade exceeded US$142 billion. This figure was roughly twice as large as Japanese trade with the European Community, and 80% the size of all American trade transactions with the entire

European Community. In addition, since the 1980s, there has been significant United States-Japan cross-investment in high-growth, knowledge-
intensive sectors, with a major portion of it being research and service-
trade related. For instance, Japan participated in the multibillion-dollar
supercollider to be built in north Texas.

As Calder (1992) explains:

> [This growing economic interdependence between the United States and
> Japan] greatly strengthened private groups, such as distributors, agricultural
> exporters, and multinational corporations, that specialized in such activi-
> ties. Interdependence gave such groups strengthened incentives to public
> activism in support of free trade. Interdependence conversely eroded the
> strength of organized labor and inland regions that politically resisted the
> open global economic order. (p. 128)

Politically, the resistance of the American political economy to protectionism was also aided by the so-called Sunbelt shift of the 1970s and
1980s: Southern and western areas of the United States, in fundamentally
symbiotic relationships to Japan (predominately relying on the agricultural, defense, and construction sectors, as opposed to basic manufactures, for their livelihood), gained influence in U.S. politics.

Calder (1992) further argues that once the U.S. recession is over, and
once the politically dictated need for transition assistance to the gravely
ill American automobile industry is past, bilateral trade issues will de-
serve far less priority in future high-level discussions than they are
accorded now by the mass media and even by policymakers. Instead,
attention will be focused on long-term economic interdependence, cooperative projects in high-technology areas, and geopolitical alliance in
regional and global organizations.

Geopolitical Alliance

With the rapid relaxation of tensions and accelerating disarmament
in Europe, East Asia becomes, together with the Middle East, the most
armed region of the world, featuring two local nuclear powers—China
and Russia—together with nuclear uncertainties in North Korea. As
such, Calder (1992) contends that there is a strong strategic argument
for Japan to find an alliance partner. Among potential alliance partners,

China and Russia are improbable because of their socialist heritage. Because economic interdependence with the United States is so great, there is a powerful impetus to push for a United States-Japan security alliance on nuclear grounds alone.

Although a strong strategic rationale for a United States-Japan alliance will likely continue to persist throughout the 1990s, its viability within the American and Japanese societies seems problematic. The U.S. public and Congress demanded more burden-sharing from Japan, and the Japanese public complained about the high cost of an American security presence in Japan. Nevertheless, Calder (1992) suggests that these conflicts are not irreconcilable. To reinforce the long-term political viability of the United States-Japan security alliance, Calder proposes: (a) that both sides hold burden-sharing, with respect to U.S. forces in Japan, to a 50-50 sharing of relevant costs; (b) the continuation and extension of coproduction arrangements of high-tech weapons; (c) that the United States would encourage Japan to participate more actively in broadened regional security discussions in East Asia; and (d) greater emphasis on the nonmilitary dimensions of the United States-Japan bilateral security treaty.

Obviously, by the 1980s, after Japan achieved the status of a "quasi hegemon in economic dimension" (Yoon, 1990), it earned both the awe and the respect of the United States. Does this imply that Japan will replace the United States as the next hegemon in the capitalist world economy?

WILL JAPAN BE THE NEXT HEGEMON?

Cumings (1987) points to the importance of a setting up a "grand area," in which nations within that area orient themselves toward the hegemon. Following Cumings's argument, it is clear that Japan must first demarcate East Asia as its grand area before it becomes a serious contender with the United States for hegemonic domination of the capitalist world economy.

But so far, Japan has failed to create an Asian yen bloc to challenge the United States and the EC. Despite Japan's strong economic presence in Asia, this region is still under the dual economic domination of the United States and Japan, and it still falls under a unilateral American security network. Furthermore, lingering suspicions remain from World War II, such that other Asian states view Japanese regional power with alarm. Thus, although Japan was reported to be keen on creating the APEC (Asia-Pacific Economic Cooperation) Conference to unite Asia, most ASEAN states initially were strongly opposed to such an idea. Their concern was that Japan would dominate the APEC, and they agreed to participate in the APEC only after the United States was to be included as a full member and the leader of the conference (Crone, 1992).

Japan, of course, could revive its previous Greater East Asian Co-Prosperity Sphere project and conquer the region militarily. However, this is a very unlikely outcome, because although Japan has developed considerable military capabilities, it remains subordinate to the U.S. military. In addition, due to the legacy of World War II, pacifism remains a powerful current in Japanese domestic politics, as can be seen in 1990 by the massive disapproval of the prime minister's efforts to send Japanese Self-Defense Force personnel to the Persian Gulf for noncombat purposes. Even dispatching a small peacekeeping force to Cambodia was hotly contested. Hence, the reestablishment of a full-scale Japanese military force is unlikely to proceed without a fundamental reorientation in Japanese political culture and policy. As a result, Japan still has to depend on the security provided by the United States and accept an American military presence in the Asian region.

In the interim, then, Japan is likely to continue being an economic giant with only a modest political and military influence in East Asia. Although the trade war between Japan and the United States may intensify, a United States-Japan partnership in global and regional security and diplomatic affairs seems to be more likely than an outright confrontation between the economic powers. As such, it may take a fairly long time before Japan will assume the hegemonic responsibility to dominate the affairs of the world economy.

Aside from United States-Japan hegemonic rivalry, another critical event that will speed up the centrality of East Asia in global capital accumulation is the national reunification project among mainland China, Taiwan, and Hong Kong. This project will the focus of discussion in the next chapter.

10. The Chinese Triangle of Mainland-Taiwan-Hong Kong

B efore China was incorporated into the capitalist world economy at the turn of the 19th century, there was only one Chinese state. The Qing empire ruled over both Taiwan and Hong Kong. Nevertheless, the Chinese nation, after its incorporation into the American-led world economy since 1945, became divided into three separate political entities: the socialist state on the mainland, the authoritarian state in Taiwan, and the colonial state in Hong Kong.

Between the 1960s and the 1970s, these three states pursued different strategies of semiperipheral development: revolutionary socialism on the mainland, developmental authoritarianism in Taiwan, and positive non-interventionist policy in Hong Kong. However, by the end of the 1970s, mainland China, Taiwan, and Hong Kong had run into various kinds of developmental problems.

On the mainland, the socialist state experienced a slowdown in the economy. Its economic productivity reached a plateau and could not be substantially increased through mass mobilization; its industrial technology grew outdated; its industrial bureaucracy became ossified; and its state workers had few motivations to work hard. Mainland China also suffered from very serious unemployment problems, as the mainland

AUTHORS' NOTE: This chapter is a revised version of an earlier paper coauthored by Hsiao and So (1993).

population doubled from around 500 million in 1953 to 1,000 million in 1980 (Riskin, 1987).

On the other hand, the two NIEs, Taiwan and Hong Kong, began to experience the limitations of export-led development. Internally, as a result of their economic successes, there were labor shortages, escalating land prices, and the emergence of environmental protests—all of which served to raise the costs of production. Externally, Taiwan and Hong Kong faced stiff competition from Southeast Asian states and socialist China in exporting goods to the capitalist core, particularly due to the emergence of protectionism in the core since the 1970s. Furthermore, Taiwan was forced by Western core states to increase the value of the Taiwan dollar, due to its huge foreign currency reserves, thus reducing its competitiveness in the world economy (Chen, 1980; Gold, 1987).

Their dilemmas were a reflection of the contradictions facing semiperipheral development in the capitalist world economy. As the world economy began its downward phase and the global market contracted in the 1970s, the semiperipheries were squeezed in the middle by both the protectionism in the core and the stiff competition from the peripheries. In this respect, mainland China, Taiwan, and Hong Kong had all reached a critical juncture in their developmental trajectories in the late 1970s. Their previous developmental policies—Maoist socialism, developmental authoritarianism, and positive noninterventionist policy—had run into difficulties, and they needed to formulate new strategies to overcome their problems. What kind of developmental options were then available to them?

One strategy to overcoming the above developmental barriers is national integration. For Wallerstein (1979), the key to a semiperipheral breakthrough is that a country must have a large enough market to justify an advanced technology, which it must produce at a lower cost than the existing producers. This market enlargement and cheapening of production can be achieved by expanding political boundaries and thereby promoting economic integration with the state's neighbors. Because most of the citizens of mainland China, Taiwan, and Hong Kong still look upon themselves as Chinese and identify their political entities as integral parts of a single Chinese nation, national integration becomes a feasible developmental strategy to them.

This chapter will examine how the Chinese triangle of socialist mainland, authoritarian Taiwan, and colonial Hong Kong developed specific strategies of economic integration with one another in order to achieve semiperipheral breakthrough in the world economy. In particular, this chapter will focus upon the actors who formulated the integration strategy; the economic and political complexities of integration; and the profound impact of integration strategy on mainland, Taiwan, and Hong Kong development.

MAINLAND CHINA'S STRATEGY SINCE THE 1980s

Open-Door Policy

Mainland China's initial strategy of national upward mobility was reincorporation into the world economy. Subsequently, in addition to calling for increasing privatization and deregulation, there was an open-door policy toward foreign investment. This open-door policy began with the establishment of four special economic zones (SEZs) in 1979, the opening of 14 coastal cities and Hainan Island in 1984, and the extension of the SEZs to three delta areas in 1985 (So, 1988).

This open-door policy was aimed at attracting large-scale, high-tech capital investment from U.S. and Japanese transnational corporations. The preferred form of operation was joint-venture prospects between the mainland Chinese government and the transnationals, so that Chinese managers could acquire advanced technology, Western management know-how, and information about world market conditions from their foreign partners. It was hoped that these joint-venture projects would invigorate aging state enterprises, raise industrial production to levels comparable to those of core states, help Chinese industries enter the world market, and earn the needed foreign currency through export-industrialization.

In order to attract foreign investment, mainland China tried hard to improve the investment climate. More than 200 pieces of joint-venture legislation were passed in the 1980s; the socialist state spent enormous amounts of capital in infrastructure construction; and special privileges, such as cheap factory sites, low rates of taxation, low wages, and tariff exemptions, were granted to the transnationals (Simon, 1990).

Nevertheless, these Chinese concessions failed to impress the transnationals. There were frequent complaints about the Chinese bureaucracy's

244

CENTRALITY

unnecessary regulations and numerous layers of required permits. Projects that had been formally approved at upper levels did not always receive cooperation at lower levels. In addition, there were many complaints about operational problems, including labor laws that prevented the transnationals from freely hiring and firing Chinese workers, difficulties in getting reliable supplies of high-quality raw materials, a lack of enterprise autonomy, and an inability to remit foreign currency profits out of China. Finally, the transnationals expressed concerns about the closed Chinese market. Even though the transnationals had invested on the mainland, their products were still not allowed to enter the Chinese market. Because the transnationals could invest in other peripheral states that provided a better investment and business climate, they did not need to limit their ventures to mainland China. Thus, the transnationals generally tended to invest just enough to maintain a foothold in mainland China (Battat, 1991). In this respect, the open-door policy failed to achieve its goals to attract high-tech capital investment from the transnational corporations.

National Reunification Drive

Side by side with the open-door policy was the drive toward Chinese national reunification. The old generation of CCP leaders perceived national reunification as a historical mission that they were duty-bound to accomplish in their lifetime. As they got older and older, they expressed a sense of urgency and listed reunification as one of the great tasks of the 1980s (Nathan, 1990).

The CCP used a two-step approach to promote national reunification. It began with the strengthening of civil society contacts with Taiwan, such as family reunions, tourism, academic meetings, sports events, trade, and investments. Beginning in 1979 the CCP proposed the "three communication" (San Tong) policy, hoping to develop trade, postal service, and transportation relationships between mainland China and Taiwan. In the early 1980s the CCP granted special favors to Chinese capitalists from Hong Kong. Whenever Hong Kong's big capitalists were in Peking [Beijing], they would be asked to hold highly publicized meetings with high-ranking CCP leaders (like Vice Premier Deng Xiaoping and Party Secretary Hu Yaobang), including "heart-to-heart" talks for a couple of hours, photo sessions, news conferences, and grand banquets. Those Hong Kong capitalists, who had failed to receive patronage from the colonial government, were especially impressed by the renewed friendship of the CCP, feeling a sudden elevation in their social status and influence.

After civil society contacts, the next step was to push for reunification talks. In the early 1980s the CCP formulated a "One Nation, Two Systems" model for reunification. In this model, the capitalist economies and lifestyles of Hong Kong and Taiwan would remain unchanged after national reunification with the socialist mainland. As special administrative regions (SARs) of the mainland, the Hong Kong and Taiwan governments would have a high degree of autonomy, with self-governance in administrative, legislative, and judicial matters. For Taiwan, the GMD would even be allowed to retain its military forces and conduct an independent foreign policy.

The national reunification drive was highly successful. In the early 1980s Great Britain was lured into reunification talks with mainland China, which resulted in the signing of the Joint Declaration to return sovereignty over Hong Kong to the mainland in 1997. Mainland China also won numerous diplomatic battles with Taiwan, forcing most of the core states to sever ties with Taiwan in order to set up diplomatic links with the mainland (Gold, 1987).

In light of the success of the reunification drive and the failure of the open-door policy, a new strategy of national upward mobility was formulated by the CCP in the late 1980s. On one hand, the transnationals kept complaining about the mainland's investment climate, and they were not willing to bring in high-tech capital investment. On the other hand, Hong Kong capitalists developed a cordial relationship with the CCP, and their investments were expanding very rapidly. As such, the CCP calculated that it was better to reorient its trade policies to favor capitalists from Hong Kong and Taiwan rather than the transnationals. The rationale was that increasing economic integration with Hong Kong and Taiwan would strengthen their dependence on the mainland's labor, natural resources, and markets, by which a vested interest group within their civil societies could be developed that would push their states toward political unification.

Coastal-Development Strategy

In 1988, a 22-point regulation was approved by the CCP to encourage Taiwanese investment in production and land development in Hainan Island, Guangdong, Fujian, Zhejiang, and other coastal provinces. It was guaranteed that Taiwanese establishments would not be nationalized, exported goods from Taiwanese investments would be free from export tariffs, Taiwanese management would have complete autonomy in running their firms in mainland China, and Taiwanese investors would be granted multiple entry visas. The same privileges, of course, had already been granted to the Hong Kong investors (Chen, 1993).

There were several crucial differences between this coastal-development strategy and the previous open-door policy. First, instead of appealing to American, European, and Japanese investors, the coastal-development strategy was targeted at the investors from Taiwan and Hong Kong. Second, instead of aiming to attract large-scale investments from the transnationals, the present strategy was targeted at small investment projects from the small and medium-sized firms in Taiwan and Hong Kong. Third, instead of demanding high-tech, capital-intensive investment and the utilization of local materials, the present strategy allowed investment in labor-intensive industries that relied solely on raw material imports. Assembly-line industries would help solve the serious unemployment problem, and foreign raw-materials imports would help ease the shortage of raw materials in mainland markets. Fourth, instead of getting approval from such central government agencies as the Ministry of International Economic Relations and Trade, the present strategy decentralized investment decisions. Municipal and county government officials were authorized to sign contracts with foreign investors. Fifth, instead of encouraging joint-venture contracts, the present strategy preferred wholly owned foreign investment because of capital shortages. Finally, although previous policies sought to confine China's foreign interaction to officially limited areas, such as the special economic zones, the coastal-developmental strategy sought to involve the bulk of China in the world economy. It was hoped that the coastal provinces would provide a major engine for China's economic growth (Battat, 1991; Nathan, 1990).

It seems that this coastal-development strategy has been successful in attracting direct foreign investment (DFI) from the capitalists of Hong

Kong and Taiwan. By 1990 more than 60% of all DFI in mainland China was from Hong Kong, which amounted to US$10 billion out of a total of US$16 billion actual investment. The capitalists of Hong Kong also employed an estimated two million industrial workers on the mainland, about twice more than the number they employed in Hong Kong (Battat, 1991, p. 1; Lall, 1991, p. 3). Taiwanese direct investment in mainland China increased from US$100 million in 1987 to US$1 billion in 1989, and to US$2 billion in 1990. By mid-1992, investment by Taiwan companies in China was estimated at US$4 billion, and in 1992 alone, Taiwan companies were expected to invest some US$1.5 billion (FEER, September 19, 1992, p. 12). As a result of the accelerated investment, by the 1990s, Hong Kong and Taiwan became the number one and number two investors on mainland China, respectively, surpassing even the United States and Japan.

What then explains the success of this coastal-development strategy? It seems that the CCP officials were more comfortable in dealing with the Hong Kongers and Taiwanese than with the Americans and Japanese. This may be due to the fact that mainlanders, Taiwanese, and Hong Kongers are all "Chinese," sharing similar customs, habits, language, and other cultural traits, and used to the "Chinese" way of doing business (Battat, 1991). On one hand, capitalists from Hong Kong and Taiwan frequently invoked their kinship and community ties (through generous donations to the local schools, sports arenas, etc.) so as to strengthen their social bonds with mainlanders. On the other, CCP officials were more flexible in enforcing labor practices, foreign currency policies, and tariffs toward their Hong Konger and Taiwanese compatriots, because these favors could be legitimized through appeals for national reunification. But if the same favors were granted to Western businessmen, the officials would be condemned for betraying national interests. This differential treatment of Western businessmen and Taiwanese and Hong Kongers helps to explain why mainland China was able to attract investments from Taiwan and Hong Kong but failed to attract Western transnationals.

In addition, the ethnic ties of the Chinese capitalists from Taiwan and Hong Kong enabled them to exercise more effective managerial control over the mainland workforce. Thus, the Taiwan and Hong Kong capitalists had faced fewer labor disciplinary problems than the transnationals when they set up branches in an alien environment.

Finally, the coastal-development strategy also developed at the right time because it coincided with the outflow of capital from Taiwan and Hong Kong that resulted from their continued growth in exports and trade surpluses. The capitalists in Taiwan, in particular, were eager to invest outward in the late 1980s after the United States forced their currency to appreciate a big margin.

Industrialization and Regional Differentiation

This coastal-development strategy had a significant impact on the mainland. First, it led to industrialization of the coastal provinces, especially in the SEZs and the Pearl River Delta in South China. By the late 1980s the coastal provinces had become centers of investment for Taiwan and Hong Kong, providing the latter with a cheap and docile labor force, natural resources, and investment opportunities.

Second, the very success of industrialization in the coastal provinces, nevertheless, led to crucial regional differentiation within the mainland. While the rest of the heartland provinces remained relatively unaffected, the coastal provinces rapidly moved toward capitalism—leading to higher rates of economic growth, better standards of living, and democratic movements on one hand, and to such social problems as prostitution, juvenile delinquency, and crime on the other. Consequently, the coastal provinces such as Guangdong became the core of the mainland, taking advantage of their peripheral heartland provinces.

Third, these regional imbalances were manifested in the factional conflicts between "conservatives" and "reformers" inside the CCP. Although the reformers wanted to achieve full-blown market socialism (i.e., more opening for the world market and greater liberalization), the conservatives remarked that there was already too much "spiritual pollution" and that they wanted to return to state socialism. As a result, there was a showdown between market and state socialist forces between 1987 and 1989.

The Showdown Between Market and State Socialism

Emboldened by the prospect of overseas investment from Hong Kong and Taiwan, as well as by the significant economic growth up to the mid-1980s, the "liberals" in the CCP decided to push forward enterprise reform, price reform, and political reform. The objective of enterprise reform was to turn enterprises into independent economic units responsible for their own gains and losses, to sever the ties between the state and the enterprises. For price reform, the state would end all price controls within 4 to 5 years, so that only market prices would remain. This was an attempt to eliminate the "political corruption" by party officials who bought resources at low state-set prices and sold them at high market prices. In addition, political reforms—such as an end to lifetime tenure in office for political leaders, constitutional definition of the scope of individual autonomy, and the vesting of true political supremacy in the National People's Congress—were proposed (So, 1992).

The assault by the "liberal reformers" on state socialism created all kinds of economic and political problems. First of all, after foreign trade decentralization was implemented through the coastal-development strategy, foreign trade companies at the county level mushroomed, leading to keen competition for raw materials and foreign buyers, to lack of control over the quality of export products, to a new influx of foreign imports, and to foreign exchange speculation. In addition, enterprise reform encountered so much resistance that it was quickly discarded. Party officials opposed the reforms because they threatened their authority and vested interests, and state workers opposed them because they undermined their job security and entitlement.

The highly publicized price reform met a similar fate. As soon as prices were decontrolled in the summer of 1988, inflation accelerated to 20.7%, resulting in panic buying by consumers and enterprises. To allay inflationary fears, the CCP was forced to declare, in September of 1988, that price reform would be indefinitely postponed, that capital construction be sharply reduced, and that ideological rectification be pursued.

The wholesale market reforms triggered the serious political unrest that almost blew the CCP apart in 1989. Urban residents generally were highly dissatisfied due to the high inflation rate and rising cost of living; state workers complained about the gradual loss of entitlement, and new workers had no entitlement at all; and the influx of rural surplus labor into the cities led to serious unemployment problems and criminal activities. In addition, members of the new middle class, after being exposed to a Western lifestyle, were no longer satisfied with the CCP's authoritarianism; they demanded freedom, autonomy, status, high salaries, job mobility, and drastic political reforms (including democratic elections, a multiparty system, and protection of human rights).

These structural conflicts in the economy and society, coupled with the succession crisis and intraparty conflict, converged in the 1989 Tiananmen Incident. Precipitated by the death of Hu Yaobang (the party secretary who endorsed wholesale mercantilism), triggered by students demanding democratic reforms and seizing the opportunity during Gorbachev's visit to China, joined by the urban masses, and supported by the Western media, the hunger strike of the students was quickly turned into a large-scale urban protest that challenged the CCP's legitimacy. Because the CCP was unable to resolve this crisis by peaceful dialogue, it resulted in violence and bloodshed (So & Hua, 1992).

Since then, the CCP has been rethinking its strategy of reforms. Moving toward wholesale market reforms would, the CCP knew, direct it down the path of the Eastern European socialist states, which would have led to its downfall. Conversely, moving back toward revolutionary socialism would certainly alienate the capitalists of Hong Kong and Taiwan, thus threatening the prospects for national reunification. These contradictory signals explain why the CCP decided to create a hybrid called a "socialist commodity economy." The ideal was to obtain an optimum combination of market and state socialism, to allow for the coexistence of the state sector and the private sector, and to strengthen a strong authoritarian state in order to promote export-led industrialization (just like state capitalism in South Korea and Taiwan). As a result, there were an increasing number of administrative controls over the economy and a continuation of political repression over dissent.

In addition, nationalism was used as a unifying force to generate solidarity among the Chinese population, so that intraparty disputes and class differences could be put aside in the struggle for national reunification with Taiwan and Hong Kong. As well, the concept of "Greater China" was formulated, stressing that the economies of China, Taiwan, and Hong Kong were complementary to one another. Economic integration among the three Chinese states makes them a core nation in the world economy utilizing the following comparative assets: China's abundant cheap labor, raw materials, and market; Taiwan's capital and technology-intensive industries; and Hong Kong's established worldwide financial and trading network.

TAIWAN'S STRATEGY SINCE THE 1980s

In the early 1980s, when the Taiwanese state confronted the developmental problems of rising production cost and worldwide protectionism, it did not pursue a policy of national integration. Instead, it adopted such policies as industrial restructuring (moving from labor-intensive to capital-intensive and high-tech industries), diversification of trade in the world market, and transferring some labor-intensive industries to the Southeast Asian region (Chiu, in press).

In addition, the Taiwanese state promoted democratic reforms from above. After Western core states severed diplomatic ties with Taiwan, and after the GMD was criticized by Amnesty International for human rights violations, there was a crisis of legitimacy in the early 1980s. In order to regain legitimacy in the interstate system, the GMD lifted martial law, legalized the formation of opposition parties, tolerated dissent, and allowed social movements to spread (Cheng, 1989; Hsiao, 1993; So & May, 1993). After winning elections and feeling less threatened by the mainland's reunification drive, the GMD began to formulate a new strategy of national upward mobility in the capitalist world economy.

Beginning to Play the China Card

In 1985 the GMD announced its "Three Nos" policy regarding mainland China: no direct trade, no contact with mainland officials and agencies, and no interference in indirect trade. Couched in obscure language, this policy actually suggested that the GMD, though still prohibiting citizens of Taiwan from having any "direct" contact with mainland China, would permit "indirect" trade between Taiwan and mainland China through an intermediary like Hong Kong.

In November 1987, after the GMD won the first election against the newly established Democratic Progressive Party (DPP), it further liberalized its mainland policy. The GMD announced that mainland-born Taiwan residents would be permitted to visit the mainland for family reunions, and other Taiwan citizens would be allowed to visit the mainland for tourism and other civilian purposes (such as sports and academic conferences). These civil society contacts helped accelerate "un-official" economic links between Taiwan and mainland China. In 1988 the Taiwanese business community was further attracted by mainland's coastal-development strategy, which encouraged direct investment in Fujian and Guangdong provinces.

In the beginning, Taiwanese small capitalists were the first group to engage in "unofficial" trade and investment with the mainland. They risked their property and faced the danger of punishment by the GMD to explore the mainland's labor market, so they could survive and pro-long the life cycle of their sunset labor-intensive industries. Although the GMD legally prohibited such direct trade and investment on the main-land, it did not impose severe punishment on firms found investing in the mainland, except for minor harassments like restrictions on bank loans and closer scrutiny of tax returns. Because trade and investment in the mainland were so profitable, Taiwanese investment increased rapidly in the late 1980s.

With respect to investment, Taiwanese capital ranked second to Hong Kong capital among all foreign investors in the Fujian province; but in the Xiamen SEZ, Taiwanese investment topped Hong Kong's as the largest outside capital source. Although two thirds of Taiwanese investment was in manufacturing industries, the Taiwanese also in-vested in real estate, tourism, resource extraction, and chemical indus-tries.

Although Taiwan's indirect trade (via Hong Kong) with mainland China was only US$1.47 billion during the 5-year period from 1979 to 1983, this expanded to US$2.61 billion during the 3 years from 1984 to 1986. After the Taiwanese state declared that there would be no interfer-ence in indirect trade, this volume jumped to US$7.72 billion during a 3-year span from 1987 to 1989, almost twice the combined total of the previous two periods, and an annual average of US$2.54 billion (Li, 1991, p. 26). Industrial materials and parts, such as man-made fibers, clothes, machine equipment, electronic parts, and plastic raw materials, emerged as major export items to mainland China. Imported items from the mainland included traditional herb medicines, animal by-products, fish and sundry goods, leather, iron, and so on. In sum, this rapid expansion of "unofficial" trade and investment set the stage for a new strategy of national upward mobility in the world economy in 1991.

Economic Integration But No Political Reunification

In 1991 the GMD finally recognized the reality of active Taiwanese trade and investment on the mainland. Consequently, it relaxed its ban on direct trade and investment beginning in 1991. Only those corporations that had invested in mainland China and failed to file a report with the government would be punished. By June 1991 some 2,600 Taiwanese companies had reported their investments in mainland China. In addition, the GMD also modified its mainland policy. A quasi-cabinet-level Commission on Mainland Affairs was established and a semigovernmental Straits Exchange Foundation was organized; they were both responsible for future policy making and implementation at official and civilian levels. The Straits Foundation, in particular, was charged by the GMD with a mission of "frontline" contact with mainland officials in dealing with civilian and business disputes that had occurred or might occur in the future.

What explains this official endorsement of economic integration with mainland China? In retrospect, the GMD may just have been following the Taiwanese big capitalists' initiatives. It was only after the big capitalists entered into mainland investment and developed vested interests there, and only after they had begun to exert pressures on the GMD, that the GMD shifted to more pragmatic mainland policies. Unlike President Jiang Jingguo's [Chiang Ching-Kuo] antibusiness ideology, the present president, Li Denghui [Lee Teng-Hui], is known for his favorable attitude toward business. President Li has a list of close Taiwanese business friends whom he often consults on various economic issues. The close relationship between the GMD and big business is also revealed by the fact that many influential capitalists are the donors to the Straits Exchange Foundation and serve on its board. These Taiwanese big capitalists are the ones pushing the GMD toward a more flexible mainland policy, with more economic, cultural, and civilian contacts between the two states. As a result of the influence of these big businessmen, in April 1993 the chairman of the Straits Exchange Foundation of Taiwan held the first official talk with mainland officials in Singapore. One key issue discussed at this historical meeting was Taiwan's demand for improved legal protection for its businessmen's huge and increasing investments on the mainland (FEER, May 6, 1993, pp. 11-12).

Therefore, economic integration with the mainland can be seen as a pragmatic strategy for the GMD and the capitalists to solve Taiwan's developmental bottlenecks in order to achieve national upward mobility in the capitalist world economy. However, economic integration should not be taken as a definite step toward political reunification with mainland China. Taiwan has held the status of a de facto state for the past 40 years; nonetheless, because of its small size and relatively weak political and military strength, it would not be in a strong enough bargaining position to have an equal share in the ultimate unification structure. Consequently, political reunification would not be a good deal for the Taiwanese state.

In this respect, economic integration can be interpreted as the politics of deferral, a tactic by which the GMD gains more room to maneuver vis-à-vis the mainland by not upsetting the CCP. The latter wishes to incorporate Taiwan by means of economic integration, but the former wishes to use economic integration to defer and halt the threat of political reunification with mainland China. The GMD now perceives, or at least rationalizes, a higher level of economic integration as an offensive against mainland China's reunification drive. Under the slogan of "Uniting China with the Three People's Principles," Taiwanese trade and investment with China then became a device to spread capitalism in China, speeding up the "peaceful evolution" of China and the CCP.

In mid-1991 the Taiwanese state formulated a model in its "National Unification Guideline" to counteract mainland's "One Nation, Two Systems" model. It pointed out that the timing and the methods of national reunification should first consider the benefits, rights, security, and welfare of Taiwanese residents, according to rational, peaceful, equal, and mutually beneficial principles. Taiwan proposed three stages of reunification: (a) In the short term, the first stage is mutually beneficial communication, aimed at lessening the hostility of each side. Each side should also recognize the other as a legitimate political entity. (b) In the middle term, the second stage is mutual trust and cooperation. Direct mail, direct transportation, and direct trade are to be developed. In particular, both states should jointly develop the mainland's coastal region so as to bridge the existing gap in living standards between the two sides. And both sides should assist each other by participating in international organizations. (c) In the long term, the third stage is reunification talks, which should be governed by the principles of political democracy, economic freedom, social justice, and the compliance with the wishes of people in both Taiwan and mainland China. Because the GMD defines the present period as still the first stage, it is, of course, unwilling to engage in any political reunification talks with the mainland.

Impact on Taiwanese Society

Because it was only in 1988 that Taiwan started to trade and invest with mainland China on a large scale, it is too early to draw any solid conclusions on how this economic integration may affect Taiwan's development. However, integration with the mainland should strengthen Taiwan's competitiveness in the world economy, because it provides new opportunities for Taiwanese capitalists to obtain cheap labor and raw materials, to escape environmental regulations, and to utilize their huge foreign currency reserves.

The late 1980s also saw the rise of a new "Taiwan Identity." Through the experience of mainland visits, the residents of Taiwan suddenly realized that they shared much in common: their contempt of the mainland's economic backwardness, their suspicion of the Communists' united front tactics, their pride in Taiwan's modernization, their "Taiwan compatriots" label assigned by the CCP, their common Taiwanese lifestyles, and so on. Again, trying to cash in on this newly emerging "Taiwan Identity," the mass media started to promote native Taiwanese folk songs, movies in the indigenous Taiwanese language, and magazines and trade books that discussed local Taiwanese history, literature, politics, and customs (Hsiao, 1990).

This new "Taiwan Identity" reshaped the independence movement. Before the late 1980s the Taiwan independence movement was promoted by the dissidents against the GMD. It was a political struggle waged by the ruled majority (the Taiwanese) against the ruling minority group (the mainlanders) in Taiwan. However, in the late 1980s, with the emergence of the provincial "Taiwan Identity," and with massive recruitment of Taiwanese into the GMD, the old political conflict of Taiwan-Taiwanese versus Taiwan-mainlanders became less important. As a result, the dissenting group, now united under the umbrella of the opposing DPP, needed to articulate a new political platform in order to pose a challenge to the ruling GMD. Consequently, the DPP redefined the political content of the Taiwanese independence movement: Instead of anti-GMD, it was now anti-mainland China. Thus, the Taiwan independence movement was charged with the new mission of protecting Taiwan from mainland domination. In 1991 the DPP openly endorsed the title of "Republic of Taiwan" in defiance of the GMD's "Republic of China." Later that year the DPP wrote in its party charter that the issue of Taiwan independence should be democratically decided by a referendum of all the residents of Taiwan. What the DPP wanted was to turn the Taiwanese election into an issue of independence versus unification.

The mainland question also served to divide the GMD. In the late 1980s the GMD was no longer a Leninist party enforcing democratic centralism over its members. Instead, it was split into a Taiwan wing and a "one-China" wing. The Taiwan wing, composed mostly of local Taiwanese, stressed that first priority should be given to the interests of the 21 million people in Taiwan. Though agreeing in principle that there is only one China, the Taiwan wing stressed that China had in fact been a divided nation since 1949. Thus the Taiwan wing advocated that reunification should not be rushed, and the status quo should be maintained until mutual trust and respect are established between Taiwan and mainland. However, the "one-China" wing, which consisted mostly of second-generation mainlanders, argued that such a passive attitude on reunification could lead to a permanent division. The "one-China" wing pointed out that mainland investment in recent years had created new opportunities to intensify relations and avoid this outcome (FEER, December 24-31, 1992, p. 25).

As a result of this internal factionalism, the GMD could no longer ban the DPP from pursuing an independence platform in late 1991. At first, the GMD threatened to enforce sedition laws against advocating separatism and to dismantle the DPP. Then the GMD framed the DPP's platform as advocating "hasty independence," charging that it would immediately provoke a mainland military invasion. Cooperating with these GMD scare tactics, mainland China subsequently issued a warning that "those who play with fire should know the dire consequences." This heightened tension between mainland China and Taiwan helped to bring some 71% of the 8.5 million voters to the ballot box in December 1991. The result for the DPP was a disappointing 24% of the popular vote, well below the 30% it won in the 1989 election (Hsiao & So, 1994).

However, the DPP made a comeback in the December 1992 legislature election. Although still running on the platform of Taiwan independence, the DPP also raised bread-and-butter issues, condemning the GMD for corruption, money-politics, and vote buying. Consequently, the GMD won only 53% of the population vote (the lowest on record), and the DPP scored a record high 31% (FEER, January 7, 1993, p. 14). In 1993 the emboldened DPP criticized the GMD for not including its members in the historical talk with mainland officials in Singapore; the DPP further warned that the fate of Taiwan should be determined by its 21 million residents, not by a small group of GMD members (*China News Digest*, May 11, 1993). Perhaps due to these political pressures from both inside and outside the state, the GMD has so far been reluctant to remove its ban on direct trade and investment on the mainland.

HONG KONG'S STRATEGY SINCE THE 1980s

National Separation

Before the 1980s the government of Hong Kong pursued a strategy of national separation. It was argued that the economic prosperity and political stability of Hong Kong owed much to its status as a British colony, because the colonial government was efficient and committed to economic growth. Indeed, its separation from mainland China enabled Hong Kong to avoid the economic chaos of the Great Leap Forward and the political turmoil of the Cultural Revolution. For the sake of Hong Kong's economic prosperity and political stability, therefore, the colonial government wanted to maintain the status quo of national separation from mainland China (Castells et al., 1990).

However, although Hong Kong Island and the Kowloon Peninsula were permanently ceded to Great Britain, the hinterland of Hong Kong (the New Territories) was only leased to Britain for 99 years. Because the lease of the New Territories was going to expire in 1997, capitalists were reluctant to make long-term investments in the colony. Hence, the Thatcher government was pressured to enter into negotiations with mainland China for the renewal of the lease in order to boost business confidence in the colony. However, Britain was shocked to find out that mainland China wanted to take back not just the New Territories but also Hong Kong Island and the Kowloon Peninsula.

Finally, Britain was forced to back down and drop its strategy of national separation. After Mrs. Thatcher's high-handed policy got nowhere, she asked diplomats in the Foreign Office to conduct the negotiations. These diplomats were more pragmatic, and they put the Hong Kong issue at a lower priority than the development of a long-term relationship between Britain and China (Scott, 1989). Moreover, colonialism was not popular in the 1980s, and the British colonial policy did not receive much support from the Hong Kong Chinese. Although the Hong Kong Chinese did not like the socialist mainland government, they also wanted the right to self-determination and an end to colonialism (So, 1993).

Decolonialization Policies

In late 1984 Britain signed the Joint Declaration with mainland China, agreeing to return sovereignty over Hong Kong by 1997. As such, the colonial government was immediately turned into a lame duck. No longer pursuing the strategy of national separation, the colonial government quickly adopted the strategy of decolonialization, promising democratization, the construction of infrastructure projects, and the right of abode in Great Britain to many residents in Hong Kong (Cheek-Milby & Mushkat, 1989).

First, the colonial government sped up democratization in Hong Kong. Successive plans were announced to reform the political structure and introduce more popular elements. Democratization could be interpreted as a means for the British government to rebut criticism that it had sold Hong Kong out to the Communists. If democratization was successful, the Hong Kong government would be run by the people of Hong Kong in 1997. Then the British government could claim that it had retreated in an honorable manner and returned sovereignty to the people of Hong Kong rather than to Peking.

Second, in order to boost business confidence in Hong Kong, the colonial government unveiled a proposal of massive state expenditures in new infrastructure projects. There was a US$16-billion proposal to construct a new airport with subways, railways, and an expanded container port. There was also a proposal to foster higher education by adding a new Science and Technology University, increasing the enrollment of the two universities in Hong Kong, and upgrading several private colleges to university status (Shive, 1990).

Third, after the 1989 Tiananmen Incident, the British government proposed a nationality package to grant the right of abode in Britain for 50,000 Hong Kong families. The aim of the nationality package was to provide insurance to the bureaucrats in Hong Kong so that they would remain in their posts until 1997, and it was aimed at attracting Hong Kong entrepreneurs and new middle-class professionals to Britain. Another apparent objective of the package was also to deflect claims by all locally born Hong Kong citizens who could legally claim British nationality.

However, these decolonialization policies failed to attain their goals. First, there was a setback to the democratization process. Faced with strong opposition from Hong Kong capitalists (who feared that democratization would bring about more taxes, more state regulation, and less business freedom) and the mainland government (which feared that democratization would lead to a truly autonomous local government that could not be controlled), the lame-duck colonial government suddenly withdrew its promise to have direct elections in 1988. This angered the new middle-class professionals who were the strongest supporters of the democracy movement, causing them to emigrate rapidly from Hong Kong—with the number of emigrants rising from 20,000 in 1984 to 40,000 in 1988, then to 60,000 in 1989 (Skeldon, 1990).

In addition, the proposed infrastructure projects and the nationality package also backfired because they were challenged by mainland China. These policies were perceived by the government of the mainland as British conspiracies to weaken mainland control after 1997. For instance, mainland China complained that the post-1997 Hong Kong government would be in deep financial straits if the British used up all the monetary reserves of the Hong Kong government on the expensive airport package. Furthermore, mainland China accused the British of wanting to extend its colonial influence in Hong Kong after 1997. The nationality package ensured that most high-ranking officials in Hong Kong would hold British passports after 1997, ensuring their loyalty to Britain rather than to mainland China. As a result of these policy disputes, hostility between mainland China and Great Britain has increased since 1989, serving to intensify the crisis of confidence and hasten the flight of the new middle class.

Under the shadow of the 1997 issue, however, a new actor was emerging within Hong Kong. The Chinese capitalists in Hong Kong, irrespective of their previous political affiliations, began to formulate a strategy of forging mainland connections, to enhance their economic and political power in Hong Kong (Rafferty, 1991).

Strengthening the Mainland Connections

Because the colonial government pursued a positive nonintervention policy and failed to expand scientific and research facilities in Hong Kong, and because most of the Hong Kong firms were small or medium-sized, there was little possibility of upgrading industries from labor-intensive to technology-intensive or information-intensive enterprises. Due to this structural characteristic of the economy, local manufacturing firms pursued a "walking with two legs" strategy. On one hand, at home they made full use of their flexibility in responding to volatile market trends, reducing lead time in production, and employing a peripheral workforce (outworkers and part-timers). This strategy indeed allowed the local firms to thrive in the 1980s. On the other, Hong Kong manufacturing firms also strived to develop connections in the mainland, to relocate their labor-intensive industries to the nearby Pearl River Delta. With local wages continuing to rise, only after the Hong Kong firms get access to the cheap and docile labor forces of the mainland will their labor-intensive industries remain competitive in the world economy (Chiu & Lui, unpublished; Lui & Chiu, 1993; Sit, 1989; So & Kwok, in press).

Besides geographical relocation, Hong Kong capitalists also hope to develop Hong Kong into a service center for mainland China. Having been involved in international trade for more than a century, Hong Kong is well known for its strengths in entrepot trade, financial connections, and other services. Thus, it could be developed as a facilitator or intermediary for mainland trade and investment, providing valuable channels of information to China, "serving as a contact point for China's trade, financing China's modernization, acting as a conduit for technology transfer, and providing a training ground where China can learn and practice capitalist skills in a market environment" (Sung, 1985, p. iii).

Deepening economic connections with the mainland have empowered Chinese capitalists in Hong Kong. Though a handful of "red capitalists" connected to the CCP were treated as nobodies and discriminated against by the colonial government in the past, they became VIPs of the mainland government. They were appointed to represent Hong Kong in the National People's Congress, the highest political organ of mainland China; they were asked to draft the Basic Law—the mini-constitution of Hong Kong; and they were frequently asked to be honored guests at the National Day Celebration in Peking. What is more, the CCP also extended lucrative business privileges to other Hong Kong Chinese capitalists who were not close to the mainland, owing to the consideration that their high-profile investment projects in China would serve to boost business confidence not just in the future of Hong Kong but also in the commitment of the CCP toward market reforms. As a result, there developed an "unholy" political alliance between Chinese capitalists in Hong Kong and the socialist government on the mainland (Lau, 1988).

With backing from the mainland government, the Chinese capitalists began to participate in Hong Kong politics (S-l. Wong, 1992). In the recent elections of the District Board and Legislative Council, the "Leftist" newspapers, banks, department stores, and unions mobilized their support for the election of these pro-mainland capitalists into office. Thus pro-China capitalists, together with various traditional "patriotic" organizations, emerged as new political forces along side the "liberal" middle-class professionals, challenging the hegemonic domination of the pro-British ruling class (which were usually recruited from big British corporations) in Hong Kong.

Impact on Hong Kong Society

Economically, the mainland connections promoted the economic growth of Hong Kong. Despite the shadow of 1997, Hong Kong still achieved a respectable average annual growth rate of around 7% throughout the 1980s (Asian Development Bank, 1990, p. 51). Its exports kept rising; its real estate market and stock market remained highly robust; and Hong Kong experienced not unemployment but a labor shortage, despite its export of millions of industrial jobs to mainland China.

However, economic growth in Hong Kong happened side by side with the emergence of an ethnic identity. A new political identity among the Hong Kong residents emerged: A survey shows that only 29% now regard themselves as "Chinese," with the majority identifying themselves as

"Hong Kong people" (Lee, in press). Furthermore, proud of their material wealth and urban sophistication, many Hong Kong people tend to look down on the relatively less developed mainland Chinese. Many of these "country cousins," when they first arrived in Hong Kong as migrants, frequently received rough treatment in low-paid menial jobs; those who came as representatives of mainland business organizations were often taken in by deception and dubious deals.

In addition, the prospect for national reunification with the mainland has produced a political typhoon that will be at its height in 1997. The decolonialization policies of democratization, infrastructure projects, and the nationality package produced unintended consequences of increasing tensions between Hong Kong and mainland China, a crisis of confidence, and new middle-class emigration. In magazines, newspapers, books, and speeches, members of the middle class constantly condemned the violations of human rights, the anti-intellectual line, the rampant corruption and profiteering, and the incompetence of the CCP. They predicted that a crisis will erupt in Hong Kong after the mainland takeover in 1997, because the inexperienced mainland officials will not know how to run the Hong Kong economy properly. It was this worry about mainland domination that prompted the middle-class proposal of installing a responsible, autonomous state in Hong Kong that could safeguard its existing free lifestyle. Trying to capitalize on this Hong Kong ethnic sentiment, the middle-class democrats began to campaign on an anti-mainland line in the early 1990s, and many of them won elections and were recruited to the legislative council (Chan, in press).

The tension between Hong Kong and China reached a climax with the outbreak of the 1989 Tiananmen Incident. Stirred by the zeal and courage of the Peking students, the people of Hong Kong, irrespective of class and political affiliation, mobilized to support the Chinese pro-democracy movement. At the height of it, more than 1 million people were marching on the streets of Hong Kong to demonstrate their sympathy for the students. The subsequent military crackdown disheartened many Hong Kong people and sparked another wave of emigration. Although the CCP, through its "unholy alliance" with the Chinese capitalists, has since rebuilt a solid organizational base in Hong Kong, the local people have become highly suspicious of China's so-called commitment to Hong Kong's autonomous self-government and civil liberties after 1997.

Just when the memories of Tiananmen began to fade, the coming of Chris Patten, the former chairman of the British Conservative Party, as Hong Kong's new governor, triggered off another political crisis. Patten brought with him a comprehensive package of political reform, but the Chinese government steadfastly opposed it, seeing it as a British conspiracy to erode China's sovereign authority over Hong Kong after 1997 (Ching, 1993). A series of protracted negotiations between the British and Chinese governments have so far failed to resolve the differences between them, and there seems to be little sign that a smooth political transition to 1997 will be realized (So, in press).

THE FUTURE OF THE
CHINESE NATIONAL REUNIFICATION PROJECT

The prospects for the national reunification project among the three Chinese states are highly uncertain, because it produced significant political divisions within mainland China, Taiwan, and Hong Kong. On the mainland, economic integration led to regional differentiation, democratization, and serious policy conflicts within the CCP. In Taiwan, the prospect for political reunification deepened the division between the right-wing GMD conservatives and the radical Taiwan independence faction. In Hong Kong, the 1997 issue led to massive emigration and a crisis of confidence.

In addition, the prospect for a unified Chinese triangle is endangered by the political rivalries among mainland China, Taiwan, and Hong Kong. Mainland China is always suspicious of the GMD (which may promote Taiwan's independence) and the Hong Kong government (which may lay the groundwork for the continuation of British rule after 1997). On the other hand, the people of Taiwan and Hong Kong tend to distrust the mainland's promise of establishing highly autonomous special administrative zones after national reunification. Therefore, the Taiwanese government has been reluctant to enter into any substantial negotiations with the mainland over national reunification, and the new middle class in Hong Kong has emigrated in protest of the mainland takeover.

Nevertheless, from an economic viewpoint, the national reunification project among the three Chinese states is mutually beneficial and has greatly enhanced the competitiveness of the mainland, Taiwan, and Hong Kong in the world economy. On one hand, mainland China helped solve the developmental problems of Taiwan and Hong Kong by providing them with cheap labor, resources, and investment opportunities. On the other, Taiwan and Hong Kong have contributed to mainland development by providing employment opportunities, market stimuli to local enterprises, and vital information and contacts for reentering the world market. In the late 1980s, state managers of mainland China successfully developed close business partnerships with the capitalists of Hong Kong and Taiwan, and this "unholy alliance" will most likely continue toward the next century.

If mainland China, Taiwan, and Hong Kong are not merely political rivals but also significant economic partners, what then is the future of the Chinese national reunification project? It seems that there are two possible scenarios.

First, there is the political chaos scenario, which predicts that political rivalries among mainland China, Taiwan, and Hong Kong will be intensified in the 1990s. As a result, there will be not only a political crisis but also an economic crisis in Hong Kong as 1997 approaches. Seeing what mainland China is doing to the Hong Kong economy, the Taiwanese state will be determined to slow the outflow of capital to the mainland. Subsequently, political rivalry will threaten the prospect for stronger economic integration among the three Chinese states.

Second, there is the economic prosperity scenario, which predicts that economic integration among mainland China, Taiwan, and Hong Kong will be intensified in the 1990s. As a result, there will not only be an economic boom in the three Chinese states, but their political hostility against each another will substantially subside. Hong Kong's economy will continue its rapid economic growth rate after 1997. Seeing that mainland China has not harmed Hong Kong, the state in Taiwan will be willing to hasten the outflow of capital to the mainland. Subsequently, stronger economic ties will lay the foundation for national negotiation talks between mainland China and Taiwan in the 1st decade of the 21st century.

From a world-system angle, if we locate the Chinese triangle in the wider context of the world economy, it seems that national economic integration is the best strategy for the three Chinese states to not only remain competitive in the world market but also overcome being squeezed in the middle by the core's protectionism and the periphery's intense competition. Therefore, although the political chaos scenario may occupy newspaper headlines in the short run, structural dynamics in the world economy will likely induce the three Chinese states, classes, and people to favor the economic prosperity scenario in the long run. If economic integration of the Chinese triangle should continue toward the next century, this reunification project may transform the Chinese nation into a new regional economic power, and it may further speed up the transformation of East Asia into a new epicenter of capital accumulation in the world economy.

11. Conclusion

Compared to that of other regions, East Asian development has possessed the following distinctive features since the region's incorporation into the capitalist world economy in the 19th century. First, East Asia is the only region to produce a non-European state (Japan) that not only escaped colonization but also became an economic power challenging U.S. hegemony. Second, the largest state in East Asia (China) not only successfully transformed itself from an Asian empire to a Communist state but also attained rapid industrialization in the late 20th century. Third, East Asia is the only region where nation-states (Mainland China and Taiwan; South Korea and North Korea) still divide along old Cold War lines, thus prompting the pressing problem of national reunification. Finally, in just a half century, the entire East Asian region has attained national upward mobility. Not only are Taiwan, South Korea, and Hong Kong transformed into newly industrializing economies (NIEs), but the entire region has also turned into an economic powerhouse in the world economy.

This book attempts to explain this peculiar pattern of East Asian development, namely, Japanese corization, Chinese communism, NIEs' industrialization, hegemonic rivalry, and regional integration. Current theories of East Asian development—the neoclassical economic perspective, the cultural perspective, the statist perspective, and the dependency perspective—are unable to provide a satisfactory account explaining the above-cited peculiar pattern of East Asian development. Although neoclassical economists highlight the crucial role played by market and private enterprises; although culturists bring out the impact of Confucianism on education, family enterprises, and corporate management; although the statist perspective underscores the strategic industrial policies of the developmental state; and although the dependency perspective reveals the dark side and the crises of East Asian industrialization, these four perspectives nevertheless tend to be unidisciplinary and adopt short historical time spans. In addition, these four perspectives generally fail to study the socialist states in East Asia, seldom bring world-systems dynamics into their analysis, overlook the historical legacy of pre-World War II development, and neglect to address how common people reacted to the changing paths of East Asian development.

This book adopts a world-systems analysis to interpret the peculiar path of East Asian development. It argues that world-systems analysis provides a methodological break with 19th-century social science inquiry by offering a new mode of thinking that stresses large-scale, long-term, and holistic (the complex interplay of politics, economics, and culture) methodology. In addition, world-systems analysis formulates many innovative concepts, such as incorporation, semiperiphery, regionalization, socialist state withdrawal and reintegration, hegemony and rivalry, and antisystemic movements, to examine the structure and dynamics of the capitalist world economy. Building upon the studies of researchers close to the world-systems school (Arrighi et al., 1993; Cumings, 1987; Gereffi, 1992; McMichael, 1987), this book argues that East Asian development since the 19th century can best be examined through the historical periodization of incorporation, regionalization, ascent, and centrality.

First of all, the decline of the Chinese empire and the great escape of Japan from colonization were greatly related to the mode of market incorporation of East Asia into the capitalist world economy in the mid-19th century. Before that time, China was able to resist incorporation because of Western awe of the Chinese empire, and a strong alliance between the Chinese state and its landed upper class. It took Great Britain's waging the Opium War in 1839 to incorporate East Asia into the world economy. Great Britain was the most likely agency because it was the hegemon during this period, with a virtual monopoly in industrial production and military technology. Promoting a free trade doctrine, Great Britain was more interested in opening China for trade and investment than for territorial annexation. Nevertheless, after losing the Opium War, the Chinese Qing government was forced to pay indemnities, cede Hong Kong, and open treaty ports for foreign trade. The relocation of foreign penetration from South China to Central China further triggered the Taiping Rebellion, which almost tore the Chinese empire apart in the 1850s. This mode of Chinese incorporation into the world economy greatly alarmed the young samurai bureaucrats in early Meiji Japan. If the great Chinese empire could not defend itself from foreign invasion, how could Japan avoid such a fate? In response to this threat of foreign colonialism, the young samurai quickly evoked the emperor symbol, merged Confucianism with Shintoism, and promoted far-ranging Meiji reforms to restructure the state and the economy. In retrospect, Japan benefited immensely from its geopolitical position in East Asia. Because Japan was the farthest removed from the reach of the great European naval powers, the core states' attention was drawn to China as they found Japan's resources or market unattractive. As a result, Japan was given breathing space in which to work out the complications of the Meiji reforms, and eventually became incorporated into the world economy as a semiperiphery rather than as a colony/periphery of the core states.

After incorporation, the next phase of East Asian development was regionalization. By the late 19th century, Great Britain was no longer a hegemon, as its industrial and military supremacy were increasingly challenged by rival core powers. In order to overcome stagnation in the world economy, core states competed with one another for new colonies and investment rights in the periphery. Observing this global trend toward colonialism, the Japanese state developed a regionalization strategy of empire-building in East Asia to overcome the constraints of its small domestic market and poor resources. Disguised through the ideology of anti-Western-imperialist Pan-Asianism, Japan developed a regionalization strategy of empire-building. After Japan won the Sino-Japanese War in 1894, its economy got a boost from the huge Chinese indemnity as well as from its colonization of Korea and Taiwan. On the other hand, the war led to the scramble for concessions in China, the weakening of the Chinese economy, the retreat of Confucianism, and finally the collapse of the Chinese empire. Japan's regional dominance, however, was challenged by the United States—the rising hegemon of the world economy—in the early 20th century. The United States' new hegemonic ideology of democracy led to a brief era of Taisho democracy in Japan and a short civilian rule in Korea and Taiwan; and it even allowed a unified Guomindang (GMD) regime to emerge in China. The 1930s global depression and subsequent dislocations in Japan's economy nevertheless prompted Japan to move toward ultranationalism, end the modest liberal reforms in its colonies, and invade Manchuria, mainland China, and Southeast Asia, leading to a head-on confrontation with the United States. Japan was eventually defeated in World War II, followed by the U.S. Occupation in the late 1940s. In China, on the other hand, the war stripped bare the contradictions of the GMD regime, aggravated the peasant problem in the countryside, enhanced the nationalist calling of the Communists, and finally sped up the triumph of the antisystemic Communist movement.

After World War II the world economy was in an upward phase, and the United States was the hegemon during this period. The main concern of the United States toward East Asia in the late 1940s was how to prevent the further spread of communism from mainland China to other parts of the region. This specific geopolitical context led to a polarized region and three different paths of ascent—socialist semiperiphery, capitalist core, and capitalist semiperiphery—in East Asia. First, mainland China, after building up a strong Leninist party-state, pursued a mercantilist strategy of heavy industrialization. However, after the Sino-Soviet dispute and the intensification of the Cold War, mainland China shifted to a strategy of revolutionary socialism. At the height of the Cultural Revolution, the ideology of Maoism called for self-reliance, mass mobilization, rural development, and absolute egalitarianism.

This Communist Revolution had a profound impact on the capitalist development of other East Asian states. In order to contain the spread of communism, the United States not only reversed its postwar Occupation policies in Japan but also started to build Japan up as its junior partner in East Asia. The United States' special concessions to Japan—such as procurement during the Korean War, U.S. aid, access to U.S. markets, and the relief of the burden of defense—were instrumental in promoting Japan's economic success. Japan's developmental state and capitalist class seized this opportunity, as well as the favorable postwar upward turn of the world economy, to promote state industrial and financial policies; incorporate labor into enterprise unionism; install an ideology of consensus, paternalism, and sexism; and engage in transborder expansion to speed up the corization of Japan. This transborder expansion of Japan, together with special U.S. concessions and the influx of refugee capital and labor from mainland China, laid the foundation for the semiperipheral ascent of Hong Kong, South Korea, and Taiwan. Although they vary in state and industrial structure, the three NIEs evoked sexism and GNPism to facilitate the social subordination of labor, to keep their labor-intensive industries competitive in the world market. The economic success of Japan and the NIEs, in turn, lured mainland China back to pursue a reintegration strategy, in the late 1970s, to achieve upward mobility in the world economy.

By the mid-1970s the golden era of postwar economic expansion came to an end and the United States became a declining hegemon. It was during this period that the East Asia region was turned into a new epicenter of capital accumulation in the world economy. This can be seen from the fact that Japan had grown from a regional to a global economic power, challenging the hegemony of the United States. Technologically, Japan's high-tech sectors were closing up their gaps with the United States, and Japanese manufacturers outsold their American competitors. As a result, Japan accumulated a sizable trade surplus and became the largest creditor of the world. Japan also started to play a leadership role in global affairs, and its flying-geese model of development began to attract followers from the peripheries. In response, the United States imposed protectionist measures against Japanese imports, sought to open up the Japanese market for U.S. imports, and forced the Japanese yen to appreciate, and the U.S. mass media started Japan-bashing. Another event with implications for the centrality of the East Asian region is the Chinese national unification project. Economic integration among the three Chinese semiperipheries proceeded rapidly in the 1980s as mainland China, Taiwan, and Hong Kong faced bottlenecks in their economic growth. The massive relocation of labor-intensive industries from Taiwan and Hong Kong to mainland China led to changing industrial structures, democratization, and new ethnic and national identities. Should this national unification succeed, the Chinese triangle of mainland China-Taiwan-Hong Kong may further speed up the centrality of East Asia in global capital accumulation.

In sum, East Asia since the 19th century has gone through phases of incorporation, regionalization, ascent, and centrality in the capitalist world economy. What, then, is the future of the East Asian region? Will the present trends of economic growth and regionalization continue? Will East Asia move from centrality to a new phase of hegemony?

EAST ASIA IN THE 21ST CENTURY

Will Economic Growth Continue?

In the early 1990s there are indicators that the strong economic growth of East Asia may come to an end. First, the pace of economic growth has slackened in the NIEs. The maturity of these NIEs' economies would make it impossible to duplicate or better the high-speed growth of the previous decades. Second, Japan has recently experienced its longest recession since World War II. The burst of the "bubble economy" in the late 1980s caused a major crisis in the Japanese financial system and a slump in domestic demand. Third, the surge of protectionism in the West, the consolidation of the European Community as an economic bloc, and the formation of NAFTA spelled trouble for the East Asian region, because trade with the West still contributed significantly to the region's economic growth. Finally, the United States in the early 1990s threatened not to renew China's most-favored-nation status because of its poor human rights record.

However, there were also signs of revitalization of the East Asian economy as the region moved toward the 21st century. First, the NIEs began to relocate their labor-intensive industries outward, hoping to capitalize on lower production costs abroad. Subsequently, NIEs' economic structures were upgraded to high-tech and capital-intensive industries. Domestic demand also played a more significant role in promoting economic growth, especially in the larger economies of Japan, Taiwan, and South Korea. The tertiary service and financial sectors also figured more prominently in the distribution of national products.

Second, there was the rapid economic growth of mainland China and the ASEAN countries. China, in particular, with its population of 1 billion and a fledgling middle class, enjoyed the potential for keeping Japan and the NIEs' exports soaring to higher levels. For example, by 1994, China should overtake the United States as Hong Kong's main market for the first time (FEER, December 30, 1993). In addition, China's domestic consumer demand burgeoned as its exports continued to grow; and Chinese currency (Renmenbi) was made convertible at the beginning of 1994. Furthermore, China applied for membership in GATT, signifying the accelerated integration of the Chinese economy into the capitalist world economy. In the future, China may become the locus of economic dynamism of the East Asian region (Jones et al., 1993).

Third, because the world economy has been in a downward phase for almost 3 decades, an upward phase should soon occur as East Asia moves toward the 21st century. Though this new upward phase may not be as strong as that in the aftermath of World War II, it still should bring the recovery of the American and European economies. As such, it may create another wave of export booms for the East Asian economies.

Given the East Asian region's industrial relocation and upgrading, the growing Chinese economy, and the upward phase of the world economy, East Asia's economic growth will probably continue in the next century. As such, will East Asia move into a new phase of hegemony?

Toward East Asian Hegemony?

In order to be hegemonic, it is necessary to set up a grand area, in which states within that area orient themselves toward the core hegemon. Because Japan has not developed the military strength to conquer other parts of the world, it needs to develop the East Asian region as its grand area if it wants to be the next hegemon of the world economy. By the 1980s Japan had already emerged as a regional economic power in East Asia. As discussed in Chapter 10, Japan has become the largest exporter to East Asian states, and its companies also dominate the exports from the East Asian states to Japan. In terms of investment and foreign aid, Japanese corporate investment in the Asia-Pacific region amounts to nearly twice the investment of American companies.

Nevertheless, judging from the Japanese effort toward East Asian regionalization in the past 2 decades, the prospects for moving East Asia into a new phase of hegemony are not bright. First, the Japanese state has yet to make a firm commitment toward the project of hegemony. After a relatively successful peacekeeping mission in Cambodia, the Japanese government remains divided over assuming more international responsibilities, especially on the matter of whether to commit a Japanese peacekeeping force in former Yugoslavia. This is because pacifism remains a powerful current in Japanese domestic politics after World War II. In addition, the Japanese state is still unwilling to open up its domestic market to its East Asian neighbors. Even the recent partial (and temporary, according to the Japanese government) liberalization of rice imports has been sharply criticized by Japanese politicians. The recent slowdown in the economy also reduced the ability and willingness of the Japanese government and capitalists to open up the domestic market further to consumer imports from Asia.

Second, there is the historical legacy of the Japanese empire. Memories from World War II make it difficult for other East Asian countries to accept Japan's hegemony. Mainland China, for instance, remains highly skeptical of the revision of Japanese textbooks on the subject of World War II history; subregional integration among mainland China, Taiwan, and Hong Kong competes with Japan for regional dominance. Moreover, the ASEAN states are reluctant to join any Asian regional organization that calls for sole Japanese leadership.

Third, the United States continues to try to suppress Japan's hegemonic emergence. Despite Japan's strong economic presence in Asia, the region is still under the dual economic domination of the United States and Japan and is still held by a unilateral American security network. The United States formed the APEC organization as a means of retaining its leadership role in the East Asia region; this explains why the Japanese government has been, so far, reluctant to support APEC wholeheartedly. What is more, the United States will continue to resort to trade and financial measures to slow down Japan's hegemonic advance. For example, the United States might want to appreciate the yen still further and install more fair-trade measures in Japan.

However, instead of heading toward outright confrontation, the United States and Japan will probably work out some sort of power-sharing arrangement. Due to significant U.S.-Japanese cross-investment in high-tech industries, and due to their strategic geopolitical alliance, the United States and Japan will continue to be political allies in the midst of severe economic competition. As such, Japan is unlikely to overtake the United States as the next hegemon in the world economy in the near future.

What seems more likely to happen in the next decade, then, is the continuation of the present trend toward interregional economic integration among Japan, mainland China, and the NIEs on one hand, and the Southeast Asian states on the other. So, by the early 21st century, researchers may speak of a Greater East Asia region that links East and Southeast Asian states together economically.

From a theoretical standpoint, what are the merits of the above interpretation of East Asian development over more traditional development theories in the past 2 centuries?

THEORETICAL REPRISE

World-systems analysis has been credited for providing a new research agenda to examine the capitalist world economy at a global level. Focusing on the East Asian region, this book shows that world-systems analysis can be applied to examine regional dynamics as well. Using the large-scale, holistic, and long-time span heuristic devices of world-systems analysis, this book highlights the crucial role played by geopolitics in East Asian development.

Toward a Geopolitical Explanation

In terms of large-scale analysis, this book studies interstate dynamics in the East Asian region. Due to the geopolitics of their strategic locations in East Asia, China (mainland China, Taiwan, and Hong Kong), Japan, and Korea (North Korea and South Korea) greatly influenced one another's development. In the mid-19th century, Japan was able to escape from colonization largely because it was far away from European trade routes, and because the core states were attracted to the huge Chinese hinterland. The rise of Japan in the early 20th century, in return, led to the colonization of South Korea and Taiwan as well as the acceleration of the Communist Revolution's triumph in mainland China. Then, the 1949 Chinese Communist Revolution caused the United States to reverse its Japanese Occupation policy so as to build up its former enemy as a junior partner in dominating East Asia. The corization of Japan and the transborder expansion of its industries in the early 1970s accelerated the economic growth of Hong Kong, South Korea, and Taiwan, which, in turn, prompted mainland China to reenter the capitalist world economy.

Through holistic analysis, this book shows that geopolitics is often intertwined with emerging cultural constructs and changing regional dynamics. For instance, when Japan started to develop a regionalization project to conquer East Asia in the early 20th century, there emerged a robust nationalist ideology in the Japanese colonies in reaction to the ideology of anti-imperialist Pan-Asianism in Japan proper. When mainland China was forced to withdraw from the capitalist world economy due to the Cold War in the mid-20th century, Maoism and revolutionary socialism were at their height, preaching selflessness, mass mobilization, and self-reliance. And when mainland China pushed for national reunification in the 1980s and the 1990s, new ethnic identities quickly arose among the residents of Taiwan and Hong Kong, revealing their political distrust of the reunification project.

Through long-term analysis, this book shows that contemporary East Asia must be understood in terms of its pre-World War II geopolitical development. For instance, the rapid growth of Japanese heavy industry in the 1960s and 1970s had historical origins in the wartime munitions industry in the 1930s and 1940s. Links between big Japanese factories and small businesses that developed in the munitions industry became the basis for the postwar subcontracting system. Administrative guidance by government ministries—a fundamental characteristic of the postwar developmental state—was a legacy of wartime controls. As for mainland China, its rapid economic development in the late 20th century seems less surprising, given the fact that it experienced such rapid economic growth during the 2 decades before 1937. Had China not gone through the world depression and World War II, it might have escaped the trend toward communism and become a capitalist semiperiphery by the mid-20th century. As for South Korea, its robust *minjung* movement owes much to the strong nationalist resistance movement against Japanese colonial rule in the early 20th century. As Koo (1993, p. 237) points out, "Antistatism became a deeply ingrained Korean intellectual orientation during this period, and this antistatist tradition has continued."

Contextualizing Current Theories

The above emphasis on geopolitics factors, needless to say, is not aimed at refuting entirely the current economic, cultural, statist, and dependency perspectives in the literature on East Asian development. Obviously, market and private enterprises, Confucianism and corporate management, the developmental state, and the dark side of dependent development are all important factors of East Asian development. What this book hopes to contribute, however, is the often-neglected geopolitical context necessary for reinterpreting these important factors.

First, although developmental states were instrumental in promoting industrialization in South Korea and Taiwan, they owed much to the repressive and exclusive policies of the Japanese colonial governments in the early decades of the 20th century, to the purging of leftist forces in South Korea and local Taiwanese elites in the late 1940s, to hyper-militarism during the Cold War, as well as to the strong influence of American advisers in the 1950s.

Second, although market and private enterprises provided the dynamics for East Asian exports, their existence depended very much on special privileges granted to the East Asian states by the United States to get access to their market, on the alliance for profit between the South Korean state and the *chaebols*, on the monopolization of the state sector by the GMD in Taiwan, and on the influx of refugee entrepreneurs into Hong Kong.

Third, although Confucianism was a common cultural trait in the East Asian region, it was fused with Japanese Shintoism in the late 19th century, severely criticized during the 1919 May Fourth Movement and the Chinese Cultural Revolution in the 1960s, evoked in Japan in the 1950s when the *zaibatsu* faced serious challenges from the labor movement, and existed side by side with sexism, GNPism, anticommunism, the Three People's Principles, and the refugee mentality in the NIEs.

Finally, although East Asian economic growth did indeed have a dark side, the NIEs were able to overcome their dependency and move into the semiperipheral zone, largely because of the upward phase of the world economy and generous U.S. aid and advice in the 1950s, the influx of foreign earnings into the NIEs during the Vietnam War, the NIEs' privileged access to the U.S. market in the 1960s, and the cheap credits offered by U.S. banks and the transborder expansion of the Japanese subcontracting system in the 1970s.

Through its emphasis on geopolitical factors, this book not only has contributed to supplementing the current theories of East Asian development, but also enriches world-systems analysis.

Enriching World-Systems Analysis

World-systems analysis has been accused of overstressing external factors at the expense of internal factors, presenting an inaccurate picture of passive victims in the peripheries, and formulating a reified concept of the world system. However, focusing on geopolitics, antisystemic movements, and the large-scale, long-term, and holistic methodology enables this book to overcome these criticisms.

First, this book helps resolve the debate on external versus internal factors. Tracing the long-term transformation of East Asia over the past 2 centuries, this book points out that certain external factors in a *previous* phase of development became *internal* factors in the present phase of development. For instance, this sedimentation of external factors can be illustrated by the fact that although the overdeveloped state in colonial Korea and Taiwan was externally imposed by Japan in the early 20th century, this same overdeveloped state became an internal factor in promoting rapid economic development in postwar South Korea and Taiwan. In this respect, instead of artificially separating external factors here and internal factors there, a more fruitful approach would be to trace the internalization of external forces and the externalization of internal forces through a long-term historical analysis.

Second, by highlighting the embeddedness of antisystemic movements in geopolitics, this book shows that the people in East Asia are not merely passive victims of the world economy. For example, the Chinese landed upper class and the peasantry invoked antiforeign sentiment to prevent the British from entering Canton and South China in the early 19th century; the young samurai revived the emperor symbol and Shintoism to unite Japan against foreign invasion in the mid-19th century; Korean students and intellectuals united to wage a resistance movement against Japanese colonial rule in the early 20th century; the Red Guards harnessed Maoism during the Cultural Revolution to prevent the restoration of capitalism in mainland China; and a new generation of intellectuals in Taiwan used the spirit of ethnic identity, in the 1970s, to challenge the authoritarianism of the GMD. These antisystemic movements may not have succeeded, their ideals may have been fantasies, and their proponents may even have later turned into defenders of the world economy, but still they represented historical efforts through which the East Asian people rose up as human agency and asserted themselves in times of rapid social change caused by incorporation into the capitalist world economy. In this respect, this book contends that the latest world-systems analysis includes the study of antisystemic movements so that history from the top down is studied interactively with history from the bottom up.

Third, this book highlights the salience of *regional analysis* as the interface between global and national analysis. It shows that the regional context is the medium through which world-system dynamics become articulated in the form of geopolitics, which in turn shape national development. For example, the global dynamics of the world depression and World War II manifested themselves in East Asia as the dislocation of the Japanese economy, the spread of ultranationalism and militarism in Japan proper, the reversal of democratic reforms in the Japanese colonies, the weakening of the economy and GMD rule, and the rise of Maoism amidst rural bankruptcy in China. On the other hand, through the regional context, the nation-state and subnational forces articulate themselves before transcending into global dynamics. For example, after the Communists gained control over rural China in the early 1940s, captured the Chinese state in the late 1940s, and spread to other regions in East Asia in the 1950s and 1960s, East Asian revolutionary socialism became a worldwide antisystemic movement challenging U.S. hegemonic domination in the postwar era. In this respect, this book illustrates that the capitalist world economy, rather than being a reified entity, worked through the geopolitics of East Asia to shape the development of mainland China, Japan, South Korea, North Korea, Taiwan, and Hong Kong.

Finally, this book can be considered a pioneer study of regional development in the capitalist world economy. We hope that our approach to these issues on East Asia will encourage future researchers to apply world-systems analysis to the study of other regional dynamics. To attain this goal, we need to apply the large-scale, long-term, and holistic heuristic devices of world-systems analysis, as well as emphasize the crucial role played by geopolitics in regional development. Only when there are enough studies along this line can we accumulate sufficient knowledge about the richness and complexity of regional dynamics, and only then can we hope to build theories of regional development in the capitalist world economy.

References

Abegglen, J. (1973). *Management and worker: The Japanese solution.* Tokyo: Kodansha International.

Abu-Lughod, J. L. (1989). *Before European hegemony: The world system AD 1250-1350.* New York: Oxford University Press.

Akita, G. (1992). The Meiji restoration. In M. Borthwick (Ed.), *Pacific century* (pp. 127-140). Boulder, CO: Westview.

Allen, G. C. (1962). *A short economic history of modern Japan.* New York: Praeger.

Allen, G. C. (1981). *The Japanese economy.* New York: St. Martin's Press.

Allen, G. C., & Donnithorne, A. G. (1954). *Western enterprise in Far Eastern economic development.* London: Allen & Unwin.

Amsden, A. (1989). *Asia's next giant: South Korea and late industrialization.* New York: Oxford University Press.

Arrighi, G. (1990). The three hegemonies of historical capitalism. *Review, 8,* 365-408.

Arrighi, G. (1991). World income inequalities and the future of socialism. *New Left Review, 189,* 39-65.

Arrighi, G. (1994a). *The long twentieth century.* London: Verso.

Arrighi, G. (1994b, October 6-8). *The rise of East Asia: World-system and regional aspects.* Paper prepared for the conference "L'economia mondiale in transformazione," Rome.

Arrighi, G., Ikeda, S., & Irwan, A. (1993). The rise of East Asia: One miracle or many? In R. A. Palat (Ed.), *Pacific-Asia and the future of the world-system* (pp. 41-65). Westport, CT: Greenwood.

Asian Development Bank. (1990). *Asian development outlook.* Manila: Author.

Awanohara, S. (1989). Japan and East Asia: Toward a new division of labor. *The Pacific Review, 2*(3), 198-208.

Awanohara, S. (1991, December 5). And the winner is . . . *Far Eastern Economic Review,* 46-47.

Azumi, K. (1974). Japanese society. In A. Tiedemann (Ed.), *An introduction to Japanese civilization* (pp. 515-535). New York: D. C. Heath.

Balassa, B. (1988). The lessons of East Asian development: An overview. *Economic Development and Cultural Change, 36* (third supp.), S273-S290.

Bank of Korea. (1962). *Monthly statistical review.*

Banister, T. R. (1931). *A history of the external trade of China, 1834-1881.* Shanghai: Inspector General of Chinese Customs.

Battat, J. (1991, March 26-28). *DFI in China in the 1980s and prospects for the 1990s within the Asian context.* Paper presented at the Conference on Foreign Direct Investment in Asia and the Pacific in the 1990s, East-West Center.

Beasley, W. G. (1963). *The modern history of Japan.* New York: Preager.

Beasley, W. G. (1987). *Japanese imperialism: 1984-1945.* Oxford, UK: Clarendon.

Bello, W., & Rosenfeld, S. (1990). Dragons in distress: The crisis of the NICs. *World Policy Journal, 7,* 431-468.

Bello, W., & Rosenfeld, S. (1992). *Dragons in distress: Asia's miracle economies in crisis* (3rd rev. ed.). San Francisco: Institute for Food and Development Policy.

Berger, P. (1986). *The capitalist revolution.* New York: Basic Books.

Bergesen, A. (1982). Economic crisis and merger movements: 1880's Britain and 1980's United States. In E. Friedman (Ed.), *Ascent and decline in the world-system* (pp. 27-40). Beverly Hills, CA: Sage.

Bergesen, A. (1992). Godzilla, Durkheim, and the world-system. *Humbolt Journal of Social Relations, 18,* 195-216.

Bhagwati, J. (1991). *Political economy and international economics.* Cambridge: Massachusetts Institute of Technology Press.

Bian, Y. (1994). *Work and inequality in urban China.* Albany: State University of New York Press.

Bianco, L. (1971). *Origins of Chinese revolution, 1915-1949.* Stanford, CA: Stanford University Press.

Blecher, M. (1986). *China: Politics, economics and society.* London: Lynne Rienner.

Blomstrom, M., & Hettne, B. (1984). *Development theory in transition.* London: Zed.

Boltho, A. (1975). *Japan: An economic survey.* Oxford, UK: Oxford University Press.

Borden, W. S. (1984). *The Pacific alliance.* Madison: University of Wisconsin Press.

Borthwick, M. (Ed.). (1992). *Pacific century: The emergence of modern Pacific Asia.* Boulder, CO: Westview.

Borton, H. (1938). *Peasant uprisings in Japan of the Tokugawa period.* Tokyo: Transactions of the Asiatic Society of Japan.

Bowen, R. W. (1980). *Rebellion and democracy in Meiji Japan: A study of commoners in the popular rights movement.* Berkeley: University of California Press.

Brenner, R. (1977). The origins of capitalist development: A critique of neo-Smithian Marxism. *New Left Review, 104,* 25-92.

Brown, S. (1979). The Ewo filature: A study in the transfer of technology to China in the nineteenth century. *Technology and Culture, 20,* 550-568.

Brudnoy, D. (1970). Japan's experiment in Korea. *Monumenta Nipponica, 25,* 172-174.

Calder, K. (1992). The United States-Japan relationship: A post-cold war future. *The Pacific Review, 5*(2), 125-134.

Cardoso, F. (1973). Associated-dependent development: Theoretical and practical implications. In A. Stephen (Ed.), *Authoritarian Brazil* (pp. 142-176). New Haven, CT: Yale University Press.

Cardoso, F. H., & Faletto, E. (1979). *Dependency and development in Latin America.* Berkeley: University of California Press.

Castells, M., Goh, L., & Kwok, R.Y-W. (1990). *The Shek Kip Mei syndrome: Economic development and public housing in Hong Kong and Singapore.* London: Pion.

Cathie, J. (1989). *Food aid and industrialization.* Aldershot, UK: Avebury.

Chan, M. K. (in press). All in the family: The Hong Kong-Guangdong link in historical perspective. In R.W-Y. Kwok & A. Y. So (Eds.), *The Hong Kong-Guangdong link: Partnership in flux*. Armonk, NY: M. E. Sharpe.

Chang C-l. (1955). *The Chinese gentry*. Seattle: University of Washington Press.

Chang C-l. (1962). *The income of the Chinese gentry*. Seattle: University of Washington Press.

Chang, Y-S. (1971). Colonialism as planned change: The Korean case. *Modern Asian Studies, 5,* 161-186.

Chase-Dunn, C. (1982). *Socialist states in the world-system*. Beverly Hills, CA: Sage.

Chase-Dunn, C. (1989). *Global formation: Structures of the world-economy*. Cambridge, UK: Basil Blackwell.

Chase-Dunn, C. (1990). Resistance to imperialism: Semiperipheral actors. *Review, 13,* 1-31.

Cheek-Milby, K., & Mushkat, M. (1989). *Hong Kong: The challenge of transformation*. Hong Kong: University of Hong Kong, Centre of Asian Studies.

Chen, E.K.Y. (1980). The economic setting. In D. Lethbridge (Ed.), *The business environment in Hong Kong* (pp.1-50). Hong Kong: Oxford University Press.

Chen, G. (1982). The reform movement among intellectuals in Taiwan since 1970. *Bulletin of Concerned Asian Scholars, 14*(3), 32-47.

Chen, H-s. (1936). *Landlord and peasant in China*. New York: International Publishers.

Chen, X. (1993). China's growing integration with the Asia-Pacific economy. In *What is in a rim? Critical perspectives on the Pacific region idea* (pp. 89-119). Boulder, CO: Westview.

Cheng, T-j. (1989). Democratizing the quasi-Leninist GMD regime in Taiwan. *World Politics, 41,* 471-499.

China News Digest. [News Global, available on internet.]

The Chinese Repository. (1832-1851). Volumes 1-20. Canton.

Ching, F. (1993). Politics, politicians and political parties. In P-k. Choi & L-s. Ho (Eds.), *The other Hong Kong report 1993* (pp. 23-39). Hong Kong: Chinese University Press.

Chiu, S.W.K. (1992). *The state and the financing of industrialization in East Asia*. Unpublished doctoral dissertation, Princeton University, NJ.

Chiu, S.W.K. (in press). The changing world order and the East Asian newly industrialized countries. In D. Jacobson (Ed.), *Old nations, new world: The evolution of a new world order*. Boulder, CO: Westview.

Chiu, S.W.K., & Lui, T-L. (unpublished). Hong Kong: Unorganized industrialism. In G. L. Clark & W. B. Kim (Eds.), *Asian NIEs and the global economy*.

Cho, L-J. (1994). Culture, institutions, and economic development in East-Asia. In L-J. Cho & Y-H. Kim (Eds.), *Korea's political economy* (pp. 3-41). Boulder, CO: Westview.

Choi, J. J. (1989). *Labor and the authoritarian state: Labor unions in South Korean manufacturing industries, 1961-1980*. Seoul: Korea University Press.

Chossudovsky, M. (1986). *Towards capitalist restoration? Chinese socialism after Mao*. New York: St. Martin's Press.

Cohen, P. A. (1963). *China and Christianity*. Cambridge, MA: Harvard University Press.

Cohen, P. A. (1970). Ch'ing China: Confrontation with the west, 1850-1900. In J. B. Crowley (Ed.), *Modern East Asia* (pp. 29-61). New York: Harcourt Brace World.

Consular Report. (1886). Volume 20. Washington, DC: Government Printing Office.

Consular Report. (1889). Volume 23. Washington, DC: Government Printing Office.

Craig, A. M. (1961). *Choshu in the Meiji restoration*. Cambridge, MA: Harvard University Press.

Crone, D. (1992). The politics of emerging Pacific cooperation. *Pacific Affairs, 65,* 50-83.

Cronin, R. (1992). *Japan, the United States, and prospects for the Asia-Pacific century.* New York: St. Martin's Press.

Crowley, J. (1966). From closed door to empire. In *Modern Japanese leadership: Transition and change* (pp. 267-273). Tucson: University of Arizona Press.

Crowley, J. (1970). A new deal for Japan and Asia. In J. Crowley (Ed.), *Modern East Asia* (pp. 235-264). New York: Harcourt.

Cumings, B. (1984). The legacy of Japanese colonialism in Korea. In R. Myers & M. Peattie (Eds.), *The Japanese colonial empire* (pp. 478-496). Princeton, NJ: Princeton University Press.

Cumings, B. (1987). The origins and development of the Northeast Asian political economy: Industrial sectors, product cycles, and political consequences. In F. Deyo (Ed.), *The political economy of the new Asian industrialism* (pp. 44-83). Ithaca, NY: Cornell University Press.

Cumings, B. (1993). The political economy of the Pacific rim. In R. Palat (Ed.), *Pacific-Asia and the future of the world-system* (pp. 21-37). Westport, CT: Greenwood.

Dai, G-H. (1985). *Taiwan shi yanjiu* [Studies of Taiwan history]. Taipei: Yuan Liu Chubanshe.

Das, P. (1993). *The yen appreciation and the international economy.* London: Macmillan.

Dernberger, R. T. (1975). The role of the foreigners in China's economic development, 1840-1949. In D. H. Perkins (Ed.), *China's modern economy in historical perspective* (pp. 19-47). Stanford, CA: Stanford University Press.

Deyo, F. (1989). *Beneath the miracle: Labor subordination in the new Asian industrialism.* Berkeley: University of California Press.

Dixon, C. (1991). *South East Asia in the world-economy.* Cambridge, UK: Cambridge University Press.

Dower, J. (1993). Peace and democracy in two systems. In A. Gordon (Ed.), *Postwar Japan as history* (pp. 3-33). Berkeley: University of California Press.

Duara, P. (1988). *Culture, power and the state: Rural North China, 1900-1942.* Stanford, CA: Stanford University Press.

Duus, P. (1968). *Party rivalry and political change in Taisho Japan.* Cambridge, MA: Harvard University Press.

Duus, P. (1976). *The rise of modern Japan.* Boston: Houghton Mifflin.

Duus, P. (1984). Economic dimensions of Meiji imperialism: The case of Korea, 1895-1910. In R. Myers & M. Peattie (Eds.), *The Japanese colonial empire* (pp. 128-171). Princeton, NJ: Princeton University Press.

Duus, P. (1988). Introduction. In P. Duus (Ed.), *The Cambridge history of Japan: Vol. 6. The twentieth century* (pp. 1-54). Cambridge, UK: Cambridge University Press.

Eccleston, B. (1989). *State and society in post-war Japan.* Oxford, UK: Polity Press.

Eckert, C. J. (1991). *Offspring of empire.* Seattle: University of Washington Press.

Eckert, C. J. (1992). Korea's economic development in historical perspective, 1945-1990. In M. Borthwick (Ed.), *Pacific century* (pp. 289-308). Boulder, CO: Westview.

Eckes, A. (1992). Trading American interests. *Foreign Affairs, 71,* 135-154.

Economic Planning Bureau, Ministry of Finance, Japan. (1994). *White paper on the economy.* Tokyo, Japan: Author.

Elvin, M. (1973). *The pattern of the Chinese past.* Stanford, CA: Stanford University Press.

Encarnation, D. (1992). *Rivals beyond trade.* Ithaca, NY: Cornell University Press.

Eng, R. Y. (1986). *Economic imperialism in China: Silk production and exports, 1861-1932.* Berkeley, CA: Institute of East Asian Studies.

Engels, F. (1972). Persia and China. In K. Marx & F. Engels (Eds.), *On colonialism* (pp. 120-126). New York: International Publishers.

Esherick, J. (1972). Harvard on China: The apologetic of imperialism. *Bulletin of Concerned Asian Scholars*, 4(4), 9-16.

Evans, P. (1979). *Dependent development*. Princeton, NJ: Princeton University Press.

Evans, P. (1987). Class, state, and dependence in East Asia: Lessons for Latin Americanist. In *The political economy of the new Asian industrialism* (pp. 203-227). Ithaca, NY: Cornell University Press.

Fairbank, J. K. (1958). *The United States and China*. New York: Viking.

Fairbank, J. K., Reischauer, E. O., & Craig, A. (1978). *East Asia: Tradition and transformation*. Boston: Houghton Mifflin.

Far Eastern Economic Review (FEER). (1991-1993, various). Hong Kong: Review Publishing.

Feuerwerker, A. (1958). *China's early industrialization: Sheng Hsuan-Huai (1844-1916) and Mandarin enterprise*. Cambridge, MA: Harvard University Press.

Feuerwerker, A. (1968a). China's modern history in Chinese communist historiography. In A. Feuerwerker (Ed.), *History in communist China* (pp. 216-246). Cambridge: Massachusetts Institute of Technology Press.

Feuerwerker, A. (1968b). *The Chinese economy, 1912-1949* (No. 1). Ann Arbor: Michigan Papers in Chinese Studies.

Feuerwerker, A. (1969). *The Chinese economy, ca. 1870-1911* (No. 5). Ann Arbor: Michigan Papers in Chinese Studies.

Feuerwerker, A. (1976). *The foreign establishment in China in the early twentieth century* (No. 29). Ann Arbor: Michigan Papers in Chinese Studies.

Feuerwerker, A. (1977). *Economic trends in the republic of China, 1912-1949* (No. 31). Ann Arbor: Michigan Papers in Chinese Studies.

Foster-Carter, A. (1978). North Korea: Development and self-reliance. In G. McCormack & M. Selden (Eds.), *Korea North and South: The deepening crisis* (pp. 115-152). New York: Monthly Review.

Friedland, J. (1994, June 9). The regional challenge. *Far Eastern Economic Review*, 40-42.

Friedman, D. (1988). *The misunderstood miracle*. Ithaca, NY: Cornell University Press.

Frobel, F., Heinrichs, J., & Kreye, O. (1980). *The new international division of labour*. Cambridge, UK: Cambridge University Press.

Fukui, H. (1992). The Japanese state and economic development: A profile of a nationalist-paternalist capitalist state. In R. P. Appelbaum & J. Henderson (Eds.), *States and development in the Asian Pacific rim* (pp. 199-226). Newbury Park, CA: Sage.

Gates, H. (1979). Dependency and the part-time proletariat in Taiwan. *Modern China*, 5, 381-408.

Gereffi, G. (1992). New realities of industrial development in East Asia and Latin America: Global, regional, and national trends. In R. P. Appelbaum & J. Henderson (Eds.), *State and development in the Asian-Pacific rim* (pp. 85-112). Newbury Park, CA: Sage.

Gereffi, G., & Korzeniewicz, M. (Eds.). (1994). *Commodity chain and global capitalism*. Westport, CT: Greenwood.

Gerschenkron, A. (1962). *Economic backwardness in historical perspective*. Cambridge, MA: Harvard University Press.

Gibney, F. (1992). Introduction: Arrival of the black ships. In M. Borthwick (Ed.), *Pacific century* (pp. 119-127). Boulder, CO: Westview.

Gilpin, R. (1987). *The political economy of international relations*. Princeton, NJ: Princeton University Press.

Gold, T. B. (1986). *State and society in the Taiwan miracle.* Armonk, NY: M. E. Sharpe.

Gold, T. B. (1987). The status quo is not static: Mainland-Taiwan relations. *Asian Survey, 27,* 300-315.

Gold, T. B. (1988). Colonial origins of Taiwanese capitalism. In E. Winckler & S. Green-halgh (Eds.), *Contending approaches to the political economy of Taiwan* (pp. 101-120). London: M. E. Sharpe.

Gordon, A. (1985). *The evolution of labor relations in Japanese heavy industry, 1853-1955.* Cambridge, MA: Harvard University, Council on East Asian Studies.

Gordon, A. (1991). *Labor and imperial democracy in prewar Japan.* Berkeley: University of California Press.

Griffin, E. (1938). *Clippers and consuls: American consular and commercial relations with Eastern Asia, 1845-1860.* Ann Arbor, MI: Edward Bros.

Grimwade, N. (1989). *International trade.* London: Routledge & Kegan Paul.

Haddon-Cave, P. (1984). Introduction. In D. Lethbridge (Ed.), *The business environment in Hong Kong* (pp. xv-xx). Hong Kong: Oxford University Press.

Haggard, S. (1990). *Pathways from the periphery: The politics of growth in the newly in-dustrializing countries.* Ithaca, NY: Cornell University Press.

Halliday, J. (1975). *A political history of Japanese capitalism.* New York: Pantheon.

Halliday, J., & McCormack, G. (1973). *Japanese imperialism today.* Harmondsworth, UK: Pelican.

Hambro, E. (1955). *The problem of Chinese refugees in Hong Kong.* Leyden: A. W. Sijthoff.

Harvey, D. (1989). *The condition of postmodernity.* Cambridge, UK: Basil Blackwell.

Hata, I. (1988). Continental expansion, 1905-1941. In P. Duus (Ed.), *The Cambridge history of Japan: Vol. 6. The twentieth century* (pp. 271-314). Cambridge, UK: Cambridge University Press.

Havens, J. (1987). *Fire across the sea: The Vietnam War and Japan, 1965-1975.* Princeton, NJ: Princeton University Press.

Henderson, G. (1968). *The politics of the vortex.* Cambridge, MA: Harvard University Press.

Higashi, C., & Lauter, P. (1990). *The internationalization of the Japanese economy.* Boston: Kluwer.

Higgins, R. (1992). The tributary system. In M. Borthwick (Ed.), *Pacific century* (p. 30). Boulder, CO: Westview.

Hinton, W. (1993). Can the Chinese dragon match pearls with the dragon god of the sea? *Monthly Review, 45*(3), 87-104.

Hirata, A., & Osada, H. (1990). Transformation of industrial structure and the role of trade and investment. In T. Fukuchi & M. Kagami (Eds.), *Perspectives on the Pacific basin economy* (pp. 93-106). Tokyo: Institute of Developing Economies.

Hirschman, A. (1981). Rise and decline of development economics. In A. Hirschman, *Essays in trespassing* (pp.1-14). New York: Cambridge University Press.

Hirschmeier, J. (1964). *The origins of entrepreneurship in Meiji Japan.* Cambridge, MA: Harvard University Press.

Ho, H.C.Y. (1979). *The fiscal system of Hong Kong.* London: Croom Helm.

Ho, S.P.S. (1978). *Economic development of Taiwan, 1960-1970.* New Haven, CT: Yale University Press.

Ho, S.P.S. (1984). Colonialism and development: Korea, Taiwan and Kwantung. In R. Myers & M. Peattie (Eds.), *The Japanese colonial empire* (pp. 348-398). Princeton, NJ: Princeton University Press.

Hong, S-H. (1980). Bureaucracy in Korea. *Korea Journal, 20,* 4-13.

Hsiao, H-H. M. (1990). Emerging social movements and the rise of a demanding civil society in Taiwan. *Australian Journal of Chinese Affairs, 24*, 1-17.

Hsiao, H-H. M. (1993). Discovering East Asian middle classes: Formation, differentiation, and politics. In H-H. M. Hsiao (Ed.), *Discovery of the middle classes in East Asia* (pp. 1-22). Taipei: Institute of Ethnology, Academia Sinica.

Hsiao, H-H. M., & So, A. Y. (1993). Ascent through national integration: The Chinese triangle of mainland-Taiwan-Hong Kong. In R. Palat (Ed.), *Pacific-Asia and the future of the world-economy* (pp. 133-150). Westport, CT: Greenwood.

Hsiao, H-H. M., & So, A. Y. (1994). *Taiwan-mainland economic nexus: Socio-political origins, state-society impacts, and future prospects* (Occasional Paper No. 37). Hong Kong: Hong Kong Institute of Asia-Pacific Studies, Chinese University of Hong Kong.

Hsiao, K-c. (1967). *Rural China: Imperial controls in the nineteenth century*. Seattle: University of Washington Press.

Huang, P.C.C. (1990). *The peasant family and rural development in the Yangtze delta, 1350-1988*. Stanford, CA: Stanford University Press.

Hughes, H. (1988). *Achieving industrialization in East Asia*. New York: Cambridge University Press.

Huntington, S. (1976). The change to change: Modernization, development, and politics. In C. Black (Ed.), *Comparative modernization* (pp. 25-41). New York: Free Press.

Ike, N. (1969). *Beginning of political democracy in Japan*. New York: Greenwood.

Iriye, A. (1970). Imperialism in East Asia. In J. Crowley (Ed.), *Modern East Asia* (pp. 122-150). New York: Harcourt.

Iriye, A. (1974). The failure of economic expansion: 1918-1931. In B. Silberman & H. D. Harootunian (Eds.), *Japan in crisis* (pp. 237-269). Princeton, NJ: Princeton University Press.

Ito, T. (1992). *The Japanese economy*. Cambridge: Massachusetts Institute of Technology Press.

Jacoby, N. (1966). *U.S. aid to Taiwan*. New York: Praeger.

Jansen, M. B. (1970). The Meiji state: 1868-1912. In J. Crowley (Ed.), *Modern East Asia* (pp. 95-121). New York: Harcourt.

Japan External Trade Organization (JETRO). (1994). *U.S. and Japan in figure III*. Tokyo: Author.

Johnson, C. (1962). *Peasant nationalism and communist power*. Stanford, CA: Stanford University Press.

Johnson, C. (1982). *MITI and the Japanese miracle*. Stanford, CA: Stanford University Press.

Johnson, C. (1987). Political institutions and economic performance: The government-business relationship in Japan, South Korea, and Taiwan. In F. C. Deyo (Ed.), *The political economy of the new Asian industrialization* (pp. 136-164). Ithaca, NY: Cornell University Press.

Jones, E., Frost, L., & White, C. (1993). *Coming full circle: An economic history of the Pacific rim*. Boulder, CO: Westview.

Jones, L., & Sakong, I. (1980). *Government, business and entrepreneurship in economic development: The Korean case*. Cambridge, UK: Cambridge University Press.

Kahng, G-H. (1991). North Korea in the era of decaying communism. *Korea Observer, 22*, 65-74.

Kaifu, T. (1990). *Foreign Policy, 80*, 28-39.

Kang, M-K. (1989). Industrial management and reforms in North Korea. In S. Gomulka et al. (Eds.), *Economic reforms in the socialist world* (pp. 200-211). London: Macmillan.

Kang, M-K., & Lee, K. (1991, June 29-30). *Industrial systems and reform in North Korea: A comparison with the case of China.* Paper presented to the Far Eastern Meeting of the Econometric Society, Seoul.

Kaple, D. A. (1994). *Dream of a red factory: The legacy of high Stalinism in China.* New York: Oxford University Press.

Kim, H-K. (1973). The Japanese colonial administration in Korea: An overview. In A. Nahm (Ed.), *Korea under Japanese colonial rule* (pp. 41-53). Kalamazoo: Western Michigan University, Center for Korean Studies.

Kim, K-D. (1979). *Man and society in Korea's economic growth.* Seoul: Seoul National University Press.

Kim, K-H. (1980). *The last phase of the East Asian world order: Korea, Japan, and the Chinese empire, 1860-1882.* Berkeley: University of California Press.

Kim, W. B. (1993, May 17-18). *China and the NIEs: Emerging symbiotic relations.* Paper presented to the International Conference on Emerging Patterns of FDI in East Asia, Shanghai.

Kitagawa, J. (1966). *Religion in Japanese history.* New York: Columbia University Press.

Kobayashi, H. (1983). *Sengo Nihon Shihon Shugi To Higashi Ajia Keizaiken* [Postwar Japanese capitalism and the East Asian economic sphere]. Tokyo: Ocha no Mizu Shobo.

Koike, K. (1988). *Understanding industrial relations in modern Japan.* London: Macmillan.

Koo, H. (1984). World systems, class, and state in third world development. *Sociological Perspectives, 27,* 33-52.

Koo, H. (1993). Strong state and contentious society. In H. Koo (Ed.), *State and society in contemporary Korea* (pp. 231-249). Ithaca, NY: Cornell University Press.

Koo, H., & Kim, E. M. (1992). The developmental state and capital accumulation in South Korea. In R. P. Appelbaum & J. Henderson (Eds.), *State and development in the Asian-Pacific rim* (pp. 121-149). Newbury Park, CA: Sage.

Kraus, R. C. (1979). Withdrawal from the world-system: Self-reliance and class structure in China. In W. L. Goldfrank (Ed.), *The world-system of capitalism* (pp. 237-259). Beverly Hills, CA: Sage.

Krause, L. (1989). Changes in the international system: The Pacific basin. *Annals of the American Academy of Political and Social Science, 505,* 105-116.

Kublin, H. (1949). The "modern" army of early Meiji Japan. *Far Eastern Quarterly, 9,* 20-41.

Kumao, K. (1993). An analysis of Japanese capability of playing a security role in Asia. In L. Kuang-sheng (Ed.), *The new international order in East Asia* (pp. 29-52). Hong Kong: Chinese University of Hong Kong, Hong Kong Institute of Asia-Pacific Studies.

Kurian, G. (1979). *The book of world rankings.* New York: Facts on File.

Lai, T-h., Myers, R., & Wou, W. (1991). *A tragic beginning: The Taiwan uprising of February 28, 1947.* Stanford, CA: Stanford University Press.

Lall, S. (1991, March 26-28). *Emerging sources of FDI in Asia and the Pacific.* Paper presented to the conference on Foreign Direct Investment in Asia and the Pacific in the 1990s, East-West Center, Honolulu.

Landsberg, M. (1979). Export-led industrialization in the third world: Manufacturing imperialism. *Review of Radical Political Economics, 11,* 50-63.

Lasek, E. (1983). Imperialism in China: A methodological critique. *Bulletin of Concerned Asian Scholars, 15*(1), 50-64.

Lau, M. (1988). The early history of the drafting process. In P. Wesley-Smith & A. Chen (Eds.), *The basic law and Hong Kong's future* (pp. 90-106). Hong Kong: Butterworths.

Lee, C-S. (1973). *The politics of Korean nationalism.* Berkeley: University of California Press.

Lee, M-K. (in press). Community and identity in transition in Hong Kong. In R.Y.W. Kwok & A. Y. So (Eds.), *The Hong Kong-Guangdong link: Partnership in flux.* Armonk, NY: M. E. Sharpe.

Levin, D., & Chiu, S.W.K. (1993). Trade unions in Hong Kong. In S. Frenkel (Ed.), *Organized labor in the Asia-Pacific region* (pp. 187-222). Ithaca, NY: ILR Press.

Levine, S. (1989). Japanese industrial relations: An external perspective. In Y. Sugimoto & R. Mouer (Eds.), *Constructs for understanding Japan* (pp. 296-320). London: Routledge & Kegan Paul.

Levy, M. (1955). Contrasting factors in the modernization of China and Japan. In S. Kuznets et al. (Eds.), *Economic growth: Brazil, India, Japan* (pp. 496-536). Durham, NC: Duke University Press.

Li, J. (1991, Jan. 28-Feb. 3). Mainland-Taiwan trade: Look back and into future. *Beijing Review, 34,* 26-29.

Liao, K-S. (1990). *Antiforeignism and modernization in China.* Hong Kong: Chinese University Press.

Lie, J. (1991). Review: Rethinking the "miracle"—Economic growth and political struggles in South Korea. *Bulletin of Concerned Asian Scholars, 23*(4), 66-71.

Lie, J. (1992a). The concept of mode of exchange. *American Sociological Review, 57,* 508-523.

Lie, J. (1992b). The political economy of South Korean development. *International Sociology, 7,* 285-300.

Lim, Y. (1985). *Government policy and private enterprise: Korean experience in industrialization.* Berkeley: University of California Press.

Lin, C-Y. (1973). *Industrialization in Taiwan, 1946-72.* New York: Praeger.

Liu, K-C. (1980). Foreword. In K-H. Kim, *The last phase of the East Asian world order* (pp. vii-xx). Berkeley: University of California Press.

Livingston, J., Moore, J., & Oldfather, F. (1973). *Imperial Japan.* New York: Pantheon.

Lockwood, W. (1954). *The economic development of Japan.* Princeton, NJ: Princeton University Press.

Lui, T-l., & Chiu, S. (1993). Industrial restructuring and labour-market adjustment under positive noninterventionism: The case of Hong Kong. *Environment and Planning A, 25,* 63-79.

Lui, T-l., & Gong, Q-S. (1985). *Cheng Shi Zong Heng* [Urban movements]. Hong Kong: Guang Jiao Jing.

Magaziner, I., & Reich, R. (1982). *Minding America's business.* New York: Harcourt Brace Jovanovich.

Martin, W. G. (1990). *Semiperipheral states in the world-economy.* Westport, CT: Greenwood.

Martin, W. G. (1994). The world-systems perspective in perspective. *Review, 17,* 145-185.

Mason, E., et al. (1980). *The economic and social modernization of the Republic of Korea.* Cambridge, MA: Harvard University Press.

Mazarr, M. (1991). Orphans of Glasnost: Cuba, Korea, and U.S. policy. *Korea and World Affairs, 15,* 58-84.

McCormack, G. (1990). Capitalism triumphant? The evidence from "number one" (Japan). *Monthly Review, 42*(1), 1-13.

McMichael, P. (1987). Foundations of U.S./Japanese world-economic rivalry in the Pacific rim. *Journal of Developing Societies, 3,* 62-77.

McMichael, P. (1992). Tensions between national and international control of the world food order: Contours of a new food regime. *Sociological Perspectives, 35*, 343-366.

Meisner, M. (1964). The development of Formosan nationalism. In M. Mancall (Ed.), *Formosa today* (pp. 147-162). New York: Praeger.

Meisner, M. (1970). Yenan communism and the rise of the Chinese People's Republic. In J. Crowley (Ed.), *Modern East Asia* (pp. 265-297). New York: Harcourt.

Michael, F. (1964). State and society in nineteenth century China. In A. Feuerwerker (Ed.), *Modern China* (pp. 57-69). Englewood Cliffs, NJ: Prentice Hall.

Minami, R. (1986). *The economic development of Japan*. London: Macmillan.

Ministry of International Trade and Industry (MITI). (1992). *White paper on international trade 1992* (Summary). Tokyo: Author.

Moon, C-i. (1991). Managing regional challenges: Japan, the East Asian NICs, and new patterns of economic rivalry. *Pacific Focus, 6*, 23-47.

Moore, B., Jr. (1966). *Social origins of dictatorship and democracy*. New York: Penguin.

Moore, J. (1983). *Japanese workers and the struggle for power: 1945-1947*. Madison: University of Wisconsin Press.

Moulder, F. (1977). *Japan, China, and the modern world-economy*. Cambridge, UK: Cambridge University Press.

Mu, T., & Sun, Z-K. (1992). *Daihan Minguo Linshizhengfu Zai Zhongguo* [Korean provisional government in China]. Shanghai: Shanghai Renmin Chubanshe.

Murphey, R. (1977). *The outsiders: The western experience in India and China*. Ann Arbor: University of Michigan Press.

Muto, I. (1986). Class struggle in postwar Japan. In G. McCormack & Y. Sugimoto (Eds.), *Democracy in contemporary Japan* (pp. 114-137). Armonk, NY: M. E. Sharpe.

Myers, R. H. (1991). How did the modern Chinese economy develop? *Journal of Asian Studies, 50*, 604-628.

Myers, R., & Peattie, M. (Eds.). (1984). *The Japanese colonial empire: 1895-1945*. Princeton, NJ: Princeton University Press.

Nahm, A. (1988). *Korea: Tradition and transformation*. Elizabeth, NJ: Hollym International Corporation.

Najita, T., & Harootunian, H. D. (1988). Japanese revolt against the West: Political and cultural criticism in the twentieth century. In P. Duus (Ed.), *The Cambridge history of Japan: Vol. 6. The twentieth century* (pp. 711-774). Cambridge, UK: Cambridge University Press.

Nakamura, T. (1981). *The postwar Japanese economy*. Tokyo: University of Tokyo Press.

Nakamura, T. (1983). *Economic growth in prewar Japan*. New Haven, CT: Yale University Press.

Nakamura, T. (1988). Depression, recovery, and war, 1920-1945. In P. Duus (Ed.), *The Cambridge history of Japan: Vol. 6. The twentieth century* (pp. 451-493). Cambridge, UK: Cambridge University Press.

Nathan, A. (1990). *China's crisis*. New York: Columbia University Press.

Naughton, B. (1991). Industrial policy during the cultural revolution: Military preparation, decentralization, and leaps forward. In W. A. Joseph, C. Wong, & D. Zweig (Eds.), *New perspectives on the cultural revolution* (pp. 153-182). Cambridge, MA: Harvard University, Council on East Asian Studies.

Nester, W. (1992). *Japan's growing power over East Asia and the world economy: Ends and means*. London: Macmillan.

NHHC [Nan-hai Hsien-chi]. (1873). [The local gazetteer of the Nan-Hai district]

Norman, E. H. (1975). *Origins of the modern Japanese state*. New York: Pantheon.

Onis, Z. (1991). Review article: The logic of developmental state. *Comparative Politics, 24*, 109-126.

Ozawa, T. (1993). Foreign direct investment and structural transformation: Japan as a recycler of market and industry. *Business and the Contemporary World, 5*(2), 129-150.

Palat, R. A. (1993). Introduction: The making and unmaking of Pacific-Asia. In R. A. Palat (Ed.), *Pacific-Asia and the future of the world-system* (pp. 3-20). Westport, CT: Greenwood.

Palat, R. A. (1994). *Pacific century: Myth or reality.* Unpublished paper, Department of Sociology, University of Auckland, New Zealand.

Park, H-C. (1986). *Development and state autonomy: South Korea, 1961-1979.* Unpublished doctoral dissertation, Indiana University.

Patrick, H. (1971). The economic muddle of the 1920s. In J. Morley (Ed.), *Dilemmas of growth in prewar Japan* (pp. 211-266). Princeton, NJ: Princeton University Press.

Peattie, M. (1988). The Japanese colonial empire, 1895-1945. In P. Duus (Ed.), *The Cambridge history of Japan: Vol. 6. The twentieth century* (pp. 217-270). Cambridge, UK: Cambridge University Press.

Perkins, D. H. (1969). *Agricultural development in China, 1368-1968.* Chicago: Aldine.

Perkins, D. H. (1991). China's industrial and foreign trade reform. In A. Koves & P. Marer (Eds.), *Foreign economic liberalization* (pp. 269-282). Boulder, CO: Westview.

Perry, J. C. (1990). Dateline North Korea: A communist holdout. *Foreign Policy, 80*, 172-191.

Petras, J. (1978). *Critical perspectives on imperialism and social class in the third world.* New York: Monthly Review Press.

Pfeffer, R. M. (1972). Serving the people and continuing the revolution. *China Quarterly, 52*, 620-653.

Phipps, J. (1991). North Korea—Will it be the great leader's turn next? *Government and Opposition, 26*, 44-55.

Prestowitz, C., Jr. (1988). *Trading places.* Tokyo: Charles Tuttle.

Putterman, L. (1993). *Continuity and change in China's rural development.* New York: Oxford University Press.

Pye, L. (1991). *China: An introduction.* New York: HarperCollins.

Pyle, K. (1987). In pursuit of a grand design: Nakasone between the past and the future. In K. Pyle (Ed.), *The trade crisis* (pp. 5-32). Seattle, WA: Society for Japanese Studies.

Rafferty, K. (1991). *City on the rocks: Hong Kong's uncertain future.* New York: Penguin.

Rapp, W. (1975). Japan's industrial policy. In I. Frank (Ed.), *The Japanese economy in international perspective* (pp. 37-66). Baltimore, MD: Johns Hopkins University Press.

Rawlinson, J. (1967). *China's struggle for naval development, 1839-1895.* Cambridge, MA: Harvard University Press.

Rawski, T. G. (1978). *China's republican economy: An introduction* (Discussion Paper No. 1). Toronto: University of Toronto.

Rawski, T. G. (1989). *Economic growth in prewar China.* Berkeley: University of California Press.

Reischauer, E. O. (1988). *The Japanese today.* Cambridge, UK: Belknap.

Reuschemeyer, D., & Evans, P. (1985). The state and economic transformation: Toward an analysis of the conditions underlying effective intervention. In P. Evans, D. Rueschemeyer, & T. Skocpol (Eds.), *Bringing the state back in* (pp. 44-77). Cambridge, UK: Cambridge University Press.

Rhee, S-W. (1991). North Korea in 1990: Lonesome struggle to keep chuch'e. *Asian Survey,* *31,* 71-78.

Riskin, C. (1987). *China's political economy.* Oxford, UK: Oxford University Press.

Robinson, J. (1965). Korean miracle. *Monthly Review, 16*(9), 541-549.

Rowley, A., & Sakamaki, S. (1992, August 6). Facts of friction. *Far Eastern Economic* *Review,* 53.

Rozman, G. (1992). The Confucian faces of capitalism. In M. Borthwick (Ed.), *Pacific* *century* (pp. 310-318). Boulder, CO: Westview.

Russett, B. (1988). U.S. hegemony: Gone or merely diminished, and how does it matters? In T. Inoguchi & D. Okimoto (Eds.), *The political economy of Japan: Vol. 2. The* *changing international context* (pp. 83-107). Stanford, CA: Stanford University Press.

Salaff, J. (1981). *Working daughters of Hong Kong.* Cambridge, UK: Cambridge University Press.

Samuels, R. (1987). *The business of the Japanese state.* Ithaca, NY: Cornell University Press.

Sanderson, S. K. (1994). The transition from feudalism to capitalism: The theoretical significance of the Japanese case. *Review, 17,* 15-55.

Sato, K. (1981). Senkanki Nihon no makuro keizai to mikuro keizai [The macro- and micro-economy of interwar Japan]. In N. Takafusa (Ed.), *Senkanki no Nihon keizai* *bunseki* [Economic analysis of interwar Japan] (pp. 3-30). Tokyo: Yamakawa Shup-pansha.

Schell, O., & Esherick, J. (1972). *Modern China.* New York: Random House.

Schram, S. (1969). *The political thought of Mao Tse-Tung.* New York: Praeger.

Scott, I. (1989). *Political change and the crisis of legitimacy in Hong Kong.* Honolulu: University of Hawaii Press.

See, C-s. (1919). *The foreign trade of China.* New York: Columbia University Press.

Selden, M. (1966). The guerilla movement in Northwest China. *China Quarterly, 28,* 63-81.

Selden, M. (1979). Introduction. In M. Selden (Ed.), *The People's Republic of China* (pp. 1-168). New York: Monthly Review Press.

Selden, M. (1983). Imposed collectivization and the crisis of agrarian development in socialist states. In A. Bergesen (Ed.), *Crises in the world-system* (pp. 227-252). Beverly Hills, CA: Sage.

Selden, M. (1988). City versus countryside? The social consequences of development choices in China. *Review, 11,* 533-568.

Selden, M. (1993). The social consequences of Chinese reform: The road to Tiananmen. In R. Palat (Ed.), *Asia-Pacific and the future of the world-economy* (pp. 151-168). Westport, CT: Greenwood.

Senkyu Hyakku Niju Nendaishi Kenkyukai (SHNN Kenkyukai). (1983). *Senkyu hyakku niju* *nendai no Nihon shihonshugi* [A social history of Japan in the 1920s]. Tokyo: Tokyo University Press.

Shannon, T. R. (1989). *An introduction to the world-system perspective.* Boulder, CO: Westview.

Sheldon, C. (1958). *The rise of the merchant class in Tokugawa Japan, 1600-1868.* Locust Valley, NY: J. J. Augustin.

Shieh, G. S. (1992). *Boss island.* New York: Peter Lang.

Shimada, H. (1980). *The Japanese employment system.* Tokyo: Japan Institute of Labor.

Shiraishi, T. (1989). *Japan's trade policies: 1945 to the present day.* London: Athlone.

Shive, G. (1990). Hong Kong's brain drain: Can education stem the flow? *Centerviews* (East-West Center), *7*(33), 1-6.

Short, R. P. (1984). The role of public enterprise: An international statistical comparison. In R. H. Floyd, C. S. Gray, & R. P. Short (Eds.), *Public enterprises in mixed economies* (pp. 110-194). Washington, DC: International Monetary Fund.

Silver, B. (1992). Class struggle and Kondratieff waves, 1970 to the present. In A. Kleinknecht, E. Mandel, & I. Wallerstein (Eds.), *New findings in long-wave research* (pp. 279-296). New York: St. Martin's Press.

Simon, D. F. (1990, June 23-24). *The economic activities of western nations in mainland China.* Paper presented to the conference on Trade and Investment in the Mainland, Taipei.

Sit, V.F.S. (1989). Industrial out-processing—Hong Kong's new relationship with the Pearl River Delta. *Asian Profile, 17,* 1-13.

Skeldon, R. (1990). Emigration and the future of Hong Kong. *Pacific Affairs, 63,* 500-523.

Skinner, G. W. (1964). Marketing and social structure in rural China. *Journal of Asian Studies, 24,* 3-43.

Skocpol, T. (1977). Wallerstein's world capitalist system: A theoretical and historical critique. *American Journal of Sociology, 82,* 1075-1090.

Skocpol, T. (1979). *States and social revolutions.* Cambridge, UK: Cambridge University Press.

Smith, B. (1986). Democracy derailed: Citizens' movements in historical perspective. In G. McCormack & Y. Sugimoto (Eds.), *Democracy in contemporary Japan* (pp. 157-172). Armonk, NY: M. E. Sharpe.

Smith, D., & Lee, S-H. (1990). Limits on semiperipheral success story? State dependent development and the prospects for South Korean democratization. In W. Martin (Ed.), *Semiperipheral states in the world-economy* (pp. 79-96). New York: Greenwood.

Smith, J., Collins, J., Hopkins, T. K., & Muhammad, A. (Eds.). (1988). *Racism, sexism, and the world-system.* Westport, CT: Greenwood.

Smith, T. C. (1955). *Political change and industrial development in Japan.* Stanford, CA: Stanford University Press.

Smith, T. C. (1959). *The agrarian origins of modern Japan.* Stanford, CA: Stanford University Press.

Smith, T. C. (1961). Japan's aristocratic revolution. *Yale Review, L 3,* 370-383.

So, A. Y. (1981). Development inside the capitalist world-system: A study of the Chinese and Japanese silk industry. *Journal of Asian Culture, 5,* 33-56.

So, A. Y. (1984). The process of incorporation into the capitalist world-system: The case of China in the nineteenth century. *Review, 8,* 91-116.

So, A. Y. (1986a). The economic success of Hong Kong: Insights from a world-system perspective. *Sociological Perspectives, 29,* 241-258.

So, A. Y. (1986b). *The South China silk district.* Albany: State University of New York Press.

So, A. Y. (1988). Shenzhen special economic zone: China's struggle for independent development. *Canadian Journal of Development Studies, 9,* 313-324.

So, A. Y. (1990a). Japan as the number 1: Insights from a world-system perspective. *Asian Profile, 18,* 217-226.

So, A. Y. (1990b). *Social change and development.* Newbury Park, CA: Sage.

So, A. Y. (1992). The dilemma of socialist development in the People's Republic of China. *Humboldt Journal of Social Relations, 18,* 163-194.

So, A. Y. (1993). Hong Kong people ruling Hong Kong! The rise of new middle class and negotiation politics, 1982-1984. *Asian Affairs: An American Review, 20,* 67-87.

So, A. Y. (in press). New middle class politics in Hong Kong: 1997 and democratization. *Swiss Asian Studies.*

So, A. Y., & Hua, S. (1992). Democracy as an antisystemic movement in Taiwan, Hong Kong, and China: A world system analysis. *Sociological Perspectives, 35,* 385-404.

So, A. Y., & Kwitko, L. (1990). New middle class and the democratic movement in Hong Kong. *Journal of Contemporary Asia, 20,* 384-398.

So, A. Y., & Kwitko, L. (1992). The transformation of urban movements in Hong Kong, 1970-90. *Bulletin of Concerned Asian Scholars, 24*(4), 32-44.

So, A. Y., & Kwok, R. (in press). Socio-economic core, political periphery: Hong Kong's uncertain transition toward 1997. In R. Kwok & A. Y. So (Eds.), *Hong Kong-Guangdong link: Partnership in flux.* Armonk, NY: M. E. Sharpe.

So, A. Y., & May, S-H. (1993). Democratization in East Asia in the late 1980s: Taiwan breakthrough, Hong Kong frustration. *Studies in Comparative International Development, 28*(2), 61-80.

The southward invasion of Japanese idols into Taiwan. (1994). [Special issue] *Japan Digest, 9*(3), 20-47.

Stites, R. (1982). Small-scale industry in Yingge, Taiwan. *Modern China, 8,* 247-279.

Stockwin, J.A.A. (1975). *Japan: Divided politics in a growth economy.* New York: Norton.

Storry, R. (1961). *A history of modern Japan.* Baltimore, MD: Penguin.

Sung, Y-W. (1985). *The role of Hong Kong and Macau in China's export drive* (Working Paper No. 85/11). Australian National University, National Center for Development Studies.

Szczepanik, E. (1958). *The economic growth of Hong Kong.* Oxford, UK: Oxford University Press.

Tai, H-C. (1989). The oriental alternative: An hypothesis on culture and economy. In H-C. Tai (Ed.), *Confucianism and economic development: An oriental alternative* (pp. 6-37). Washington, DC: Washington Institute Press.

Taira, K. (1970). *Economic development and the labor market in Japan.* New York: Columbia University Press.

Tawney, R. H. (1932). *Land and labour in China.* London: Allen & Unwin.

Thomas, S. C. (1984). *Foreign intervention and China's industrial development, 1870-1911.* Boulder, CO: Westview.

Turner, H. A., et al. (1981). *The last colony: But whom?* Cambridge, UK: Cambridge University Press.

van Wolferen, K. (1989). *The enigma of Japanese power.* London: Macmillan.

Vogel, E. (1991). *The four little dragons.* Cambridge, MA: Harvard University Press.

Wade, R. (1992). Review article: East Asian economic success: Conflicting perspectives, partial insights, shaky evidence. *World Politics, 44,* 270-320.

Wakeman, F., Jr. (1966). *Strangers at the gate: Social disorder in South China 1839-1861.* Berkeley: University of California Press.

Wallerstein, I. (1976). *The modern world system: Capitalist agriculture and the origins of the European world economy in the sixteenth century.* New York: Academic Press.

Wallerstein, I. (1979). *The capitalist world-economy.* Cambridge, UK: Cambridge University Press.

Wallerstein, I. (1982a). Fernand Braudel, historian. *Radical History Review, 26,* 105-119.

Wallerstein, I. (1982b). Socialist states: Mercantilist strategies and revolutionary objectives. In E. Friedman (Ed.), *Ascent and decline in the world-system* (pp. 289-300). Beverly Hills, CA: Sage.

Wallerstein, I. (1984). *The politics of the world-economy.* Cambridge, UK: Cambridge University Press.

Wallerstein, I. (1986). Braudel on capitalism and the market. *Monthly Review, 37*(9), 11-19.

Wallerstein, I. (1987). World-system analysis. In A. Giddens & J. H. Turner (Eds.), *Social theory today* (pp. 309-324). Stanford, CA: Stanford University Press.

Wallerstein, I. (1988). Development: Lodestar or illusion. *Economic and Political Weekly, 23*(39), 2017-2023.

Wallerstein, I. (1989). *The modern world-system III.* Cambridge, UK: Cambridge University Press.

Wallerstein, I. (1990). Antisystemic movements: History and dilemmas. In S. Amin et al. (Eds.), *Transforming the revolution: Social movements and the world-system* (pp. 13-52). New York: Monthly Review Press.

Wallerstein, I. (1991a). *Report on an intellectual project: The Fernand Braudel Center, 1976-1991.* Binghamton: State University of New York, Fernand Braudel Center.

Wallerstein, I. (1991b). *Unthinking social science: The limits of nineteenth-century paradigms.* Cambridge, UK: Polity Press.

Wallerstein, I. (1992). America and the world. *Theory and Society, 21,* 1-28.

Wallerstein, I. (1993). Foes as friends. *Foreign Policy, 90,* 145-157.

Waswo, A. (1982). In search of equity: Japanese tenant unions in the 1920s. In T. Najita & J. V. Koschmann (Eds.), *Conflict in modern Japanese history* (pp. 366-411). Princeton, NJ: Princeton University Press.

Weng, J-Y. (1992). *Taiwan shehui yundong shi* [A history of Taiwan's social movement]. Taipei: Daoxiang Chubanshe.

White, G. (1983). The postrevolutionary Chinese state. In V. Nee & D. Mozingo (Eds.), *State and society in contemporary China* (pp. 27-52). Ithaca, NY: Cornell University Press.

Wilson, G. (1969). *Radical nationalist in Japan: Kita Ikki, 1883-1937.* Cambridge, MA: Harvard University Press.

Wong, J. Y. (1976). *Yeh Ming-Chen: Viceroy of Liang-Kuang.* Cambridge, UK: Cambridge University Press.

Wong, R. B. (1992). Chinese economic history and development: A note on the Myers-Huang exchange. *Journal of Asian Studies, 51,* 600-611.

Wong, S-l. (1988). *Emigrant entrepreneurs.* Hong Kong: Oxford University Press.

Wong, S-l. (1992, December 16-19). *Business and politics in Hong Kong during the transition.* Paper presented at the Conference on 25 Years of Social and Economic Development in Hong Kong. Hong Kong: University of Hong Kong, Centre of Asian Studies.

World Bank. (1992, 1994). *World bank.* Baltimore, MD: Johns Hopkins University Press.

Wormack, B. (1984). Modernization and democratic reform in China. *Journal of Asian Studies, 43,* 417-439.

Woronoff, J. (1984). *Japan's commercial empire.* Armonk, NY: M. E. Sharpe.

Wright, T. (1986). Imperialism and the Chinese economy: A methodological critique of the debate. *Bulletin of Concerned Asian Scholars, 18,* 36-45.

Wright, T. (1992). Introduction. In T. Wright (Ed.), *The Chinese economy in the early twentieth century* (pp. 1-28). New York: St. Martin's Press.

Wu, C. (1992). A brief account of the development of capitalism in China. In T. Wright (Ed.), *The Chinese economy in the early twentieth century* (pp. 29-43). New York: St. Martin's Press.

Yamamura, K. (1974). The Japanese economy, 1911-1930. In T. Najita & J. V. Koschmann (Eds.), *Conflict in modern Japanese history* (pp. 299-329). Princeton, NJ: Princeton University Press.

Yamamura, K. (1980). The agricultural and commercial revolution in Japan, 1550-1650. In R. Uselding (Ed.), *Research in economic history* (Vol. 5, pp. 85-107). Greenwich, CT: JAI Press.

Yamamura, K. (1987). Shedding the shackles of success: Saving less for Japan's future. In K. Pyle (Ed.), *The trade crisis* (pp. 33-60). Seattle, WA: Society for Japanese Studies.

Yanagihara, T., & Emig, A. (1991). An overview of Japan's foreign aid. In S. Islam (Ed.), *Yen for development* (pp. 37-69). New York: Council on Foreign Relations Press.

Yanaihara, T. (1956). *Riben Diguozhuyi xia zhi Taiwan* [Taiwan under Japanese imperialism]. Taipei: Bank of Taiwan.

Yang, D. (1991). China adjusts to the world economy: The political economy of China's coastal development strategy. *Pacific Affairs, 64,* 42-64.

Yoon, Y-K. (1990). The political economy of transition: Japanese foreign direct investments in the 1980s. *World Politics, 43,* 1-27.

Yoshinaga, I. (1994, August). *The "contradictory" nature of twentieth-century Japanese labor: Integrating western ideology into Japanese society.* Paper presented to the Annual Meeting of the American Sociological Association, Los Angeles.

Young, E. (1970). Nationalism, reform, and republican revolution. In J. Crowley (Ed.), *Modern East Asia* (pp. 151-179). New York: Harcourt.

Yu, S. R. (1987). Recent developments in North Korea and inter-Korean relations. *Korean Journal of International Studies, 18,* 351-370.

Zarrow, P. (1991). Review essay: Social change and radical currents in republican China, 1912-49. *Bulletin of Concerned Asian Scholars, 23*(1), 49-60.

Zarrow, P. (1994). Review essay: Nationalism and alienation in modern China. *Bulletin of Concerned Asian Scholars, 26*(1-2), 93-110.

Zeitlin, M. (1984). *The civil wars in Chile (or the bourgeois revolutions that never were).* Princeton, NJ: Princeton University Press.

Zo, K-Z. (1978). Korean industry under the Japanese colonial rule. In C. Shin-Yong (Ed.), *Economic life in Korea* (pp. 145-167). Seoul: International Cultural Foundation.

Index

Agriculture:
  early 1900s Japan, 101-102
  East Asian NIEs, 19
  modern China, 155
Amnesty International, 251
Amsden, A., 12-14
Ancestor worship, 10
Antisystemic movements, 25-26, 29, 140,
    278-279
  anti-Japanese resistance, 96-97, 126
  antimissionary movement, 48
  in China, 39-42, 48, 126, 121-123, 154,
    250, 278
  in Hong Kong, 210-211
  in modern Japan, 182-184
  in South Korea, 208-209
  in Taiwan, 209-210, 255-257
  Japan as anticolonial model, 92
  Korean development and, 276
  See also Labor movements
Arms industry, 49, 111, 276
Asia-Pacific Economic Cooperation
    (APEC) Conference, 240, 274
Asian Development Bank (ADB), 231
Authoritarian developmentalism, 201

Bakufu system, 59
Balance of trade, 161, 166, 190, 214, 219,
    226-227, 233

Balassa, B., 5-7
Bank of Japan, 172
Banks and financial institutions:
  early 20th century China, 120
  Hong Kong colonial state and, 206
  Japanese developmental state, 172, 174-
    175
  Japanese global financial power, 227-
    228
  zaibatsu and, 100, 103
Bello, W., 17-20
Bolshevik Revolution, 122
Borrowing:
  early 20th century Japan, 100
  modern China, 151-152
  postwar Japanese developmental state,
    174-175
  Qing dynasty China, 46, 114
  South Korean, 197
  U.S. trade deficits and, 220
Boxer rebellion, 113
Boycotts, 121-122
Braudel, Fernand, 23
Britain, 32, 268
  hegemonic decline, 84, 98, 269
  Hong Kong reunification talks, 245
  Opium War, 37-40, 54, 268
  support for Chinese independence, 119
  Taiping rebellion, 40
Bushido, 60

About the Authors

Alvin Y. So received his Bachelor of Social Sciences degree from the Chinese University of Hong Kong, and his M.A. and Ph.D. degrees from UCLA. From 1983 and 1984, he taught at the University of Hong Kong. He is now a professor and graduate chair of Sociology at the University of Hawaii, where he received a Regents' Medal for Excellence in Teaching in 1989. His research interests are in development, class theory, and East Asia. He is the author of *The South China Silk District* and *Social Change and Development*. He is coauthoring a book with Hsin-Huang Michael Hsiao, titled *The Chinese Triangle and the Future of Asia-Pacific*; is co-editing a book with Reginald Kwok, titled *Hong Kong-Guangdong Integration*; and is completing another book project on the new middle-class politics in Hong Kong.

Stephen W. K. Chiu received his Bachelor of Social Sciences and Master of Philosophy degrees from the University of Hong Kong, and his Ph.D. from Princeton University. The title of his dissertation is *The State and the Financing of Industrialization in East Asia: Historical Origins of Comparative Divergences*. He now teaches sociology at the Chinese University of Hong Kong. His primary research interests are in development, social movement, and industrial sociology. He has published articles and book chapters on labor unions, industrial restructuring, and East Asian NIEs. He is completing a book project with Tai-Lok Lui and K. C. Ho, comparing the divergent patterns of industrial restructuring in Hong Kong and Singapore.

3110